*DAVID LYNCH*          *SWERVES*

# DAVID

# LYNCH

# SWERVES

Uncertainty

from *Lost Highway*

to *Inland Empire*

*MARTHA P. NOCHIMSON*

UNIVERSITY OF TEXAS PRESS

AUSTIN

Requests for permission to reproduce material from
this work should be sent to:
PERMISSIONS
University of Texas Press
P.O. Box 7819
Austin, TX 78713-7819
*http://utpress.utexas.edu/about/book-permissions*

♾ The paper used in this book meets the minimum
requirements of ANSI/NISO Z39.48-1992 (R1997)
(Permanence of Paper).

Library of Congress Cataloging-in-Publication Data

Nochimson, Martha.
    David Lynch swerves : uncertainty from
Lost Highway to Inland Empire / by Martha P.
Nochimson. — First edition.
        p. cm.
    Includes bibliographical references and index.
    Includes filmography.
    ISBN 978-0-292-72295-8 (cloth : alk. paper)
1. Lynch, David, 1946– —Criticism and interpretation. I. Title.
    PN1998.3.L96N53  2013
    791.4302'3092—dc23                    2012040910

doi: 10.7560/722958

While atoms move by their own weight straight down
Through the empty void, at quite uncertain times
And uncertain places they s
                              w
                                e
                                  r
                                    v
                                      e
                                                    slightly from their course.
You might call it no more than a change of motion.
If this did not occur, then all of them
Would fall like drops of rain down through the void.
There would be no collisions, no impacts
Of atom upon atom, so that nature
Would never have created anything.

**LUCRETIUS, *ON THE NATURE OF THE UNIVERSE*;**
**TRANSLATED BY SIR RONALD MELVILLE, P. 42.**

[FORMAT ALTERED BY AUTHOR]

# CONTENTS

# PREFACE
## CRITIC ON FIRE

Ring the bells that still can ring
Forget your perfect offering
There is a crack, a crack in everything
That's how the light gets in.

**LEONARD COHEN, "ANTHEM"**

In *The Passion of David Lynch* (1997), aided by the ideas of Carl Jung, I followed Lynch up to the boundaries of ordinary cultural discourse as he looked beyond them to much larger realities. Tracing a path from Lynch's early student work to *Twin Peaks: Fire Walk with Me*, I argued that to understand the Lynchian vision we must open ourselves up to Lynch's unique depiction of an organic reality that lies beyond the limits we, as a part of a culture that obsessively draws lines, have imposed on our lives. True enough, but not quite the whole story. Although, at the end of that book, I commented briefly about *Lost Highway* as if it could be understood within the framework I had outlined, I eventually found myself faced with a need to recognize that that film and Lynch's subsequent cinema have dramatically altered the circumstances of Lynch criticism. Hence the need for *David Lynch Swerves*.

With my first book about Lynch, I became one of the pioneers of a major redirection of Lynch criticism. We moved toward an examination of his characters' interior lives in order to illuminate Lynch's originality as a cinematic storyteller.[1] I emphasized the levels of consciousness in his characters, and the optimism Lynch radiated through his portrayals of the visionary capabilities of his incandescent heroes, especially Special Agent Dale Cooper (Kyle MacLachlan). And I would have liked to say that, wielding my copy of Jung, I provided the necessary map and the flashlight for Lynch's filmography, world without end. But I can't. Although my critique provided much-needed new clarity about the Lynch work that preceded *Lost Highway* (1997), try as I might to believe otherwise, it did very little to help the critical conversation about the story of Fred Madison (Bill Pullman). My doubts grew into a nagging dissatisfaction with what I had said, or not said, about the notorious "scene on the lawn" in *Lost Highway* in which the life of the film's protagonist, Fred Madison, takes an astonishing turn. In that extraordinary and original scene, Fred undergoes a physical metamorphosis into another person, and we see it happening. There is a molecule-by-molecule interpenetration of the body of Pete Dayton (Balthazar Getty), whom Fred has never met before, by the body of Fred Madison, a moment that seriously challenges our ordinary understanding of how bodies and matter function. By the time I had seen *Lost Highway* (1997) for the third or fourth time, I knew that with this film, Lynch had undergone a crucial artistic change. He had moved beyond limits he had previously only approached, and I had to let go of old assumptions (once again) and follow him.

I stand by what I said in my first book, *as far as it went*. At the time I wrote it, given what Lynch had then revealed to me about his sense of a universal unity linking us all, Jung's ideas seemed to help explain the intriguing growth and development of Lynch's visionary protagonists in his work up to *Twin Peaks: Fire Walk with Me*. But Jung didn't have a word to say about Lynch's shifting emphasis in *Lost Highway* and in his subsequent films, in which many very disorienting images of the physical world took center stage. Then I remembered that for twenty years, Lynch had mentioned physics to me whenever we talked, and I began to investigate his cinema, especially from *Lost Highway* to the present, with quantum mechanics and relativity in mind. My more recent, post-1997, increasingly revealing conversations with Lynch have confirmed my new direction—and given me a new frame of reference.

The climactic moment came on March 18, 2010, when Lynch and I spent three hours talking in his compound in the Hollywood Hills. In a long, frank, unguarded conversation, Lynch told me about his vision of the physical world as an uncertain place that masks important universal realities, enunciated for him not by Carl Jung, but by the Holy Vedas of the Hindu religion. At the same time that Lynch told me that he is fascinated by physics, he emphasized that he knows very little about the nuts of bolts of the scientific method used by physicists. ("I barely graduated from high school.") He was more comfortable vividly describing the universal center of consciousness evoked by the Hindu holy text. His wholehearted affirmation of his Vedic map of the universe made it clear why he re-

David Lynch in his hillside retreat, the site of our March 18, 2010, interview.

mains optimistic about life even though he finds the physical landscape on which we live to be unstable.

As Lynch spoke, he burned away my Jungian ideas. Nevertheless, much that he said also corresponded remarkably with the scientific constructs relating to the disorienting, shifting plane of objects and bodies that emerged from experiments conducted by modern physicists in the 1920s, theories that since then have identified even more intense mysteries about the physical plane of life. Lynch's passionate words about the Vedas, and the specter of modern physics that haunted our discussion, generated sparks when they struck against each other in my mind. The tinder burst into flame, casting a new, more illuminating light on Lynch's films—including that mysterious night on the lawn.

In the scene on the lawn outside the Dayton house, Fred and Pete fuse physically, as Pete's parents and his girlfriend watch in shock and horror. Dreamlike and murky when we see it in this suburban setting, the metamorphosis is followed immediately by a scene in Fred's jail cell that visualizes the same transformation on a particle level, when we see the particles of Fred Madison and the particles of Pete Dayton occupy the same space at the same time. (These complex frames will be discussed in great detail in Chapter 1.) The seeming physical impossibility of this bi-level event has led many critics to interpret it as parts of a purely psychological dream or fantasy. But it is now clear to me that in so doing those critics are only putting obstacles in the way of Lynch's discourse. In short, I now argue that we must look not only at the extraordinary function of consciousness in his films, but also at the extraordinary construction of matter. Lynch's films are not about a complex internal/cosmic life lived on an easy-to-fathom, stable, solid physical plain. His films place the complications of the consciousness in a spatial/temporal terrain that is strange and mysterious by logical standards, and also connected in amazing ways to the cosmos.

In the scene on the lawn and many others like it, as we shall see in the chapters to come, Lynch provocatively offers his audience unique images of the linkage of inner and outer that must be acknowledged in its full complexity if we are to see the films that Lynch made, and not the much less interesting films that his critics have invented. A full and rich reading of Lynch must not only take into account the many levels of human interiority, but also Lynch's images that reference the many possibilities offered by the multiple levels of the external world of matter. The latter have, to date, gone virtually unremarked. The character of the external world in Lynch's filmic universes has all but eluded criticism so far. It's time for a change.

It is also time for a change about the way we explore the entirety of Lynch's work. It is now clear that with *Lost Highway*, Lynch's filmmaking altered significantly. We all sensed that there was something about *Lost Highway* quite different from anything Lynch had done previously, but no one was ready to integrate that intuition into a coherent approach to all of Lynch's cinema and television. Now that Lynch has made *The Straight Story*, *Mulholland Drive*, and *Inland Empire*, all going further in the direction that he took when he shot *Lost Highway*, it is no longer possible to trace an unbroken line of development in his work. Yes, Lynch's cinema from *Lost Highway* to his most recent film, *Inland Empire*, has much in common with what came before, but there are crucial differences that require us to regard his work in two stages. Building on *The Passion of David Lynch*, I intend, in *David Lynch Swerves*, to bring the details of both stages of his work into clear focus. Most of this study is an exploration of Lynch's second-stage cinema from *Lost Highway* to *Inland Empire*, but I will also, from time to time, discuss how what we now know of Lynch's later work casts light back on his first-stage films.

With *David Lynch Swerves*, I intend to offer a corrective to previous critical misunderstandings of Lynch, some far more serious than others, which have been rooted in part in a failure to acknowledge the post–*Lost Highway* changes in Lynch's filmmaking. Some other misprisions have been caused by critics' overdependence on psychology, both in interpreting Lynch through psychological theories and in using their personal subconscious fantasies as a way to grasp the meaning of Lynchian cinema. Moreover, in reaching for theory as a lever to understanding, too often existing criticism has rendered the films passageways to the theory rather than the reverse. This has been painfully true in the use of Lacanian psychoanalytic theory in Lynch criticism. Specifically, Todd McGowan, making a good-faith effort to open up Lynch's films, ended up selectively extracting from the texts just what he needs to support Lacan's beliefs. Thus, ignoring many aspects of Lynch's films that run counter to Lacanian thought, McGowan comments only on those scenes that he can say reflect Lacan's belief that what we consider the "real" is actually constructed and artificial, while fantasy arising from desire is a less-mediated, better way of looking into the "hidden structure of reality itself."[2] Another critic, blocking Lynch's films almost completely with his demonstrations of their purported interface with Lacanian theory, uses them as a springboard for his political ideas, and his discussion convolutedly links Lacan and *Lost Highway* with the political significance of Hitler and Stalin.[3]

If Jung's collective unconscious was not sufficient as a springboard into Lynch, relying on Freud and Lacan has proven even less successful. Lacan offers an interesting paradigm, but one that is not applicable to Lynch. Lacan's ideas grew out of his belief in intractable human limitations that preclude any possibility of direct perception of reality. These limits, according to Lacan, restrict us to bumping into the real through our fantasy lives, which are less mediated by obstructionist cultural constructs than consciousness and logic and thus more accessible to whatever is beyond them. Attempts to impose Lacan's pessimistic framework of thought on Lynch's often-expressed optimism about our infinite possibilities are problematic because Lynch's deepest commitment is to the existence of an accessible reality to which human beings can connect through a boundless capacity for receptivity. This rules Lacan out as an appropriate frame of reference for Lynch. And a new entry into the arena of Lynch criticism, Allister Mactaggart, references his own subconscious and ends up telling us more about his inner life than about Lynch's films.

Taking a tack that brings him closer to Lynch's work, Eric G. Wilson references the tradition of transcendence in American literature which, like Jungian philosophy, seeks to link the individual consciousness to a cosmic "oversoul" that envelops us all. Wilson even more importantly references traditional gnostic and negative theologians as potential lenses onto things Lynchian.[4] But even though Wilson is not overdependent on psychology, he is still too focused on human internal life and Judeo-Christian traditions. As with my use of Jung, Wilson's mobilization of the American literature of transcendence and gnostic theology as critical aids walks him toward Lynch's mysticism, but does not allow him to come as close as he needs to. It was a step forward in Lynch criticism when we began to engage with the director's mind-bending images of what happens beneath familiar surfaces. But if paradigms of internal life and Western spirituality are the first to come to mind in approaching "what lies beneath," they are not the only option; and in this case they are not comprehensive enough.

We will engage and enjoy Lynch's art more if we stretch beyond our own limits to meet him. As I now know, Lynch's paradigm of a cosmic "beyondness" comes from the Vedic tradition, not from Western thought. And his paradigms for the physical world, which Lynch depicts with as many levels as he depicts for the mind, do not come from literature or psychology. They come from his impressionistic gleaning of physics. According to modern physics, there is much more to objects and bodies than the finite images we seem to see clearly around us. On the particle level, there is another truth, the essential limitlessness of interactions among the building blocks of matter, and an uncertainty that is not visible on the surfaces of material forms. This map of matter drawn by modern physics is pertinent to Lynch's sense of important truths about materiality.

As we shall see in the succeeding chapters, there is in Lynch's cinema a partial reality to matter as it conventionally appears to us, that is to say to our perception of matter as certain and stable. But Lynch makes it clear that that reassuring way of thinking about objects and bodies can never be the whole story because on its deepest levels ordinarily invisible to the naked eye, matter is anything but solid or stable. The behavior of particles that scientists observed in physics experiments boggles all our traditional expectations; for example, physicists have seen particles that can literally be in two places at the same time. The poetry of these hidden realities of matter is very present in Lynch's cinema and has an impact upon the conscious awareness of his characters. The importance to Lynch's movies and television of the role played by the various levels of external matter, which includes a boundlessness every bit as expansive as that of the interior consciousness, is the aspect of Lynch's work that has been missing from the criticism. His is a more complex modern vision than has been attempted by any other American filmmaker.

Let us be clear here. Lynch's films are not *about* Hindu religion and/or modern physics. Lynch's films tell stories about specific characters in specific situations. His method of telling those stories profits from the vocabularies of Vedic texts and modern physics and the images those frames of reference generate for Lynch in his quest to represent both the limits and the limitlessness of human realities. The way modern physics and the Holy Vedas engage the interplay between boundaries and boundlessness inspires Lynch and gives him ways to speak about multiple levels of reality—levels we know about and levels that come as a surprise to us. Another way of putting this is that Lynch believes our existence hovers between enclosure and liberation, and his films explore human suffering, failure, and triumph from this perspective. Ordinary forms of cinematic realism do not permit him sufficient scope to voyage into what lies beyond apparent limits, and he has no interest in using conventions attached to the non-realistic genres of fantasy or horror films that give an aberrant cast to the beyond. Lynch believes the boundlessness of mind and body is an ordinary part of reality, and Vedic texts and modern physics give him ways of talking about going beyond our ordinarily limited vision of who we are and what we may be.[5]

Do we need to be Hindus or physicists to engage with Lynch's films and television? Do we need to be Catholics to read Dante? Do we need to believe in the Great Chain of Being to engage with Shakespeare? Or the Greek pantheon of gods to read Homer? The task at hand here is the same as for art works of all kinds, all of which are informed by some original combination of the beliefs of the artist who produced them and the beliefs of the society that produced the artist. So, with the cinema of David Lynch, we must excavate the complexity of the relationship between Lynch's work, the holy Vedas, and physics.

In the chapters that follow, I shall attend to consciousness as Lynch's central preoccupation in his life and work and I shall be concerned with how it manifests itself in his works not as Vedic per se, but rather as it is inflected by his exposure to Vedic wisdom. I shall also delve into an exploration of how, from *Lost Highway* on, that spiritual interest has become much more entangled with modern ideas about spatial and temporal physicality than his pre-1997 cinema was. I will put modern physics and Vedic literature forward as better references for reading Lynch than theories derived from psychology, other social sciences, Western religion, and literature, which have clouded the critical lens. My use of physics for the purposes of this book was aided substantially by my discussions with Professor David Z. Albert, Director of the M. A. Program in the Philosophical Foundations of Physics at Columbia University. I am also grateful to Professor Albert for introducing me to the work of Arthur Eddington, and particularly to Eddington's description of a physicist entering a room, which has been so helpful to me. Professor Arkady Plotnitsky, Professor of English and Theory and Cultural Studies and Director of the Theory and Cultural Studies Program at Purdue University, has also been invaluable in helping me enter into the conversation in progress today among physicists.[6]

I have included in the appendix a transcript of my extensive conversations with Professor Albert; I have also included a fragment of my conversation with Lynch on March 18, but not the whole text. Why not? Lynch felt that what he said that day was too revealing and he asked me not to print it in its entirety. As a result, this book is broken. Something I dearly wanted to include is missing. The full transcript, as I see it, reveals a wonderful kind of energy in Lynch, rarely seen by the public, and a similarly rarely seen thoughtfulness. But it is too intimate a portrait for Lynch to be comfortable with in print. I have conveyed some of his ideas in the chapters to come, but not in his specific language. Of course, the preponderance of the evidence for my interpretations comes from the films themselves, but the addition of Lynch's voice would have made the chapters to come all the richer. However, heeding Leonard Cohen in "Anthem," I will "forget my perfect offering." And hope that the crack in this book will be, as Cohen assures us, "how the light gets in."

# ACKNOWLEDGMENTS

The myth of the lone creator tantalizes American society with its pristine macho seductions, and yet in reality it describes (probably) no one's process. Certainly, whatever creativity is represented by this book has come to life because of the immense generosity of others. Lynch's films from *Lost Highway* to *Inland Empire* kept calling me, and I answered; then, every step of my journey was enlivened by the graciousness of the talented, the admirable, and the steadfast.

First, I must thank David Lynch. Often, it seems like the time I have spent in his company has taken place in a series of visions. "People don't talk like this," he told me the last time I saw him. "They talk about football; I don't talk like this with anyone but you." Surely a hyperbole, and unquestionably the stuff that dreams are made of. But, "There is always the magic," says Visitor #1 in *Inland Empire*; yes there is. In this case it translates into scholarship.

Thank you, Mindy Ramaker, David's personal assistant, who secures the perimeter, makes the connections, and keeps the ship afloat. Your sympathetic attention to my overly many requests was very much appreciated.

Thank you David Z. Albert and Arkady Plotnitsky, physicists with a real delight in art as well as in their own discipline. They taught me physics for the pure love of the subject and, I conjecture, for the pleasure of being part of a little meeting between science and the humanities.

I owe a huge debt of gratitude to Columbia University. My presentation of some of the ideas in this volume before the University Seminar on Cinema and Interdisciplinary Interpretation and my conversations with Professor Robert L. Belknap in his capacity as Director of University Seminars stimulated my thinking about my subject in very important ways. I have been fortunate to once again receive financial support from the University Seminars, for which I thank the current Director, Professor Robert Pollack; Alice Newton, the always supportive Assistant Director; and her administrative assistant Pamela Guardia. To use the prescribed language, "The author expresses appreciation to the Warner Fund at the University Seminars at Columbia University for their help in publication. Material in this work was presented to the University Seminar: Cinema and Interdisciplinary Interpretation."

I owe an equal debt of gratitude to my acquisitions editor at the University of Texas Press, Jim Burr. We go back all the way to *The Passion of David Lynch: Wild at Heart in Hollywood*, when he was my copy editor and my champion. Some things don't change. Ditto my current copy editor, Karen Backstein, who asks all the right questions; nothing gets by her. You can't buy her kind of attention and commitment. Ditto, ditto Arthur Vincie. Arthur, a filmmaker himself, has given generously of his technical expertise. Despite a hectic, crowded schedule of his own, he is always there. To everyone at the University of Texas Press who lent a hand, particularly Victoria Davis, thank you.

To my two readers, Joseph G. Kicksola and Eric G. Wilson: you illuminated the dark corners of my manuscript.

To Donna Brooks at Transcendental Meditation in New York, to whom David Lynch introduced me: thank you for teaching me how to meditate. You are a person whose camaraderie and knowledge I value enormously.

To the many writers, actors, directors, and producers over the years who shared meals, coffee, and conversation with me about all kinds of subjects over both plain and fancy tables: you have kept me grounded and inform all my thinking, including the pondering that went into this book.

To my family and friends—human and animal: to paraphrase a key line from *Lost Highway*, you'll always have me. It isn't quite the doing of specific deeds that matters, or the speaking of specific words: it's the palpable being. Especially my husband Richard, my children David and Holly, and my gloriously golden granddaughter Amara Leigh.

Lastly to absent friends. To the lost.

DAVID LYNCH                    SWERVES

# INTRODUCTION

# THE PERPLEXING
# THRESHOLD
# EXPERIENCE

I am standing on the threshold about to enter a room. It is a complicated business. In the first place I must shove against an atmosphere pressing with a force of fourteen pounds on every square inch of my body. I must make sure of landing on a plank traveling at twenty miles a second round the sun—a fraction of a second too early or too late, the plank would be miles away. I must do this whilst hanging from a round planet headed outward into space, and with a wind of aether blowing at no one knows how many miles a second through ever interstice of my body. The plank has no solidity of substance to step on; it is like stepping on a swarm of flies. Shall I not slip through? No, if I make the venture one of the flies hits me and gives me a boost up again; I fall again and am knocked upwards by another fly; and so on. I may hope that the net result will be that I remain about steady; but if unfortunately I should slip through the floor or be boosted too violently up to the ceiling, the occurrence would be, not a violation of the laws of Nature, but a rare coincidence. These are some of the minor difficulties. I ought really to look at the problem four-dimensionally as concerning the intersection of my world line with that of the plank. Then again it is necessary to determine in which direction the entropy of the world is increasing in order to make sure that my passage over the threshold is an entrance, not an exit.

Verily, it is easier for a camel to pass through the eye of a needle than for a scientific man to pass through a door.

**ARTHUR EDDINGTON, *THE NATURE OF THE PHYSICAL WORLD* (1929)**

You are being invited to enter this study of David Lynch's films from *Lost Highway* (1997) to *Inland Empire* (2006) through a discombobulating doorway because we are about to establish the perplexing threshold experience as the defining characteristic of David Lynch's four most recent films. Simply put, the Lynchian threshold is a key departure point for understanding the arc of action and meaning in each of Lynch's films, from *Lost Highway* to *Inland Empire*. As we get to know it better, we shall see that it has always been a Lynchian staple, but that it began to play a more central role in *Lost Highway* and that it has since become increasingly indispensable to Lynch's cinema. As with Eddington's threshold above, the Lynchian threshold is a passage between two perceptions of the same space, and a wake-up call for a fuller apprehension of our mind/body realities. CAUTION: amazing subatomic spaces ahead.

In Lynch's early works, some of these thresholds occur in dreams, but, from Lynch's earliest days as a filmmaker, his most provocative and evolved depictions of threshold experiences are emphatically *not* dreams or fantasies as we commonly understand them. This became increasingly true in Lynch's later work, in *Lost Highway* and the films that came afterward. The Lynchian threshold, which appears when a troubled consciousness is forced beyond the perceived limits of reality, has the strangeness of dreams. But this experience is the essence of the Lynchian real, even if, like Arthur Eddington's subatomic image of entering a room, it has a

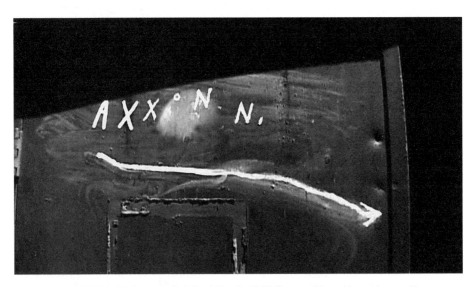

The AXXON. N. doorway in *Inland Empire* (2006), one of Lynch's most evocative perplexing thresholds. Is it easier for a rich man to walk through a needle's eye than for a scientific man to walk through a doorway?

distinctly fantastic aura. Eddington removes the blinders from our vision to reveal the alternate identity of a material world usually imagined only as a solid, stable place. Lynch does the same in his films. Thus, we can find a key to reading Lynch in the room Eddington imagines entering, even though it seems almost cartoonlike in its strangeness. Eddington is summoning up a scientific scenario, not a reverie. The familiarly solid shapes of floorboards are replaced here by the frightening (yet quasi-comical) indeterminacy of the behavior of the particles that make up the floor that Eddington would find if he looked at them in a laboratory. Clearly life is more surprising in the light of modern paradigms than it is when we wear the glasses of classical Newtonian physics, but it is no less real.

But Lynch and Eddington have different motives for surprising us. Eddington is attempting to provide a simple visible parable for complex theories developed by physicists. Lynch has much larger purposes in mind. He is, rather, channeling some paradigms from physics to enable him to talk about the fear, anger, instability, and violence of the modern world; the general problem of the negativity he sees rampant around him. As we shall see, Lynch links these problems to the materialism of American society that has led to a misperception that security abides in our possession of physical objects, and sometimes in our misprision of spiritual energies as things that can be possessed. Lynch's answer to this misunderstanding is to use images that have much in common with the vision of materiality found in modern physics to reveal that materialism can lead us only to fear and despair. At crucial points in Lynch's later films a sudden apprehension of the instability of matter meets socially conditioned eyes. Lynch's protagonists, imbued with a flawed cultural education, react anxiously when they arrive at this threshold. And that's when the stories begin to take shape.

Lynch's films do invoke a hope beyond the broken material plane, but that will be attended to later in this introductory discussion. We must begin by talking about the shattering moments when Lynch opens up thresholds among the multiple levels of the material world for his protagonists. These moments take place when problems arise for which society does not provide an answer—when his characters are struggling with impossible dilemmas or to create something new. The upshots of such Lynchian encounters vary greatly. Fred Madison, in *Lost Highway*, has increasingly disastrous confrontations with the threshold of matter because of his impossible desires concerning his wife, and, as it turns out in the film, concerning sexuality in general. Alvin Straight, in *The Straight Story*, old and ailing, grazes the threshold of matter as he forces materiality to its limits so that he can see his brother, Lyle, who is in even more fragile health; but finally he does succeed in repairing the breech between them before they die. Betty Elms, in *Muholland Dr.*, is catastrophically wounded by her threshold encounters, as her desire for certainty and security persistently leads her away from using her creative potential, while everything around her is silently screaming that she is on the wrong path. Nikki Grace, in *Inland Empire*, is alarmed as she encounters one threshold after another that grants her a spectacular display of matter's limitlessness as she creates the role of Susan Blue for a new film. But, unlike Fred or Betty, she does not retreat in fear. Rather, she accesses the deepest levels of her creativity by opening herself up to boundlessness.

These are the kinds of stories Lynch wants to tell, because of their dramatic intensity and because they reflect the problematic narrow, illusory limits of materialism that he sees as rampant in American life. And his use of images inspired by modern physics helps him to communicate many things about the ways those limits beget fear and impede valid connection with the world. When they are driven outside those illusory limits, Lynch's protagonists are not only surprised by the behavior of things and bodies around them, they also experience a kind of isolation because they are propelled by events into radical conflict with the flawed and often punishing world of "normal" transactions. These are moments that we have all experienced, usually as we suffer problems that have come (temporarily disrupting our lives) and that go in the course of events (leaving us free to scurry back to socially sanctioned normal behavior). However, Lynch's protagonists, especially from *Lost Highway* to the present, experience conflicts with established norms of perception that are so intense that they enduringly disrupt what the characters (and we) doggedly wish to think of as the whole of reality. The extreme drama of that kind of destabilization, and the way the Lynchian story speaks to our hopes for something larger and more meaningful, informs Lynch's films and gives them their power.

The impaired and dangerous view of reality from which Lynch's protagonists start is summed up by Lynch in the "marketplace," a term that will be valuable to our discussion of his films. Lynch's term "marketplace" refers to the problematic limits of ordinary domestic and public transactions. A word Lynch has borrowed from his mentor in things spiritual, the Maharishi Mahesh Yogi, "marketplace" refers to a level of reality at which illusions of stability are promoted by culture. The "marketplace" expresses the Maharishi's sense of the inadequacy of everyday transactions to support human happiness. (Interview of March 18, 2010.)

As it happens, the Lynchian vision of the marketplace significantly resembles the quantum mechanical description of things and bodies. Quantum mechanics envisions a multilevel terrain of things and bodies that involves both apparently solid surfaces and another, subatomic, uncertain level of matter that is anything but solid. So does the Maharishi. Thus the term "marketplace," which Maharishi understands as the opposite of the cosmic reality of Vedic philosophy, also eases us into a discussion of the overlap between the quantum description of the physical world and the Vedic description of the world of matter, and how these two ways of comprehending reality apply to Lynch's work.

This aspect of Lynch's cinematic zeitgeist can be understood in Vedic terms, which describes the physical world as a mask for the larger spiritual realities at the core of the universe, but it can also be understood in terms of the uncertainty principle evolved by physicist Werner Heisenberg in 1927, which offers the general proposition that we can never be in full possession of all the data about any physical event. (What it specifically states is that we can never measure both the position and the momentum of a particle at the same time, but by extension the uncertainty principle destroys earlier assumptions that we could fully understand the behavior of materiality—things and bodies.) A corollary is the assertion by quantum scientists that the harder we look at phenomena the more confused we become about what we see, which runs parallel with mystic Vedic assertion about the deceptiveness of appearances.[1] The confusion exhibited by Lynch's protagonists as they attempt to observe what is around them is a point of convergence between Lynch's cinema, quantum mechanics, and Vedic literature. *Lost Highway* was not the first of Lynch's films to examine that confusion, but it was the first where the confusion became a central aspect of the film's plot and story.

In his feature films from *Eraserhead* on, Lynch has tapped into the uncertainty of matter as a shattering reality that his characters are forced to face. Thus, to understand any of Lynch's films, it is essential to grasp that Lynch's development as a filmmaker has brought his work and his characters more fully into new levels of reality—not into dreams and fantasies—

as his plots thicken. Taking full advantage of the possibilities of cinema, Lynch allows his characters to confront the mysteries of the Lynchverse both in dreams and in their external, physical lives. When Lynch seems to drive his camera into the dark orifice of Jeffrey Beaumont's ear at the beginning of *Blue Velvet*, he is not indicating an external process. But we gain nothing by mistaking Lynch's images of external, material uncertainty for internal fantasies.

Point of conjecture: the Lady in the Radiator (Laurel Near), in *Eraserhead*. Fantasy or a reality built on the metaphor of the subatomic event? When *Eraserhead* first screened, audience reaction to protagonist Henry Spencer's (Jack Nance) unlikely object of desire was that Henry found her when he was lost in fantasy. And that remains the most common initial reaction to this film. But the Lady in the Radiator is arguably the poster girl for the long tenure in Lynch's cinema of a quantum mechanical cinematic vocabulary. The Lady—like much of what troubled or inspired Lynch protagonists see, feel, and experience—contradicts ordinary understanding of how things and bodies work. In her fusion of a Vedic-like blissful harmony with subatomic particle reality, she is more a balance of these two strands of Lynch's vision than we will find in any of his other films. As Lynch worked out the poetics of his complex view of reality, he moved away from the simplicity she represents. The vision of what happens beneath the surface of things became more disorienting and achievement of ecstasy much harder. But I propose that she stands at the very least as a challenge to widespread assumptions about the role of fantasy in Lynch's early works.[2]

For the most part, though, Lynch's early dream/fantasy moments are easy to recognize. Take for example the images that flash through the mind of a puzzled Jeffrey Beaumont (Kyle MacLachlan) in *Blue Velvet*, rising from his subconscious as he probes the dark mystery of villain Frank Booth (Dennis Hopper) and the more nightmarish aspects of the marketplace of Lumberton; and those that appear to the inner eye of Paul Atreides (Kyle MacLachlan) in *Dune*, as he transcends the negotiations of the perverse interplanetary marketplace in which he is embroiled and becomes visible as the savior of his people. These are threshold experiences of sorts, and they are captivating. But distinctive as they may be, they are less challenging than images in Lynch's early cinema that involve an external engagement with the problem of matter itself. For a sense of the difference between Lynch's internal and external narrative strategies we must turn to *Twin Peaks*, where we find not only dreams but brief appearances of perplexing external threshold experiences.

In its unforgettable first appearance, the Red Room, where Special Agent Dale Cooper (Kyle MacLachlan) sees the Little Man (Michael J. Anderson) and hears—though we don't—the name of Laura Palmer's murderer, is obviously a dream. However, by the end of the series Cooper has a full-fledged threshold experience when he finds and enters the Red Room when actually crossing an external threshold in Glastonbury Grove, a stand of trees just outside the town limits—an external event that raises many more questions than Cooper's dreams. We take a wrong turn if we refuse to recognize that the entrance to the Red Room in Glastonbury Grove is external to Cooper's imagination; after all, it is observed by the very pragmatic, non-visionary Sheriff Harry S. Truman (Michael Ontkean). Similarly, we must deal with the fact that Lynch presents as a physical, not a psychological, actuality that Laura's murderer was both BOB and Leland Palmer, two bodies unfathomably occupying the same space as a matter of external fact.

The ability to see that one is two in this case has to do with whether the character is free from conventional habits of perception. Laura bursts free of those constraints near the end of *Twin Peaks: Fire Walk with Me* as she is being sexually violated by Leland/BOB. And the room above the convenience store in *Fire Walk with Me* exists as an actual place that FBI Agent Philip Jeffries (David Bowie) has found in the marketplace where none of the expected laws of matter apply. In fact, when Jeffries makes his report to bureau chief Gordon Cole (David Lynch) in an FBI office building, he himself contradicts the laws of classical physics by both being in two places at once and, at the same time, not being present at all.

In the *Twin Peaks* mythology as well as in *Eraserhead*, Lynch attends to the special, bracketed circumstances of seeing beneath ordinary appearances. In these early instances, the stories also propose a frame of normality to which the audience and the characters may retreat, even if the breaks in ordinary perception are never explained. By neither explaining them away rationally or revealing them as someone's private reverie, Lynch takes great pains to avoid narrating these peculiar moments of external uncertainty as either mistakes in perception or dreams. It has taken great selective amnesia in Lynch's critics to avoid Lynch's definition of these moments as real. ("He *was* here," says Agent Cooper, when Jeffries's image shows up on a security videotape even though the guards at the front desk never saw him.) Here is where concepts imported from quantum physics will help us to meet these aspects of Lynch's work head-on instead of retreating into ideas about purely internal workings of the mind that don't apply.

Where quantum mechanics really comes to the rescue for the critic is when Lynch starts to make films like *Lost Highway*, which predicate an entire plot, not just an isolated event, on the dissolution of the external world into the kind of realities Arthur Eddington faced on entering a subatomically defined room. In *Lost Highway* Lynch's storytelling strategies continually challenge the usual movie definitions of reality as woefully constricted, conjuring the poetry inherent in modern physics. It doesn't take a very large leap of the imagination once we acknowledge the parallel between physics and Lynch's evocations of a multi-leveled materiality from *Lost Highway* on to comprehend why Lynch uses these images. Anyone who has contended with a self in turmoil, engaged in troubling conflicts with our surrounding society, or pushed the boundaries of his/her knowledge will, at least in theory, find that physicists' description of matter on a particle level evokes the experience of learning, discovering, and growing. Any profound revelation breaks up habit, and not in a lighthearted way; it can be a trauma akin to losing coordinates in space and time. Sometimes, and all teachers know this, the inability to deal with that kind of disorientation makes it impossible for some people ever to go beyond their limited comfort zones—that is, makes it impossible to learn, grow, and change.

Specifically, two spatial circumstances, particularly pertinent to Lynch, which can be described only through the vocabulary of uncertainty, are "entanglement" and "superposition." First there is entanglement, a phenomenon observed in the laboratory on the particle level of matter, in which multiple particles respond to stimuli as if they were they were one as well as many—whether or not they are within direct spatial reach of the stimuli or each other. In terms of everyday reality, if we try to envision entanglement on a more complex particle level, the millions of particles that go into making up human beings, we would have the following scenario: physically touching a person standing within reach of one's hand would simultaneously mean touching any number of people with whom that "touchee" was entangled—no matter how distantly located in time and space.

The physicality of entangled people would be so completely merged that in some sense they would each no longer have a completely distinct separateness, nor would the connection require any instrumentality for the connection to assert itself. Entangled people would react as if many were one; they would immediately and spontaneously be in contact with each other across long distances and even time without the help of the technology of Facebook, a smartphone, or Skype.[3] Conversely, continuing to imagine a quantum circumstance on the complex particle level of human beings, one can become many. This eerie subatomic phenomenon, called superposition, allows for one particle to be in two places at exactly the same time—making it impossible to apply pronouns as we do in the ordinary course of things. The particle is both "it" and "they."[4] If you find this hard to follow, it is. But when Betty Elms is both herself and Diane in *Mulholland Dr.*, she is both "she" and "they." And there are important narrative ramifications to this subatomic-like physicality, as we shall discover when we examine that film.

Entanglement and superposition cannot but strike a chord with anyone familiar with Lynch's films from *Lost Highway* to *Inland Empire*. In fact, they should strike a chord with those who only know his earlier, first-stage works. If we understand the workings of superposition, the Log Lady prologue to Episode 29 of *Twin Peaks* enigmatically prepares us for Cooper's final appearance at the end of the episode—which is also the series finale: "And now an ending. Where there was once one, there are now two. Or were there always two? What is a reflection? A chance to see two? When there are chances for reflection, there can always be two or more." In hindsight, we can see that these elliptical words refer to the moment at the end of the episode when protagonist Special Agent Dale Cooper is reflected in his bathroom mirror as the demonic BOB, one who is now two. Or was he always two? We do not have a chance to see this superposition play out in a full narrative, but in Lynch's second-stage films, we do.

Once Fred Madison (Bill Pullman) in *Lost Highway* is forced by misery and frustration beneath the surface of his tormented life, we watch him encounter physical mysteries that resonate of both superposition and entanglement. Fred meets the Mystery Man (Robert Blake) who is in two places at the same time (superposition) and he becomes entangled with a complete stranger, Pete Dayton (Balthazar Getty), such that Fred and Pete are both "he" and "they." By the time Lynch made *Inland Empire*, he was able to conceive of the AXXON N. door, pictured at the head of the chapter, beyond which time and space can no longer maintain conventional shape. After actress Nikki Grace (Laura Dern) opens the AXXON N. door in *Inland Empire*, she is no longer one person, but is entangled with the character she plays. She is no longer contained by one time frame, but finds herself watching herself as she was two days previously. No, if early Lynch protagonists, in films from *Eraserhead* to *Twin Peaks: Fire Walk with Me*, came to their thresholds only intermittently and at least in part as a function of their imaginations, once the protagonists from *Lost Highway* to *Inland Empire* step across the Lynchian threshold, they're completely immersed in the kinds of strange realities that physicists have been talking about for almost a century. These characters are not dreaming.

We thus need to explore anew those moments when Lynch portrays an expanded consciousness in his films and television series, and see if and how he also depicts an entwined, expanded (and uncertain) experience of materiality. In earlier Lynch works, those expansive material experiences, sometimes painful, often joyous, were not as befuddling as they are in *Lost Highway* and Lynch's subsequent films, but they are present. Dr. Frederick Treves (Anthony Hopkins) in *The Elephant Man* experiences pain and confusion of sorts when the different physicality of John Merrick (John Hurt) becomes his threshold into an expanded understanding of the world. When Agent Cooper throws stones at glass bottles in *Twin Peaks* as he is attempting to assemble the clues to the identity of Laura Palmer's murderer, Lynch adds a playful dimension to the intertwining of consciousness and matter. These early Lynchian moments of extraordinary physicality are easier to digest than the physical expansions past ordinary limits that are typical of Lynch's later films.

Ever since *Lost Highway*, Lynch has been playing hardball with the fusion of mind and matter when he tells stories, just in time for the new burst of public interest in quantum mechanics. There are a sprinkling of new books that aim to give the non-physicist a toehold on quantum physics, and even less technologically sophisticated journalistic venues like Salon.com are beginning to speak of cutting-edge science, albeit in souped-up articles with come-hither titles like "When Science Became Spooky."[5] Lynch, as always, is on the cutting edge of this trend, and he is pitching not to any presumed appetite for clever cuteness, but to our highest sensibilities and deepest need to face reality. In the spirit of quantum mechanics, Lynch sees the cultural assumptions of the essential solidity of objects and bodies as a culturally created illusion we are trained to internalize as the *totality* of reality.

Or that is what I will contend as, in the following chapters, I analyze his films from *Lost Highway* to *Inland Empire*, and cast some of this light back on his previous films. I will not disregard consciousness as a touchstone for explicating Lynch's films, since Lynch believes that at the core of being there is nothing but consciousness. But a very important aspect of Lynch's cinema is the way it depicts our flawed understanding of the material plane as an impediment to our ability to experience the heart of reality in the universal consciousness. In short, Lynch's second-stage films insistently depict the disorientation and cruelty that result from the materialist illusion that objects are the source of human security. Only by revealing the shifts of an uncertain physical world is Lynch able to point beyond to what he sees as more sustaining for human life.

## ALL ABOARD FOR THE SECOND STAGE

The main fact of Lynch's films from *Lost Highway* to *Inland Empire* is that while they are importantly concerned with the subconscious, their principal actions bring all levels of character consciousness into radically modern encounter with the world of matter. This will be true in *Lost Highway*, *Mulholland Dr.*, and *Inland Empire*, where such an engagement is intuitively obvious, and it is also true of *The Straight Story*, where nothing that would make Newton blink seems to be going on—at first glance.

*The Straight Story* appears to offer a landscape of certainty that is entirely congruent with our sunniest expectations about rural America. Thus, we might assume that the story of Alvin Straight undermines the existence of a coherently defined second stage to Lynch's cinema of the type I am proposing. However, in Chapter 2, I will show that the idyllic images in *The Straight Story* are the necessary complement to the America of the other three films just because of their seeming contradictions of the mysteries of multi-leveled materiality. A crucial aspect of today's physics is its assertion that under certain conditions the world not only *appears* to have the solidity described by Isaac Newton, but works as if it were governed by classical principles of physics. *The Straight Story* quite brilliantly embodies those conditions, at the same time as the film encourages us to ponder what other possibilities were suppressed to achieve those conditions. *The Straight Story* is told as much on its periphery as through its central action, thereby suggesting why the constrictions with which Straight lives are not problematic for him, although they are catastrophic in the life of Fred Madison and extremely problematic in the lives of the protagonists in *Mulholland Dr.* and *Inland Empire.*

But whatever destiny Lynch gives the protagonists of a particular film, he distinguishes himself among artists with insights parallel to those of contemporary physicists. Unlike the majority of his own characters, Lynch is not driven to radical insecurity or despair. In his pre-Anglican poetry T. S. Eliot expresses fears about his encounters with an uncertain universe that tends to slip and slide beyond our control, as do Samuel Beckett and Franz Kafka. In opening up the boundlessness of physical possibilities, modern physics has at least set the stage for a world depleted of comfort and unity. But Lynch has put a positive slant on a world he acknowledges is filled with frightening spectacles of uncertainty.

Lynch, like a number of contemporary physicists, believes that there is something beyond the instability and uncertain behavior of the world of objects and bodies, and that our encounter with uncertainty can become the path to a grander, absolutely positive vision.[6] Of course, Lynch does not take the experimental route to his positive understanding of the universe, as do physicists in their attempt to prove absolute realities that lie beyond the manifestations of uncertainty. Rather, Lynch fuses his understanding of the illusory qualities of the marketplace with a vision of meaning and unity at the core of existence that he finds within Vedic mysticism. Lynch holds it to be an unalterable truth that a core of unity exists beyond the marketplace and that human perception of its existence is too often blocked by an unnecessary but persistent entrapment within the marketplace. But how best to envision those obstacles as part of a larger, fully coherent cosmos? Lynch depicts the uncertainty of the marketplace using images with a family resemblance to phenomena that have been experimentally documented by physics. However, when he seeks to portray the larger unity of which that uncertainty is a part, he often opts for a model of how the world works that is more like theories proposed by physicists on the fringes of the mainstream academy, the "many worlds" theory. Whatever its deficits in the eyes of hard-nosed quantum scientists, the many worlds construct has proven in Lynch's hands to be a highly expressive metaphor for describing unity in diversity in the cosmos.[7]

While Lynch has never read any of the literature proposing "many worlds" theories, in his post-1997 films he has serendipitously arrived at his own versions of the way some hopeful modern physicists have found unity in diversity by proposing a plethora of fragmentary worlds all forming one meaningful universe. Lynch has also invoked the opposite trajectory which involves the collapse of the many worlds into a black hole that swallows and terminates all possibilities. The potential of the many worlds possible in a limitless universe are vibrantly manifest in *Lost Highway, Mulholland Dr.*, and especially in *Inland Empire*, the only second-stage film in which the possibility of enlightenment is realized. As we shall see, *Mulholland Dr.* is the film in which Lynch uses the analogy of the black hole of physics—and its attendant associations with disintegration and death—to depict the collapse of possibility within a completely corrupt cultural framework.

In Lynch's first-stage cinema, he creates some fascinating representations of *parallel* worlds, but nothing as disturbing to the traditional worldview as what emerges in his later work. For example, in *The Elephant Man* Lynch depicts the inversions of the daytime and nighttime environments in the hospital where John Merrick lives. In his *Twin Peaks* cycle, Lynch evokes the simultaneous existence of connected yet inverse parallel worlds in his depictions of the communities of Twin Peaks and Deer Meadow, which oppose each other in all particulars; what is true in one town is absolutely untrue in the other. Think of the contrasts between the sheriff's station in the two towns and between Norma Jennings's Double R Diner and Hap's Diner. But these are evocative contrasting locations, neither frightening nor in conflict with our ordinary understanding of the physical world, as the phenomena of superposition and entanglement can be. Lynch became more adventurous in *Twin Peaks* when he created spaces of disruption that seriously challenged the broader landscape of normality, such as the co-existence of Twin Peaks and the peculiar physicality of the Red Room, as well as the room over the convenience store. With *Lost Highway*, Lynch thoroughly shattered the larger terrain of the normal, or classical, world of objects through his depictions of the simultaneous, entangled worlds of Fred and Pete. Similarly, in *Mulholland Dr.* the film broke down into contradictory versions of Betty and Diane in superposition. And in *Inland Empire*, Nikki Grace exists in multiple overlapping worlds. By employing entanglement and superposition in conjunction with a "many worlds" paradigm, Lynch creates a complex of circumstances in which the world is both uncertain and also somehow unified.

In sum, Lynch has made use of the metaphorical opportunities offered by the scientifically questionable "many worlds" paradigm to give a very special kind of heft to his vision of a coherent human destiny that exists beyond the uncertain events of the marketplace.

## EDDINGTON'S DOOR, LYNCH'S VEDAS

So, Eddington's doorway leads to a thought-provoking, unrelieved insecurity, the sense of an unreliable world similar to that found in Kafka and Beckett. But for Lynch, the disorientation encountered at the threshold can be positive, a prerequisite to liberation from the false marketplace sense of security. This is the paradox at the heart of Lynch's films: the recognition of uncertainty is mandatory if one is ever to arrive at the kind of stability that some modern physicists fear they destroyed. Physicists—even those who still believe that the universe is essentially unified, despite the discoveries made in quantum science and relativity—require solid proof that beyond quantum mechanical particle behavior there is a world not based on chance, a world that makes perfect sense.[8] Lynch, on the other hand, is a poet who has faith that there exists a stable truth beyond uncertainty, a truth well beyond the cultural discourses that construct a phantom of material stability where there is none.

Lynch's first-stage cinema exhibits varying degrees of such optimism. *Eraserhead* ends in a moment of euphoric bliss just because Henry can cross over into the arguably subatomic physical level of the Lady in the Radiator. Of course, since this is the film's terminal moment, we don't know if this is a brief, temporary release from the dark marketplace of Henry's ordinary life or something more permanent. It's uncertain. Similarly, Jeffrey and Sandy (Laura Dern) are happy at the end of *Blue Velvet*, but the madness associated with "blue velvet" is alive and well, as is clear from the refrain over the image of Dorothy Vallens, who "still can see blue velvet through my tears." Ditto Sailor (Nicholas Cage) and Lula (Laura Dern) at the end of *Wild at Heart*; they have come through their trials together, but in the last image of them kissing, they are not in a particularly stable position, standing as they are on top of the hood of their car in the middle of a traffic jam. In *Dune*, Paul Atreides is portrayed as achieving an elemental stability as the recognized Kwisatz Haderach, but there is something off about the perhaps too-triumphant ending of the film—the only film for which Lynch did not have the right of final cut. Was this the ending Lynch wanted?

More typical of Lynch's originality in his first-stage works is how he expresses a belief in the possibility of fragile and/or uncertain moments of peace and happiness, while at the same time endorsing the uncertainty that rules the landscape of our lives. Lynch's second-stage films are increasingly audacious in their depiction of uncertainty, even as they are more boldly emphatic in their belief that an enduring security is possible for humanity—as long as the shattering of our illusions about matter doesn't paralyze us with fear. Beyond the uncertainty lies the unified field of consciousness at the center of the universe that he deduces from the Holy Vedas, a universe of immense power and beauty beyond the limits of human cultures. The light of that optimistic belief shines on Lynch's second stage films.

Lynch's take on the unseen unity underlying what appears to be nerve-racking fragmentation and discontinuity, then, has some resemblance to Jung's collective unconscious, which I used as a paradigm for interpreting his work in *The Passion of David Lynch*. The Lynchian combination of local fragmentation and global coherence resembles Jung's identification of a unifying set of innate mythologies beneath the fragmented variety and mutability of the world of experience. Both posit a cosmic sense of human rootedness in something larger than history, larger than the parameters of ordinary perception. But it is now clear that Lynch is not referring to Jung but to Vedic literature, and the difference is significant.

As a mystic of the Vedic variety, Lynch's faith is more stable and impervious to political and cultural perversion than was Jung's psychological model. The problem of Jung's cosmology was dramatically revealed when it was corrupted by Hitler as justification for his twisted dogma that the Germans were the Master Race with a mission to subjugate and/or kill all "inferior" people. Nazism allied Jung's concept of the collective unconscious with a belief in the "volk," which stipulated a separate collective unconscious for each culture. Thus Jung's theory about a universal human link became, in Hitler's mad mind, the basis for a vicious hierarchy of human value. It is of course true that the Vedas were the holy literature of an India afflicted for many centuries by a terrible caste system in which the lives of the lower classes, especially the "untouchables," were painfully afflicted by poverty and all manner of suffering. However, it is an explicit tenet of Lynch's cosmology of the unified field that it precedes all national cultures, all developments of civilization on earth, even the structure of matter. It is being itself and is, if human beings can access it, the source of abundant, boundless creativity, love,

15

and power for everyone. There are no racial, ethnic, national, or gender preconditions or qualifications.

Because the unified field precedes all form, it is also almost fully un-representable—at least it has been to date in Lynch's films—and thus does not take the shape of any aspect of any culture that is privileged over any other culture. What Lynch finds representable are the macro and micro visions of materiality that comprise the surfaces and lower levels of the marketplace, and this is what most characterizes the look of a Lynch work. It is also what joins the look of a Lynch work to today's physics, for which the landscape of matter comprises the doubleness of the Newtonian mac-rovision and the quantum microvison as the total picture of the world of matter.[9] At the same time, Lynch implies a space that exists beyond the marketplace. Here I will introduce another term from Lynch's vocabulary, also borrowed from the Maharishi. That term is "the Palace," and it refers to the great, radiant unity beyond the bi-leveled marketplace. What Lynch has so far integrated into his films of the Palace is only suggestive of its presence and generally makes itself visible as light or particle-like images.

Lynch's account of the relationship between the marketplace and the Palace completes his cosmology. He adheres to the standard Vedic creation story that matter initially came into existence out of the boundlessness of the Unified Field—"the Palace, being our connection to it." Lynch un-derstands the Vedas as the act of creation from which the marketplace emerged. The Vedas were originally oral not written, and, as Hindu cre-ation mythology has it, it was from the sounds, syllables, and gaps in its poetry that the solid-seeming appearances that we think of as reality emerged. Lynch pictures this process quite vividly, as a magical dynamic in which the syllables and gaps of the Vedas occur in sequence, but are, at the same time simultaneous.

Similarly, in his films, Lynch likes to evoke creation mythologies, like the "snow" on television sets that precedes the appearances of images and the pulsating field of blue at the beginning of *Twin Peaks: Fire Walk with Me* from which the film emerges. There is also the intrusion of static, col-ored lights; flashing bright white light; and the rudiments of sound that Lynch uses when he suggests the emergence of a threshold experience in his narratives. Because of that imagery, and because I know Lynch has read *The Tibetan Book of the Dead*, which is in sympathy with Vedic visions of the illusory nature of physical appearances, I would like to add it as another interesting reference for reading Lynch's work. The images in *The*

*Tibetan Book of the Dead* form a parallel with what Lynch sometimes shows onscreen during crucial moments of transition between the levels of the marketplace and between the marketplace and the Palace. I don't feel I can claim it as a definitive influence on Lynch's work, since Lynch has not spoken directly to me about it in the way we have discussed the Vedic books. But it may be heuristically helpful since it is a text that interests Lynch, and it contains images with vivid resemblances to what Lynch's protagonists experience as they go through their changes.

The *Tibetan Book of the Dead* deals with the connections between consciousness and materiality at the time of transition between life and death. While it can be helpful for understanding death scenes in Lynch's cinema, it is even more enlightening as a paradigm for Lynch's depictions of life-and-death-like transitions, such as the moment when Fred turns into Pete in *Lost Highway*. The *Tibetan Book of the Dead* details the events and images that occur in the space between two cosmic states of being, a lacuna that in the vocabulary of mysticism is called the Bardo, which means gap. In Lynch's second-stage films, traumatic transitions and the interim space between two states of being are a crucial part of his narratives and suggest what lies beyond the marketplace. Where there are visually portrayed cracks in the bi-level marketplace, we can glimpse something else.

The *Book of the Dead* describes the Bardo in ways that are tantalizingly similar to the images Lynch uses in his moments of radical transformation. In the Bardo, as recounted in the book, what the dying person perceives is the flashing of lights, and the appearance of colors, and also transitional figures who may be either consoling or frightening. Similarly, in the transitions that Lynch depicts in *Lost Highway*, *Mulholland Dr.*, and *Inland Empire*, the characters also are assaulted by lights, colors, and transitional figures. Lynch's changes never take place without sound and light in play.[10]

Another way in which the Bardo forms an enlightening parallel with Lynch's films is that in the moment of the Bardo the dying person either falls into a lower position than he/she occupies in his/her present incarnation, or grows into an evolved life form. If the person in question is too terrified to face the fearfulness of the transition, he or she will be doomed to a rebirth into an even more troubled and miserable existence than the one he/she is leaving.[11] If he or she is able to avoid paralyzing fear, and to brave the anxiety of the transition, he or she will move into a higher state of existence. As we shall see, this is also true of the characters undergoing change in Lynch's films. In his cinema from *Lost Highway* to the present, characters debilitated by fear at the moment of transition morph into circumstances of increased misery. If they can withstand the pressures at the threshold, they can move toward the Palace, the essence of security in the Lynchian universe.

A fusion of mysticism with quantum paradigms is at the very least perplexing to anyone familiar with the actual state of authoritative quantum mechanics. No mainstream physicist connects the strange effects of entanglement and superposition with the reincarnation so basic to the narratives of *The Book of the Dead*, nor with the Lynchian mythology of the marketplace and the Palace that informs his articulation of metamorphosis, inversion, and parallel existences. But this kind of synthesis is endemic to Lynch's cinematic poetry, and its blend of finite materiality and universal boundlessness is at the heart of those visual and narrative events that are most closely associated with Lynch's distinctiveness as a director.

## A VEDIC QUANTUM OF SOLACE

All told, it is counterproductive to say about Lynch's cinema, "The stuff I don't recognize as materially real is a dream, and the stuff that looks like what I expect the material world to be is reality." This formulation ignores Lynch's revolutionizing of the American cinematic vocabulary about space that brings it into line with the observations of cutting-edge science. The yearning and/or tormented consciousness of the Lynch protagonist cannot be understood unless we also understand its relationship to quantum phenomena. We should listen carefully to Lynch's formulation of the threshold encounter so crucial to his cinema: "Doors and corridors to doors can allow you not only a way toward a different room, a different place, but also a different world." (Interview, March 18, 2010) These worlds are not dreams; like the AXXON. N. doorway, they are portals into a universe beyond marketplace illusions and limitations that lead to a new apprehension of space and time. As the gift of vision is proffered, it opens up the possibility of enlightenment. Lynch's characters often misunderstand the meaning of the portal, but sometimes they successfully make their way through. Second-stage films require the lenses of physics *and* mysticism.

Why bother with something so way-out, you may be wondering. But is it? What Lynch is doing is inescapably of the world as we culturally are coming to know it. His films are an exceptionally original and important part of an evolution already in progress. Integrating modern physics into the cinematic representation of the material plane of existence is as inevitable now as integrating modern psychology into film narratives once was. Perhaps film has been slower to catch up with Albert Einstein and Niels Bohr than it was to latch onto Freud and Jung, but quantum insights are already part of cinema culture and began to be well before Lynch came onto the scene. In *The Passion of David Lynch*, I traced Lynch's interest in a Jungian kind of consciousness back to Alfred Hitchcock and Orson Welles.[12] We can also trace back to Hitchcock and Welles intimations of the macro and microvision of materiality that characterizes modern physics. For the sake of brevity, here is one example.

*Rear Window* (1954) is Lynch's favorite Hitchcock film, and interestingly it is the one in which Hitchcock most deeply undermines the possibility of the completely objective observer of classical science. Some critics have been tantalized by the theatrical artificialities of L. B. Jeffries' (James Stewart) apartment courtyard in *Rear Window*. Others have interpreted the courtyard's windows as reflexive allusions to filmmaking. However, when we consider Jeffries, confined to a chair by a broken leg as nothing but an observer, the theatricality of the urban setting begins to suggest Hitchcock's intuitive grasp of the mysteries of modern physics. Think of all the lenses involved in Jeffries' surveillance of his courtyard. Think about how at first, Jeffries seems to be objective, safely, snoozingly detached from what he sees, and how increasingly there seems to be no objectivity possible. Jeffries is increasingly involved in what he sees and his involvement changes everything about a landscape that at first seems entirely comprehensible. Or for a while it does. The sense that nothing in the material world exists detached from what is perceived by the observer, who can never be "objective," is crucial to the uncertainty principle. *Rear Window* is virtually an object lesson in how observation changes what is observed. Of course, the conventions of the detective story that Hitchcock works within bring the film back to the comfort zone of "normality." Jeffries and his lady love Lisa Fremont (Grace Kelly) ultimately do extract certainties from the situation and separate themselves from the murderer they have been watching. As Lynch narrates his stories, the marketplace never yields certainty.

This points toward the difference between what Lynch is doing with his cutting-edge sensibility and what we find in most of American pop culture, even in the films of the great Hitchcock. When pop culture visualizes the microvision of quantum mechanics in its fictions or incorporates it into its narratives, it quickly recuperates the normality of the macrovision. Arguably, the disaster movies that began in the 1960s to depict circumstances in which the mammoth, seemingly eternal structures of the modern city fly apart are flirting with a quantum mechanical sensibility. But they do not, as Lynch does, experiment with cosmic transformation as a potential result of trauma. Similarly, though the *Matrix* trilogy (Dirs. Andy and Lana Wachowski, 1999–2003) includes much greater violations of classical space and time than either Hitchcock or the basic Hollywood disaster film, they ultimately restore a comforting Newtonian normality. The world of the trilogy is *initially* lost in false images of solid materiality that are punctured by Agent Smith (Hugo Weaving), who attacks our hero, Neo (Keanu Reeves), in frightening demonstrations of superposition. But it all turns out to be a plot, not a true mystery of space, a computer error that has allowed a mere virus, Agent Smith, to create havoc. Once Smith is eradicated by Neo, in the third film of the trilogy, ordinary physicality is recuperated and all questions are answered. Cue a sigh of relief. The *Matrix* films did not trouble audiences. They ultimately did what Lynch will not do: define the instabilities of the marketplace as fixable, dreams from which we can awaken. The *Matrix* trilogy is what cinema looks like when it translates quantum insights about materiality into nothing more than interior states, dreams, and fantasies, a far cry from what Lynch is up to.[13]

But Lynch isn't completely alone as a filmmaker who, in order to deal with modern dilemmas, uses science as a part of his cinematic vocabulary without reaching a closure that invalidates the uncertain aspects of the material world. Outside of the Hollywood canon, there are independent American and European filmmakers who also—in a way that puzzles, outrages, and sometimes thrills audiences—update our understanding of space, time, and materiality. Among their creations, we may count a number of films that enduringly stand, along with Lynch's second stage films: Alain Resnais' *Last Year at Marienbad* (1961); Andrei Tarkovsky's *Solaris* (1972); Luis Buñuel's *That Obscure Object of Desire* (1977); David Kronenberg's *EXistenZ* (1999); Wong Kar-wai's *2046* (2004), and Apichatpong Weerasethakul's *Uncle Boonmee Who Can Recall his Past Lives* (2010). Resnais' spa in *Marienbad* depicts the rigid, elegant Newtonian clarity of what is representable in the space in opposition to the world outside, which is so mysterious that it can never be shown. Tarkovsky's sea of Solaris brings to a crisis of sanity all the astronauts who live with its ability to render as physical realities images it copies from inside the minds of the characters. Conchita, the seductress played by both Carole Bouquet and Angela Molina in Buñuel's *That Obsure Object of Desire*, in the tradition of quantum superposition, not only drives protagonist Mathieu (Fernando Rey) crazy with frustration and confusion, but also prefigures the explosion of the world as we know it. The fusion of game and reality in *EXistenZ* is such that, as with entanglement, it is impossible to say where the boundaries between the two exist. *Uncle Boonmee Who Can Recall His Past Lives*, Apichatpong Weerasethakul's consideration of an ancient Thai civilization that is disappearing in the face of modernity, offers another (unusual) fusion of Eastern mysticism with quantum mechanics in its presentation of the film's landscape. Although none of these filmmakers would use Lynch's terms, in fact the protagonists of all these more tentative approaches to using cutting-edge physics in cinema can be said to be trapped in the marketplace. Unlike Lynch's characters, however, for the most part, they have nowhere else to go even if they want to. David Kronenberg and Luis Buñuel intuit no Palace beyond the confusion of day-to-day negotiations.

There has already been some piecemeal critical attention paid to the unexpected behavior of external time and space in Lynch's films and television. One noteworthy fragmentary discussion of the modern representation of time in the *Twin Peaks* cycle occurs in Allister Mactaggart's *The Film Paintings of David Lynch: Challenging Film Theory*. In an early chapter, Mactaggart notes the way Lynch bends linear time at the end of *Twin Peaks: Fire Walk with Me* (1992), a prequel like no other in which earlier events dramatized after the later events have already been displayed in a preceding film fold cause and effect back in on each other, a phenomenon not possible under the rules of Newtonian mechanics but much discussed by quantum physicists. As Mactaggart says of the end of *Fire Walk with Me*, when we see Laura's body wrapped in plastic and floating in the water, soon to be discovered by Pete Martell (Jack Nance) in the opening scene of the television series that already aired, "But this ending is really a beginning, although it is the beginning of what has already been and now is no longer as it previously was, because of these closing moments, which have, in one sense, already taken place, and which predate . . . the murder of Laura Palmer and the detection of her killer. Therefore this conclusion . . . cannot be clearly delineated from the events that predate it, nor those that follow afterwards. So we do not have a clear sense of cause and effect any longer, nor closure to the story."[14] This small sound bite, which acknowledges the presence of circular time in *Twin Peaks*, is a particularly relevant example of why we need physics as a referent for critiquing Lynch's work, especially his second-stage films.

## MOVING FROM HERE TO HERE

Lynch's vision of the meeting between the enormity of consciousness and the instability of matter requires that he effect major renovations to the linear narrative. While ordinary narratives that move the protagonist toward a goal are part of both Lynch's first- and second-stage films, a more important narrative goal is to move from "here to here," to see the moment of being in an expanded way. In Lynch's early films, proceeding from "here" to "here" is only to some small extent vouchsafed by the characters. In Lynch's first feature film, *Eraserhead*, protagonist Henry (Jack Nance) is given the most latitude of any characters in Lynch's first-stage cinema. He negotiates the levels of the marketplace to arrive at where he first began, once a dark, frustrating here, now a "here" filled with light and satisfaction. Lynch's next films—*The Elephant Man*, *Dune*, and *Blue Velvet*—are more commercial, drawing back from the radical sensibility of *Eraserhead*, but there is still some sense of evolving from here to here. Dr. Frederick Treves not only has removed John Merrick from the world of the freak show, but also has an altered sense of his "here" as a scientist. At the end of *Dune*, Paul Atreides has not only become an intergalactic leader, he also sees into the heart of the universe he lives in, not just the encyclopedic facts of it we once saw him study on his computer. And, if Jeffrey has rescued Dorothy Vallens, more importantly he now sees Lumberton in its entirety, not just from a partial perspective.

The *Twin Peaks* television series achieves a far more fully articulated sense of the journey from here to here. Special Agent Cooper has satisfied his legal duties in identifying Leland Palmer as the one who killed Laura, but in the final series episode, Episode 29, he opens up many more questions than he has answered. When Cooper physically crosses the threshold in Glastonbury Grove and actually enters the Red Room he once only saw in a dream, he is greeted by a demonstration of the invisible level of matter when his coffee randomly metamorphoses from ordinary liquid to a frozen block and then into an oily substance. When the giant and the

Little Man are spoken of as "one and the same," Cooper is introduced to the concept that at base all matter is the same, no matter how different its larger manifestations may look from a macro, Newtonian perspective.

There is also a physics lesson involved when the Little Man (Michael J. Anderson) goes through a series of behaviors that have no conventional narrative connection with Cooper's presence in the Red Room—his desire to rescue his girlfriend Annie (Heather Graham). The Little Man's body and voice point toward the microvision of quantum understanding of matter. He alludes to the string theory of matter, which proposes that all materiality begins with infinitesimally small strings that vibrate. Different vibrations promote different forms of matter. The Little Man suggests that he is fundamentally a vibration, a la the string theory, in both the series' Red Room and the *Fire Walk With Me* Red Room, when he spontaneously creates a pulsating sound by tapping his mouth with his hand as he is emitting a noise. When the Little Man speaks in a palindrome—"WOW BOB WOW"—he displays language that is completely reversible, which points to another quantum theory about materiality. Modern physics theorizes the conundrum of time reversal symmetry, which says that every physical process is the same whether moving forward or backward in time, a contradiction of common-sense reality, which Lynch uses to interesting advantage, as when in *Twin Peaks: Fire Walk with Me* the sequence of eating garmonbozia (the strange Lynchian word for both sadness and creamed corn) is displayed moving forward and backward. Cooper is also introduced to the doppelganger, the sign of the presence of "many worlds," at least the parallel worlds of the negative and the positive Red Room, as he encounters two versions of the Little Man and of Laura, both the demonic and the friendly and helpful.[15]

In *Fire Walk with Me*, we find both a linear narrative movement toward the moment of Laura's murder, and Laura's non-linear progress toward a post-mortem "hereness" through the vision of her angel in the Red Room that allows her to understand the essential goodness of the universe despite the horror of her experience in the marketplace. *Wild at Heart*, sandwiched between *Twin Peaks* and *Fire Walk with Me*, also contains a harbinger of the goodness of the cosmic "here"—the goofy vision of Glinda, the Good Witch (Sheryl Lee) who persuades Sailor to open his heart to love. The direction taken by Laura and Sailor has been as much a voyage into these non-linear visions as it has been toward the linear aspects of the plot, Laura's death and Sailor's full union with Lula.

In *Lost Highway*, *Mulholland Dr.*, and especially *Inland Empire*, as we shall see, Lynch is much more innovative in the use of narrative time and space to arrive at a deeper sense of being "here." In these films, instead of simply juxtaposing linear narrative with a non-linear motion that takes the protagonist below the surface, Lynch thoroughly reshapes the linearity of the narrative structure through disruptions and narrative time that runs in a circular and curved pattern rather than in a direct motion from Point A (origin) to Point B (terminus). In these films, Point A and Point B are, paradoxically, the same—Point A, in fact—but more has been revealed by the end of the narrative of the starting point. In the second-stage films, that is, Lynch creates narrative that recalls the end of T. S. Eliot's Four Quartets: "and the end of our exploring/Will be to arrive where we started/And know the place for the first time." For example, in *Lost Highway*, the adventures of Fred Madison lead in a circular path from the announcement of the death of Dick Laurent to the same announcement in a way that suggests, paradoxically, that the future was already there before Fred began his story, as if a full understanding of the "here" would involve the scraping away of the surface of the now to arrive at the future, rather than a linear progression toward it.

The Lynchian voyage from "here" to "here" refuses to reconcile harmony and stability with the ordinary plane of physical existence, but it does acknowledge security that can be reached beyond ordinary, temporal and spatial boundaries. Once beyond, there are rewards for suffering and punishment for pain inflicted. In Lynch's first-stage films, this is clearest at the end of *Fire Walk with Me*, when Laura's suffering and struggles against BOB, unredressed in her life, are rewarded by a new form of understanding and peace when she finds her angel. In that film, Lynch, less complexly than he later will, invokes the Red Room as some form of "here" (anew) that is also an afterlife. But in the second-stage films, Lynch achieves a much more hard-won closure with characters who are literally where they always were but newly washed in the light of revelation and ethical consequences in a way that fuses Lynch's allusions to modern physics with the moral universe of the Vedas in a vividly characteristic Lynchian manner.

## REAPING WHAT WE SOW

The ethical and moral dimensions of moving from an unaware "here" to an illuminated "here" as his protagonists move beyond the illusion of a certain physical here, is where Lynch's films tap most potently into Vedic-inspired mysticism. In the discussions of the four films that are the primary subject of this study, we watch the consequences of the inability or refusal to move from here to here. But there is always the implication, and sometimes the revelation, that as the Lynchian protagonist moves more confidently away from the illusions (and corruptions) of an uncertain plane of objects and bodies, he/she can move toward a clear apprehension and experience of a just and stable universe. The reverse, of course, is also true. When we reject enlightenment we reap the wild wind of punishment for inhumane behavior. Lynch has a deep commitment to the belief that, even if it takes numerous lifetimes, we do reap what we sow because: "[W]hat you do to anyone else, you're in effect doing to yourself . . ." (March 18, 2010). *What you do to anyone else, you're in effect doing to yourself.* This is the essence of Lynch's belief in karma and the moral center of his cinema.

As we shall see, Fred Madison's perverse choice of cultural illusions over the call to him of a large, generous universe of limitless possibilities yields what looks as if it will be a long cycle of descent into painful negativity in *Lost Highway*. Similarly we shall see that Betty Elms reaps what she sows in *Mulholland Dr.* because she has allowed herself to be driven by Hollywood's marketplace culture into bitterness and despicable acts. In *The Straight Story*, by contrast, Alvin is blessed by the universe for miraculously transforming limitation into limitlessness. Similarly, but even more emphatically, in *Inland Empire*, Nikki Grace achieves karmic happiness because she is part of a magical metamorphosis within the boundaries of the Hollywood studio system that has brought her from a corrupt Hollywood "here" to a thoroughly illuminated creative "here."

All of these consequences will be discussed in the appropriate chapters in terms of what it means to pay for what you have done, to reap what you have sown, a process to which the police and courts are sometimes laughably, sometimes painfully peripheral. These discussions will be informed by the necessary references to the paradigms of modern physics and Vedic mysticism we have outlined here. The transitions and transformations on which we will focus are forms of change—*like* reincarnation, although they are not precisely that. The necessity for these reincarnation-like developments in Lynch's work is dictated by Lynch's interest in identifying what kinds of responsibilities are so indelible that they cannot be avoided, even in an uncertain world, by changes in our circumstances of any kind, and what kinds of rewards belong to us even after "the great change": death.[16]

In sum, while it is true that in Lynch's depiction of marketplace space the order of cause and effect often becomes slippery; one person can be in two places at the same time; and doorways may lead to many worlds, it is also true that his second-stage films are infused with the presence of a cosmic fair-mindedness. Lynch's stories are full of universal justice, separate and apart from the typical failures of the marketplace police and courts in his films. This sets him apart from most other artists who have explored space and time in all their quantum uncertainty, for example Franz Kafka, with whom many physicists identify. Lynch feels close to him too, but Lynch speaks not to a Kafkaesque fear and trembling, but to our desire not to be lost out here in the stars.

Kafka, and Samuel Beckett too, are among the great artists who explore the loss of the human dimensions of control, identity, and, above all, the stability of wisdom implied by uncertainty; they share with physics an intuition of the indeterminacy of our world and are often viewed by physicists as engaging the insights of quantum mechanics on its own terms. In David Albert's words, "It seems to me that what [modern] science has to offer us intellectually is exactly the opposite of wisdom. Science presents us with a picture of who we are that it's really not possible to fully take in and remain a human being. With this mechanical reduction of who we are, I think that the aesthetic sensation associated with taking in scientific theories is something like panic or something like the uncanny or the uncanny in the psychological sense of inanimate things looking animate. That's what I think science does to you if you really open yourself to it. It produces the opposite sensation of being settled." (David Albert, Appendix II, "New Age Science.") What could better sum up the relationship between physics and Kafka or Beckett?

Lynch is not of this group. Rather, although he intuits a world around him that is filled with the uncanniness of uncertainty, he creates art that is fundamentally anchored in a unified and certain Vedic universe beyond the uncertain landscape into which the characters are propelled. For Lynch, the insights of modern physics do not describe the entirety of the universe but a falsely limited, culturally created plane of existence from which there can be a release, though not all can avail themselves of the power out there, at least not within the parameters of some of the narratives. So while Lynch overlaps with Kafka, he is not completely Kafkaesque.

Moreover, whether his characters do or do not find liberation, Lynch does not tell their stories as a conscious response to the insights of modern physics. As I wrote in *The Passion of David Lynch*, by his own word, ninety percent of the time he doesn't know what he is doing when he makes films. Rather, Lynch channels images put into the zeitgeist by cutting-edge physics that empower him to visualize the reality of the marketplace as he sees it. Journeys through the marketplace appear to him and call to him to tell the story. It might be a story in which, as in *Lost Highway* and *Mulholland Dr.*, the seemingly effective control of the marketplace version of the "boss of it all" promotes the very fear its authority is supposed to cure and destroys his protagonist. Or it might be a tale as in *The Straight Story*, in which Lynch can also imagine how a steely determination can work despite the uncertainty of the world of things and bodies. Or as in *Inland Empire*, the story could revolve around a protagonist who has the courage to embrace the uncertainty that surrounds her and so discovers a benign universe beyond what she sees and succeeds on that basis. It all depends, as we shall see, on what happens at the moment of that perplexing threshold.

# CHAPTER ONE
# LOST HIGHWAY: "YOU'LL NEVER HAVE ME"

It is an inestimably deep feature of the way we approach the world conceptually . . . that something called locality is true. . . . We assume that in order for something here to have an effect on something there it needs to be the case that there is some continuous, unbroken chain of mediating subcauses and effects stretching from here to there in space and time. So for example, if waving my hand here causes somebody to be hit over there, it's because light is bouncing off my hand and traveling and causing a signal. . . . Any effect on anything that is not directly next to you is necessarily indirect. It occurs through the agency of other things between you and them. It's this principle that quantum mechanics apparently violates, that entangled particles violate. So it's much, much weirder than the effect of going fast [a high speed connection between objects not in each other's presence, which would constitute locality]. It's that the effect doesn't go at all. It's that you have a fundamental violation of this principle of locality.

**PROFESSOR DAVID Z. ALBERT, INTERVIEW, APPENDIX II**

If we analyze *Lost Highway* from what we know to be David Lynch's perspective, that we live in a universe of unbounded possibility, the first film of Lynch's second stage reads easily as an account of the ways in which protagonist Fred Madison and the society around him close themselves off from the freedom that is the natural prerogative of humanity. In this tale of violence and seduction, Lynch gives us no character with whose point of view we can identify. Rather, he sets us the task of being active spectators who do not lose ourselves in the confusion, fear, absurdity, and suffering of Fred and all those around him. They are all under enormous pressure to misread every sign of the miracle of existence through blinkered eyes. We don't have to.

To allow us to distinguish ourselves from Fred, Lynch surrounds him with astonishing events which we are free to see differently from the way he does, by referencing a reality very much like that of the non-locality at the heart of quantum mechanics. The non-locality of modern physics, as explained in the quotation of Professor David Z. Albert above, describes connections between objects and bodies that are not based on direct or indirect contact, but rather manifest as simultaneous, spontaneous links among particles. Particles are, when they are behaving non-locally, both themselves and other particles—at the same time. This state in which a particle is both one and many simultaneously has no relationship to any of the time/space causalities recognized by classical theories about matter. The non-locality that is part of modern physics infinitely and provocatively multiplies the kinds of events that are possible in the material world.

Non-locality in *Lost Highway* creates a provocative and cinematically revolutionary interplay between what is possible and what is impossible and what it means to refuse to recognize boundless possibility. At the same time that Fred early and often rejects and frets over revelations of the boundless possibilities of matter, which seem hallucinatory but are in fact real, he locks his focus onto only one option for satisfaction, and that option *is* impossible. Fred is consumed with an unreciprocated desire for his wife, Renee (Patricia Arquette). Ironically, all the while that Fred struggles in vain to win Renee's love, he is busy chasing away signs that there are many more options for him than he realizes. Life is mysterious and open. Fred is closed. Unidentified people are speaking enigmatically on his external intercom and leaving videotapes on his front steps for no apparent reason. But mystery doesn't pique Fred's interest. Fred is always in the process of creating the worst of all possible worlds for himself.

As we move through *Lost Highway*, at every turn, Fred gives a negative interpretation to all the options repeatedly revealed to him (and to us) by means of what I shall call non-local images, though Lynch would certainly not use this terminology, that uniquely depict for us the kind of instability that Lynch does in fact see in marketplace physicality. Sometimes Fred spins negativity on his own initiative and sometimes he does so because he is encouraged to think pessimistically by those around him—straight-arrow government officials, gangsters, and very peculiar strangers alike. On his own steam, Fred is annoyed rather than curious, when a couple of anonymous videotapes show up at his house. Later, when he is thrown into contact with a Mystery Man who can be in two places at once, Fred is virtually directed by the oddball stranger to be anxious when the guy presents his unusual physicality as highly sinister and threatening instead of as remarkable. It can, of course, be argued that all these oddities *do* have awful consequences, particularly a third videotape that arrives unbidden on Fred's doorstep to become the basis for the death sentence he receives after being convicted of the murder of his wife. But as the movie unfolds, the dark events that beset Fred come more and more to seem as if they have been created by the very unfortunate attitudes with which Fred and the society around him approach life.

As we explore the film we shall see that what Lynch shows us is that it isn't the strange events that lead to unfortunate consequences, but a marketplace habit of seeking certainty where there is none. There isn't any certainty that Fred's wife is dead, but the highly dubious videotape is interpreted as if it were conclusive, and Fred is convicted for murder. On the other hand, when large, uncertain energies incontrovertibly manifest themselves with such vigor that they allow Fred to be liberated from his death-row cell, neither Fred nor the penal system officials ever regard the unexpected mutability of matter with either wonder or the kind of delighted curiosity demonstrated by the incandescent FBI (Very) Special Agent, Dale Cooper in *Twin Peaks*. In this second-stage Lynchian universe, Fred, the police, and the hierarchy of the prison system are only interested in finding ways back to the old limits. The authorities and some vicious and depraved gangsters—quite as married to boundaries as the law enforcers are—define the marketplace that surrounds Fred as an environment that actively forms a barrier against all that is expansive and open.

Contrasting with the cultural inclination toward ideas of certainty and neat boilerplate order in this marketplace, Fred's "jail break" exists as a spontaneous, expansive transformational energy that demonstrates, at the very least, that there is a great deal more extra-cultural freedom possible than Fred imagines. True, the transformation is very painful for Fred, and frightening as well, but when all is said and done, isn't it likely that Lynch imagines that it wouldn't have been such an excruciating ordeal if Fred were more receptive and open to the power that sweeps him to freedom? For when Fred finds himself being transformed into Pete Dayton, a young garage mechanic who is not under sentence of death for Renee's murder, and the baffled but essentially uncurious prison authorities are, as a result, forced to release this unknown occupant from

Fred's cell, the metamorphosis is in keeping with Lynch's beliefs about a limitless universe. Perhaps Fred's unexpected arrival at a threshold experience would have been quite different if Fred had looked at his liberation through Lynch's eyes. As it is, though, Lynch stands at a distance from his protagonist. Fred's is an unreliable point of view in his story, particularly as he is unmoved by the miraculous second chance offered to him and uses his regained freedom to continue to grasp for the same old illusory form of control. (I use the term unreliable point of view the way the term "unreliable narrator" has historically been used to describe an erroneous, first person narrative perspective in a novel or short story.)[1]

Given Lynch's understanding of the world, it is fair to say that Fred's failure to understand that there is something wonderful about the boundless power that has transformed every atom of his body makes his point of view "unreliable." It doesn't get any more liberated than the non-local experience of transcending what we think of as solid matter and the usual restrictions of time and space. So while this event does not register with Fred or any of the characters as a sudden eruption of freedom, wouldn't Lynch's ideal spectator realize it is just that?

Like Fred and the forces of law and order in *Lost Highway*, most critics have not read Fred's metamorphosis into Pete as a sign of a world in which anything is possible, but as part of a dream or delusion. That perspective is based on assumptions about the limitations of matter that Lynch does not share. If we did not have access to his assumptions, the case for considering the metamorphosis a physical event would not be stronger than any other theoretical conjecture about it. But now we do have access to what Lynch thinks, and that must make all the difference. The prevalent emphasis on Fred's inner life in dealing with Fred's physical transformation, then, sets roadblocks between the Lynchian film and its audience. Yes, Lynch believes that the consciousness at the heart of cosmic being has created matter, but Fred is not the unified field. His individual consciousness, like that of all other human beings, is inevitably called upon to deal with the matter external to him that comes from the unified field, as well as with its uncertainty.[2] As Fred's transformation into Pete is dramatized, it is no dream, and if it is a fugue state, the name Lynch likes to give this transformation, it is not a simple internal psychological fugue, for Fred is not creating the transformation.[3] That his escape, in opposition to all expectations, fails to alert any of the characters to the illusions they cherish about the solidity of matter is the heart of the narrative dilemma in *Lost Highway*. Of course, Lynch is not literally suggesting that the transformation of Fred into Pete is possible. This is a movie that harnesses the power of the imagination; it is not a documentary. Lynch is using the metaphoric power of fiction to invoke the way our reductive habits of perception prohibit us from experiencing and understanding the boundlessness of our freedom.

Kicking off Lynch's second-stage cinema, *Lost Highway* is notable for the debut within its narrative of the Lynchian threshold experience. In his earlier films and in his television series, the threshold was a brief encounter. In his second-stage cinema, it takes on a new role as a narrative catalyst for a journey straight into the uncertainty of the marketplace. Miserably stuck in the marketplace, with its fabricated certainties, Fred takes a turn toward the Kafkaesque. ("Kafkaesque" is not merely a fanciful adjective here; Kafka's picture is on the cover of Lynch's shooting script of *Lost Highway*.) As with the prescient works of Kafka, Lynch's provocative pictures of the uncertain material world in *Lost Highway* enable him to speak vividly and piercingly to his audience of a particular kind of trauma, the problems of a culture lost in the illusions of how we are supposed to see things and bodies and how we are supposed to manage them.

In kinship with the literature of Kafka, with its cockroach heroes and mysteriously doomed men, in Lynch's *Lost Highway*, Fred finds himself spontaneously entering into a new relationship with physical reality. But unlike in Kafka's tales, Fred is not helplessly lacking in resources; he only thinks he is. Unlike Kafka's rudderless heroes, Fred has to work to continue on a path of misdirection. While life keeps showing him the wonders of existence, encouraged by his society, he invariably takes the wrong lesson from events, becoming more and more obsessive, more and more violent, descending to ever lower states of being.

## A SNAKE OR A COILED ROPE?

If you see a snake, you see a snake, even if it's a coiled rope. . . .
The world is as you are.

**DAVID LYNCH, INTERVIEW, MARCH 18, 2010**

The blocked perspective, Fred's perspective—in his case a perspective that sees only the snake—is defined for the spectator from the first frames of *Lost Highway*. The main title image of driving down a highway and the main title song, "I'm Deranged," immediately depict the disorientation of the world of matter in this film. The main title features the image of a highway, ordinarily understood as a passage that allows us to go places, but here it goes nowhere. It manifests as a dark terrain, through which the camera conveys us in a narrowly focused, fast-motion shot that simulates the point of view from inside a vehicle heedless of the boundaries marked out by the highway's center line. What light there is illuminates nothing but speed and intensity, and reveals neither what or who is moving, nor the goal of the motion, nor even the position of the moving matter. It's a fraught image of the material world with major resemblances to the way the uncertainty principle defines human observation of matter: if we can perceive the speed of the particles of matter, we cannot know its position—and vice versa. Modern uncertainty about the physical world means that we can never have a complete image of it, only a partial one.

This uncertain image of the road is also loaded with an emotional and sexual coloring. "I'm Deranged" infuses the highway with a masochistic helplessness through lyrics like: "The clutch of life and the fist of love/Over your head"; "I'd start to believe if I were to bleed"; and the unmistakable sexual obsessiveness of "Cruise me cruise me cruise me babe/I'm deranged." The grinding vibrations of the highway image are evocative of bad sex as well as of the alienated negativity of the film's characters, whom we will see flail about during the course of the narrative with a confused, often pornographic, intensity. Sexual abjection and helplessness takes center stage in these lyrics and will continue to do so as the action unfolds. This is not the Lynchian release of control that gives rise to creativity. This is its opposite: a compulsion born of false perceptions that gets in the way of everything authentic.

Abjection and uncertainty also shape our first meeting with Fred. His eyes full of a cruelty born of pain, Fred erupts for the viewer in darkness, adumbrated only in the lurid, red glow of his burning cigarette. When we first see him, struggling in vain to see something meaningful to him, he moves fitfully in and out of the darkened corridors of his home, corridors so murky that his body seems one with the dark, with not even a sliver of light to define the edges of his body. The embedding of this observer in the environment around him bears an interesting similarity to the observer of the physical world as physics now construes him/her. There is no room for a freely objective distance in an uncertain world.[4]

The incompleteness of what Fred can glean from his surroundings at first takes the form of one enigmatic line of dialogue, "Dick Laurent is Dead." Fred—a jazz saxophonist whose wailing solos at the Club Luna reveal that his art is patently an expression not of exuberance but desperation—uncomprehendingly hears those words over the internal speaker of his home intercom, knowing nothing of Dick Laurent (Robert Loggia) and unable to identify who is speaking over the intercom. By the time the film has reached its penultimate point, however, when Fred returns to his house after a very long journey to speak those very words into his home's exterior intercom speaker, he knows exactly who is speaking. And he knows Dick Laurent, a gangster boss whom he not only has just killed, but in fact replaced. But even though Fred is being shown that he exists in two places at the same time, both at the beginning and the end of this film—and how much more clear can life make it that he lives in an uncertain world of slippery time and undefined bodies?—he still doggedly strives to stay with the reductive program of the marketplace. Fred has traveled from here to there, from being a jazz musician soaked in depression to being a gangster on the lam from the police, but he has not traveled from "here to here." He is as obtuse about the nature of his world as he was to begin with. Hopefully the audience, which is given the necessary distance from which to observe and ponder Fred's misconceptions, can do better.

Fred's tense response to the anonymous message about the death of the unknown Dick Laurent is only the beginning. His tense response whenever he speaks with Renee is filled with an anguished antagonism sparked by what he doesn't know about her, and which washes over her with a negative energy that renders all their domestic scenes awkward and painful. Partial, inconclusive knowledge keeps Fred angry and darkens his vision. Where is Fred's wife Renee (Patricia Arquette) when he is playing at the Club Luna? Home, as she tells him? Or stepping out with Andy (Michael Massee), a very unsavory male friend, as Fred imagines when she doesn't answer his phone call from the club? What can he do about sex with Renee? It is so unsatisfying to her that her most palpable reaction to their lovemaking is pity. Fred's rage when Renee pats his back comfortingly afterwards opens the door to a very negative energy in his life.

After their bad sex, Fred has a shocking momentary sensation that a stranger has usurped Renee's place in their bed. This threshold moment of sorts is a preparation for the later, and more crucial, threshold experience when Fred morphs into Pete Dayton. Renee's brief physical transformation occurs just after Fred speaks to her about a dream he had, which Lynch visualizes for us. In the dream, Fred wanders through a dark maze— a physical manifestation of the negativity that suffuses his dream, as well as his life. In the dream darkness, Fred hears his wife's voice calling to him, and his voice calling to her. At first, as Fred tells Renee, he is unable to find her and when he does, the discovery isn't comforting. As he says, "It wasn't you, but it looked like you." Fred is even more alarmed by the final moment of his dream—so alarmed that he doesn't tell Renee about it. As the dream is coming to an end, Fred sees Renee hold up her arms defensively to ward off an attack, but he doesn't see what is attacking her. However, since his is the point of view from which Renee's terror is visible, he's pretty sure that he himself is the attacker, which terrifies him.

As if the misfired sex and the harrowing, homicidal dream were not enough, when Fred turns toward Renee in what can hardly be called afterglow, Renee is much changed. Here is the description of that moment from Lynch's script: "Fred is lying in bed with Renee, who is now backlit by her bedside lamp. Fred looks at her shadowed face, but it's *not* Renee's face. It's a face Fred has never seen before. Fred quickly turns and switches on *his* bedside lamp, and looks quickly back at Renee, whose face is now her own."[5] The face, which is not described in the script, is ghoulishly white, and male, but made up in feminine fashion around the eyes and mouth, and, bizarrely, the lips are painted with Renee's shade of lipstick. This is the Mystery Man (Robert Blake), of whom we will see a great deal in Fred's narrative.[6] Both Fred and the audience want to believe that this is a passing figment of the imagination but the film does not support that option for long.

Fred's "jailbreak" is a long way off, but Fred is already moving between the surface of ordinary appearances and the endless possibilities that lurk beneath the surface of matter. Yet the abundance of possibility that emerges in this case suggests to him only a boundless malevolence, not the joyous optimism that Lynch sees in the limitlessness of the open cosmos. Moreover, as the story continues, Fred's encounters with the largesse of life, with the signs of the threshold past the bounded conception of materiality, take on an increasingly sinister character. If we read the incidents in the early part of the film from Fred's point of view, we interpret the world Lynch is showing us as ugly and hopeless. But Fred is not telling the story, Lynch is, and Lynch does not see the world as Fred does. In a universe of glowing and infinite wonder, the ceaseless appearance of

Fred Madison (Bill Pullman) sees the face of the Mystery Man (Robert Blake) where his wife's (Patricia Arquette) face should be. At this moment, he thinks he is hallucinating, but subsequent events reveal to the spectator that this spectacle is part of physical reality.

hurt and harm is a result of an imposition on circumstances of a negative attitude, which is exactly what Lynch is showing us. Fred's oppositional attitude shapes a negative life. What is more, as we shall see, negativity breeds yet more negativity. Tuned into a perception of the large and the unexpected as malevolent, Fred becomes a magnet for destructive and sinister forces. After all, for Lynch, "the world is as you are."

Accordingly, the mysteriously appearing VHS tapes are rendered a prologue to Renee's death/murder by Fred's increasing insistence on interpreting them as a coiled snake in his path. On the first one, which arrives before the "bad sex" scene, there is only a panning shot across the exterior of the Madison house, which is rather a neutral image, but Fred is annoyed rather than curious. It is not coincidental that the second tape, more annoying to Fred, is also more disquieting. The second tape, which also begins with an exterior shot of the Madison house, adds a floating, high-angle image of the interior, terminating in a downward perspective on the sleeping bodies of Renee and Fred. In this Lynchverse, the truism that "the world is as Fred is" is a process, not a static moment. And as Fred's anger builds, he becomes part of a process by means of which his external world indeed turns darker.

The detectives assigned to the case demonstrate that the world is also as culture is. In a scene in which they investigate the Madison complaint about the videotapes, the detectives initiate a comedy of useless procedures as they graft onto a situation of extreme indeterminacy a bizarre aura of certainty. Detective Al (John Roselius) and Detective Ed (Lou Eppolito) are stolid devotees of "just the facts, ma'am," in the tradition of Sergeant Joe Friday (Jack Webb) in the old *Dragnet* television series. But where that series established Friday and his partner, Officer Frank Smith (first Herbert Ellis and then Ben Alexander), as the benchmark of absolute reality, defining facts in terms of the most classical understandings of object, bodies, and space, by the time Lou and Al appear Lynch has defined this world in such a way that this approach appears so narrow as to be absurd. "This is the bedroom?" asks Detective Al standing in a room that couldn't be anything else. "You sleep here? In this room? Both of you?" chimes in Detective Ed, tracing this and other "facts" about the house to their almost irrelevant and useless conclusions. The attitude of the detectives eggs Fred on to assert his own self-created dogma. When the detectives ask Fred if he has a video camera, ostensibly in case it can be connected to the offending videotapes, Fred, equally pointlessly, expresses his distaste for video cameras. He tells the detectives that he wants to remember events the way he remembers them, "not necessarily the way they happened." Caught in a world that Lynch has shown us is highly indeterminate, both the police and Fred want to impose different, but equally erroneous, certainties. Ironically, while the world keeps displaying the presence of boundlessness, the characters fail to notice. Limits of their own making—Fred's inclination to remember events the way he remembers them, "not the way they happened," for example—are all they focus on.

Lynch continues to follow Fred into a kind of quantum wonderland which Fred greets only with smoldering anger and anxiety. When Fred and Renee attend a party given by Renee's disreputable and vulgar friend Andy, Fred is chagrined to see that one of the guests, identified in the credits as the Mystery Man, has the same face as the one that showed up on Renee in the Madison bedroom after Fred's exasperating sexual failure.

This irritates him as much as the anonymous VHS tapes. And again, because the world is as Fred is, the reality comes to him in a sinister and actively malignant guise. While tipsy Renee is leaning all over Andy, the Mystery Man aggressively stalks Fred, taunting him with the fact of what Fred would like to dismiss as a delusion: the Mystery Man's appearance in Fred's bed where Renee was supposed to be. Moreover, the Mystery Man identifies Fred as the instigator of that event, telling Fred that he never goes anywhere he isn't invited. What's more, the link between them is ongoing: "I'm at your house now."

The eruption of the Mystery Man in Fred's life takes its form from the non-local quantum circumstance of entanglement, the connection among particles that overrides the classical physics of space and time.[7] Fred and the Mystery Man are entangled. There is no doubt that their connection fills Fred with fear. But within quantum mechanics, the phenomenon of entanglement is baffling but neutral. As Louisa Gilder writes in *The Age of Entanglement: When Quantum Physics Was Reborn*, "Any time two entities interact, they entangle. It doesn't matter if they are photons (bits of light), atoms (bits of matter), or bigger things made of atoms . . . The entanglement persists no matter how separate these entities are from each other, as long as they don't subsequently interact with anything else—an almost impossibly tall order for a cat or a person, which is why we don't notice the effect. But the motions of subatomic particles are dominated by entanglement. It starts when they interact; in doing so, they lose their separate existence. No matter how far they move apart, if one is tweaked, measured, observed, the other seems to instantly respond, even if the whole world now lies between them. And no one knows how." David Lynch creates in the relationship between the Mystery Man and Fred such a phenomenon; it's poetically employed so Lynch can tell his story, but within the world of *Lost Highway* it has all the reality that it has on the subatomic level. In itself, the entanglement is surprising but not essentially fearful. (In *Twin Peaks,* when Agent Cooper and Laura have the same dream, that similar entanglement astonishes Cooper but doesn't frighten him.)

It is the Mystery Man who defines this encounter as a negative one. He bullies Fred, who is susceptible to negativity, into calling his own home and hearing that the Mystery Man is there while he is also at Andy's party, and then laughs at his ability to drive Fred into a state of nervous agitation with this display. Any residual thought that this too is Fred's fantasy should become questionable for both Fred and the spectator when the host of the party, Andy, identifies the Mystery Man as a friend of Dick Laurent. Fred, struck by the reappearance in his life of Dick Laurent— whoever he may be—feels ever more insecure about what he thought he knew to be reality; he's never excited by the new possibilities that are being manifested. And his reaction is a kind of self-fulfilling prophecy. If one expects the new, the different, the unexplained to be frightening, it will be. Alas, all that negativity has consequences.

The first, expository segment of *Lost Highway* comes to a climax when a third videotape arrives at chez Madison, while Fred is home alone. This video shows everything on the first two tapes plus a high-angle image of Fred bending over Renee's dead body, blood spattered over both of them. The tape poses more questions than it answers, above all about whether it reflects any kind of reality. There is no external evidence that Renee Madison is dead, let alone that Fred is her murderer. Despite the peculiar insubstantiality of the images on the tape—there is no actual corpse in the film—Fred is convicted of murder and sentenced to death. Fred has conspired with the Los Angeles justice system to make his coiled snake a reality.

While everyone in *Lost Highway* wants to deal decisively with the situation, the effect of large forces and material indeterminacy are the central realities depicted in the action, producing a very different kind of murder mystery. One difference is the portrayal of Fred's trial, which is represented by nothing more substantial than two voiceovers, one by the jury spokesperson (Mink Stole) announcing the guilty verdict, the other by the judge (Leonard Termo) handing down the death sentence, as Fred is seen walking down a flight of stairs toward his death row cell. The trial has the insubstantiality of a ghost. Why?

The legal system, with its belief in cut-and-dried facts, is ghostly in this uncertain Lynchverse. *Lost Highway* makes it clear that there is no way to absolutely answer questions of guilt and innocence because reality principles are on the line. If reality is uncertain, how can courts make the kinds of determinations they are constructed to make? This leads us to the astonishing conclusion that in *Lost Highway* there will only be a probable answer to the question of whether or not Fred killed Renee. Wildly unusual in a murder mystery, especially in a culture like ours, *Lost Highway* flouts all of the conventions of the popular police procedurals that continually affirm the comprehensibility of matter and the ability

As we watch Fred (Bill Pullman) descend the stairs with two guards (Henry Rollins and Michael Shamus Wiles) to his high-security cell, we hear voiceovers of the pronunciation of a guilty verdict (Mink Stole) and a death sentence (Leonard Termo); it is to this ghostly moment that Fred's trial is reduced.

of force and intellect to subdue it.[8] Lynch here rather replicates the spirit of Franz Kafka's *The Trial*—Kafka being an artist who in 1925, as quantum physics was in its infancy, arguably intuited the future of matter with preternatural precociousness. Neither we nor Kafka ever know what he was accused of or whether he was guilty. If we interpret this using quantum mechanics as our frame of reference, ambiguity reigns because probability does not permit definitive answers. Like *The Trial*, *Lost Highway* is not a "whodunit?" so much as it is a "who, what, and, especially, *where* is it?"

In *Lost Highway*, Lynch uses both visualizations of insubstantiality, like the trial, and images of supposed solidity to make his points about the nature of the marketplace in which Fred lives. For example, the confining cells on death row, which are vividly shown, are seemingly very substantial; in every jail scene, sadistic guards over-control the space on death row. But despite this evocation of mass and impenetrability in the metal walls and barred ceiling of Fred's cell, one day, he changes into Pete Dayton, a punkish boy of twenty-four with a trivial police record, who works as a garage mechanic at Arnie's Complete Car Service (Arnie played by Dick Gregory). Both the body and the cell are sieves. Fred enters the jail through an insubstantial process and leaves the same way.

Here is where Lynch begins to evolve his second-stage vocabulary about modern uncertainty and cultural attempts to deal with it atavistically from the perspective of old, Newtonian certainties. And a dramatic revelation it is too, as in great detail Lynch depicts Fred's journey from his own body to someone else's. The metamorphosis of Fred into Pete is a threshold experience on a grand scale. If *Lost Highway* has previously suggested the malleability of matter, then the moment of Fred's transformation vividly asserts it. In one of the most confined, limited, structures one can imagine, the site of (supposed) absolute social control over the material world, Fred experiences the dissolution of the classical terrain of objects into the completely indeterminate universe of permeable substances and randomly grouped particles.

The subatomic behavior of matter—the part of the marketplace that offers intimations that there are bigger forces in life than the cultural illusions of solidity assert—when Fred transforms into Pete is a complex event that fuses three locations simultaneously through a cinematic superimposition of images: the highway of the main title, where we first see Pete standing; the lawn of the Dayton home, on which Pete, his girlfriend Sheila (Natasha Gregson Wagner), and his parents Bill and Candace (Gary Busey and Lucy Butler) are all congregated; and Fred's jail cell. These disparate sites become one. Although there should be, once the threshold experiences commence, there is no spatial distance that separates these strangers, no temporal measurement of minutes or hours that requires them to move through space at some kind of pace and/or in some kind of vehicle to interact with each other. They are simply all joined together as Fred's seemingly coherent body disintegrates into furiously speeding surges of energy. A white blast of lightning-like light crackles and the images of matter dissolved by fire erupt on the screen as the classical boundaries of Fred's body explode into sudden paroxysms, as his body thrashes from side to side while his face grimaces in agony.

This representation of a boundless human existence within time and space, despite Fred's ostensible entrapment inside death row, the stronghold of the marketplace, calls on images from the quantum mechanics of entanglement and images of the cosmic Bardo state described in *The Tibetan Book of the Dead*.[9] Thus it is not purely a reproduction of how

The stylized image of the body of Fred Madison (Bill Pullman) as he is transformed into Pete Dayton (Balthazar Getty) shows us that the metamorphosis is a physical rearrangement of Fred's molecules.

modern physics sees the world but an imaginative use of it in a cinematic fiction fused with Vedic mysticism. The upshot, however, whatever allusions we may see in it, is that this transition suggests an enormous power beyond that of culture. In fact, the penal system, for all its clanging doors, locks, and detention of people in small spaces, must acknowledge that it is down for the count—and the government officials are quite aware that they aren't dreaming. But they aren't taking into consideration the amazing aspects of what confronts them either. It is interesting for us to watch them unable to deal with behavior outside of "normal" parameters as anything but an embarrassment to the system—a system that is supposed to be foolproof against any inmate's escape, let alone an escape like this.

When Fred escapes from death row, however, he is unable to escape from his rejection of the larger forces animating his life. Fear and/or embarrassment triggered by the indeterminate Kafka-esque moment, the threshold experience, or "spooky shit," as a jail guard says to the jail warden with much less elegance, remains as part of Fred/Pete's life too.

However, the trajectory of the apprehension has been altered by the new line of action in the story. While Fred is continually alarmed by what might happen, Fred/Pete is terrified by what has *already* happened. That is, while Fred's trigger for anxiety is any foreshadowing that something's about to fire, Pete's trigger is any reminder of the threshold through which he has already passed. When Pete hears on the radio a jazz solo performed by Fred, he gets a headache. Periodically, the world blurs and shimmies before Pete's eyes when a word or a gesture reminds him of what happened. Fred has the police to encourage his fear of what might lie beyond the narrow parameters of normal, and the courts to make him a victim of society's inability to deal with whatever is out there. Fred/Pete has his neighborhood girlfriend, Sheila, and his parents, whose fears of the threshold they witnessed inflame his own retrospective fears. (All of Fred's avatars also have the Mystery Man to shape their perspective, but of that much more below.)

In the first third of *Lost Highway*, we have watched Lynch build a picture of Fred's angst about the limitless possibilities of the world. That negative construction of boundlessness is connected with a rage and anxiety about sexuality that culminates in what is judged a crime of passion. The links between marketplace negativity and sexuality persist as the film develops, opening more pervasive terrors and toxicity about the energies of the human body. Bill and Candace Dayton and Fred/Pete's girlfriend Sheila fill the air with an ominous sexually tinged silence about the transformation that took place on the lawn in front of the Dayton house which they all witnessed. Although they intend Fred/Pete no harm, what they will *not* say agitates Pete, keeping alive Fred and Fred/Pete's inclination to see a snake where there is none. Sheila, who displays more courage and more curiosity than any of Fred/Pete's family and friends, wants Pete to know about the transformation, but her potential openness is cut off by her intense jealousy, which contributes to the atmosphere of fear.

Bill and Candace Dayton's mute agitation is what most destabilizes their son. Their voiceless embarrassment about "that night" screams loudly of a murky sexual subtext. The Daytons are wracked by a deep shame tinged by a defensive sorrow, as if some terrible disgrace has befallen their son. Clearly, they read compromised manhood into what they have seen of Fred/Pete's threshold experience. Watching their son on "that night" has shaken them with paroxysms of panic, as if they had glimpsed their son involved in some sexually taboo event. Homophobic dread is in the air.

Mom and Dad Dayton speak furtively to Pete after a visit from the police, who have been asking for more information about the night that Fred disappeared. As Bill Dayton vows solemnly to Pete that they will never tell what they saw, and Candace Dayton's eyes fill with tears, it is almost as if they had witnessed him being raped.[10] "There was a man with you," says Bill, when Pete asks what happened to him, as Candace bows her head in obvious torment and Bill tears up, so moved by humiliation that he is almost unable to catch his breath. His face contorts, and he does not respond in words to Pete's entreaties. Stunned by uncertainty into vague but harrowing sexual implications, Bill Dayton silently chokes back his humiliation. The film, which has already shown us in many ways that what Dayton saw was a matter of unusually behaving particles, a phenomenon that has nothing to do with sex, stands back from him with pity but also with irony. But the ramifications for human sexuality in a culture so radically confused about the nature of the material world is not confined to Bill Dayton. One of the most terrible consequences of the blocked perspective for human sexuality is that while Fred is busy rejecting all authentic signs of the wonders of the universe, he fatally mistakes one of the most toxic materialist illusions of the marketplace for a miracle.

## SONG TO THE SIREN

Did I dream you dreamed about me?
Were you here when I was full sail?

**"SONG TO THE SIREN," THIS MORTAL COIL**

In the confused marketplace of *Lost Highway*, the complementary delusion to fearing a coiled rope as if it were a snake is mistaking the untrammeled forces of sexuality for the well-defined, glittering sexual object that can be possessed. The most intense forms of that delusion in *Lost Highway* concern Fred's obsession with Renee, and, after the metamorphosis, Fred/Pete's obsession with Alice Wakefield (also Patricia Arquette). The dangerous continuity of Fred's possessive sexuality even after he has experienced boundlessness in his metamorphosis into Pete Dayton is a key aspect of his continuous descent into worse and worse forms of existence. While both Fred and Fred/Pete run from the larger energies that if embraced would change the world from a death sentence to a life adventure, they

Pete Dayton (Gary Busey) exudes humiliation and fear as he tells Pete about "that night on the lawn."

are paralyzed by desires for Alice and Renee that express in vivid form the disastrous way in which the marketplace operates.

As they appear in *Lost Highway*, Alice and Renee, as sexualized objects, are "she" and "they" at the same time, like particles in superposition—one particle that can be in two places at the same time. This quantum image poetically serves Lynch well here because at the same time it suggests the instability of bodies in the marketplace and the interchangeability of women as objects of desire under the conditions of the marketplace. This/ These woman/women embody toxic illusions about things/bodies, giving the impression of abundant solidity, but perishing into ghostly indeterminacy with any pressure on them to yield the security of permanence. Renee and Alice do for women and women's bodies what Eddington's threshold did for the objects on which we daily stake our physical security: floors and walls. And they reveal the sad condition of sexuality in the marketplace as an ongoing betrayal constantly in peril of deteriorating into a pornographic toxicity because of the misbegotten expectations attached to it by the world of ordinary transactions. It is on Renee and Alice and the desire that they provoke, after all, that Fred and Fred/Pete stake their daily feeling of stability in the world, a trust these two women and their bodies cannot sustain. Alas for Fred and Fred/Pete, they treat Renee and Alice as if they could.

As we come to know Renee and Alice, we realize that possession of them is out of the question. The first time we see Renee, she emerges mysteriously from behind the corner of a wall in the Madison house. She is first a shadow and then seemingly an apparition of glamour: the copper-colored Cleopatra hair, slinky dress, provocatively heavy makeup, and film noir posturing. Between the time that she fills the screen like a tableau and the moment we see Fred walk toward her, the screen goes black, as if Fred were moving across empty space to get to her. (This is not a shot pattern that we see with any other male and female pair in this film.)

Indeed, there is a continuous suggestion of how elusive Renee is in Fred's life, as a physical presence. Although Renee tells Fred she wants to stay home to read while he is playing at Club Luna, when he calls her during a break, she doesn't answer the phone. Yet when he arrives home, after Lynch places another black screen between them, he observes Renee sleeping peacefully on their black satin sheets. For him, she is a maddening object whose location he cannot nail down.

Elusive Renee is at odds with Fred's desire throughout the film. Despite the exaggerated images of Renee's large, seemingly solidly fleshy breasts heaving during the "bad sex" scene, she is at the same time defined as a chimera. She is penetrated by the face of the Mystery Man and she disappears without a trace—at least for a while—as soon as a videotape arrives, suggesting in a difficult-to-read image that Fred has killed her. Renee's body is both matter and ephemera. As Fred is reaching his premature sexual climax in the bad sex scene, the resonant, magical strains of "Song to the Siren," by the group This Mortal Coil, softly begin to rise on the soundtrack, adding a new dimension to Lynch's evocation of the nature of Fred's relationship with Renee. "Song to the Siren," speaking of the insubstantiality of this irresistible creature—"Did I dream I dreamed about you?"—becomes the musical sex theme for both Renee and Alice, recasting the notion of the dangerous seductress, once narrated as the story of female evil in a certain world, now narrated in quantum science terms, as part of the dangerous illusions of the marketplace.

Alice is also characterized as a flummoxing cocktail of matter and air. Pete meets her as Mr. Eddy's consort when Mr. Eddy arrives at Arnie's

Renee (Patricia
Arquette) looms as
an object of desire.

A black frame
evokes the void
that separates Fred
(Bill Pullman) from
his object of desire.

Fred (Bill Pullman)
continues to
move toward his
wife, never quite
possessing this
object of desire.

garage, where Pete works, to have his car fixed. Alice is completely out of place in this body shop, with her platinum blonde cloud of hair surrounding her petulant, theatrically made-up face. And yet she is one with the manufactured products of the culture, a juxtaposition that is repeated even more forcefully at sunset that evening when Alice surprises Pete by showing up to ask him to take her to "dinner"—her code word for sex—at the motel. In the dusk of the Los Angeles street with its rushing taxis, she materializes in a clinging champagne-colored silk dress that displays not only her breasts but also her nipples, her pale candy cotton hair lit by the neon signs. Organic goddess, and part of the machinery of the city.

The superposition metaphor—matter that is both one and many at the same time—that is at the core of the presence and absence of Renee and Alice vivifies their solid elusiveness continually. Alice and Renee enigmatically both appear in a photograph in Andy's house that makes it so obvious that they might be the same person reproduced in the image by trick technology that Fred/Pete asks Alice whether she is both the women in the photo or only one. Alice appears to Fred/Pete in a phantom form upstairs in Andy's house while her obviously physical body is downstairs looting Andy's house. In her phantom form, Alice taunts Fred/Pete about

Alice Wakefield (Patricia Arquette) glows with her own luminous siren radiance in the urban night.

his confusion, "Did you want to talk to me? Did you want to ask me, 'Whyyyyyyyyyy?'" Phantom Alice pronounces the last word as if she were judging Pete as a pitiful whiner, an ironic judgment from a siren who has lured him into committing a terrible crime. Later, Alice disappears from Andy's photo while the police detectives are searching his house after Andy is killed. And, of course, she disappears completely, without a trace, when she walks into the desert cabin of the fence to which she and Fred/Pete hope to sell what they took from the now dead Andy. Her vanishing act is particularly colored by the incongruous combination of her solidity and her slippery elusiveness. She vanishes into thin air after she has made a spectacular display of her naked nubile body, lit magically by the headlights of their car standing outside the desert cabin as she straddles Fred/Pete voluptuously, telling him when he is wild with desire—and she ostensibly is too—that he can never have her. To seal the deal of Alice's existence as both meat and moonlight, when Fred, in his third, post Fred/Pete incarnation, comes to look for her in that cabin, he finds only the Mystery Man, speaking caustically to him. "Alice who? Her name is Renee. If she told you her name is Alice, she's lying."

Renee and Alice alter the depiction of femininity that was characteristic of Lynch's first-stage cinema. Renee and Alice, and even Sheila and Candace Dayton, are not models of feminine receptivity for men to be guided by as were Lula for Sailor in *Wild at Heart* or Sandy for Jeffrey in *Blue Velvet*, among other earlier female characters, as I asserted in *The Passion of David Lynch*. And it is true that in Lynch's first-stage films, the women are paradigms of connectedness for their lovers. Lula and Sandy are sustaining for men, models of personhood that offer more life-affirming, more imaginatively expansive possibilities than the modes of domination that men are pressured to accept as signs of their manhood. Female protagonists in Lynch's early works often signal contact with the actual limitlessness beyond what culture offers up; they are a solace for bedeviled male characters. But that doesn't happen in *Lost Highway*. In fact the reverse happens; Renee and Alice are very important parts of the trap sprung on Fred and Fred/Pete that locks them into the sharply downward cycles from which the earlier Lynchian women saved their men. In *Lost Highway*, if Fred's conviction for murder reveals the problem of law and justice in an uncertain world, Alice and Renee reveal the sexual dimensions of the problem.

Through Renee and Alice, Lynch also changes the terms of the discussion of the femme fatale from one about the evil of female sexuality into one about what happens to everyone's sexuality in the marketplace. Putting a new spin on the sexual objectification of women, in *Lost Highway* Lynch goes beyond what has come to be a feminist cliché of sorts, for in this film, any object is an illusion of solidity that can never be possessed—a catastrophic circumstance endemic to the marketplace that gets extended to male desire for women, not because female sexuality is by its nature destructive, but because of the cultural misreading of all bodies and objects. The siren call in *Lost Highway* is the erotic version of the fallacy of certainty in the marketplace. Renee and Alice are femmes fatales for the modern age.[11]

The sirens of classical culture are images of the intoxicating but deadly allure of female sexuality. They make their definitive first ancient appearance in Homer's *Odyssey* (believed to have been composed in 800 BCE). In that tale, hero Ulysses orders his men to lash him to one of the masts of his ship and stuff their own ears with wax so that Ulysses (although not the crew) can hear the ecstatic songs of the sirens without the ship crashing on the rocks from which the sirens seductively call to the sailors. The sailors are ordered by Ulysses not to release him from his restraints no matter how he makes demands or begs them because Ulysses knows that no mortal man can resist the sirens' song and that unbound he will take his ship to destruction under their influence. In conformity with the belief systems of its time and the hundreds of years that followed, this epic portrays the sirens as deviations from the resilient and sturdy limits of absolute time and space. They are a venerable feminist nightmare that specifically positions feminine sexuality as dangerous and men as the guardians of the safety of culture.

The rocks are in a specific place which can be determined by a navigator and avoided. The sturdy mast to which Ulysses is bound does not resemble the mast that Arthur Eddington might later have described in the spirit of his threshold in which all objects are composed of empty space and whirling particles. The excessive charms of the sirens are demonized in contrast with the steady, domestic, predictable presence of Ulysses' wife, Penelope, who remains constant in a completely ascertainable place to which the voyaging hero can return when his travels are finished. Her orderly life is the totality of the real, attacked periodically by deviant forces and people to be sure, but the true north to which the return can and must be made. There is a threshold indicated here by the sirens, but nothing that can destroy stable material reality. The story may fill us with a healthy respect for the capacity of human beings to fall away from ideal behavior, but, in the tradition of classical narrative, *The Odyssey* features a world around us that will not waver even if we might.

By contrast, in *Lost Highway*, a modern physics is asserted. Renee and Alice are the sign and standard of the only world we can inhabit, a difficult environment that only looks solid, but is actually elusive and impossible to connect with. In the *Odyssey*, Ulysses stands for ordinary masculinity, a definition of man as a complex organism that might want to experience delirium but owes his allegiance to the world of fact, as it was then understood. In *Lost Highway*, Fred longs for a world of fact but has only the truth of the marketplace, delirium. Fred's sexual desire for Renee is a delirium of impossible yearnings. Hoping for control and stability, he looks to this siren for security, and at every turn she produces nothing but insecurity. She is there and she is not there. She is dead and she is not dead. But in a marketplace that is always opting for certainties where there are none, Fred is punished whether or not a crime has been committed.

When the story moves forward to Fred's repetition of his initial sexual confusion when he is Fred/Pete, the protagonist's story has moved from here to here for the audience, but not for the protagonist(s). Fred and Fred/Pete do not have increased insight into the situation where they began. Alice reveals more about the siren call of marketplace illusions than Renee did, making more manifest the obscenity of this degradation of sexuality in a culture constricted by its own lies. Alice is not just an illusion of solidity masking an ephemeral indeterminacy as Renee was; the combination is patently degenerate. A bewildered Fred/Pete has allowed Alice to lead him into conflict with Mr. Eddy, a dangerous mob boss who considers Alice his property. Tempting Fred/Pete with the promise of exclusive possession of her, Alice also leads Fred/Pete into committing robbery and murder, ostensibly so they can be together. Significantly, Fred/Pete's susceptibility to her deceptive plan has nothing to do with the perils of femininity. Instead it is motivated by his already fragile relationship to the marketplace and the fear of Mr. Eddy that the Mystery Man has instilled in him during a joint phone call to Fred/Pete from the two of them. Eddy has figured out that his "moll," Alice, and Fred/Pete have been sneaking around behind his back, having sex in motels, and he means to terrorize this upstart kid. Eddy adopts a faux affability when he speaks to Fred/Pete that reveals, as no direct intimidation could, the underlying threat. He leaves it to his "friend," the Mystery Man, to supplement the message with flashier scare tactics. When the Mystery Man takes the phone, he characteristically sends Fred/Pete into a fit of anxiety by invoking the threshold that Fred/Pete dreads thinking about. "We've met before . . . at your house," he says, as he once said to Fred. After Pete splutters his denials as Fred once did, the Mystery Man recites a parable: "In the East, the Far East, when a person is sentenced to death they're sent to a place where they can't escape, never knowing when an executioner may step up behind them and fire a bullet into the back of their head."

Fred/Pete is so destabilized by how things work in the marketplace that he cannot free himself from compliance with Alice even though once the plot is in play he is horrified to find himself surrounded by disordered heaps of objects and the pornographic movie image of Alice being sexually penetrated brutally from behind. He is carried along by events until he is stranded in the desert with Alice, and, as "Song to the Siren" rises to a crescendo on the soundtrack, he learns that she will always evade his grasp, just as Renee evaded Fred's, when she whispers, "You'll never have me." At this point, Fred/Pete can go no further and Fred reappears to find only the Mystery Man, and no sign of Alice. The slippery sexualization of bodies and objects comes to a head when the Mystery Man insists that there never was an Alice, only a Renee. "And your name," the Mystery Man says to Fred. "WHAT THE FUCK IS YOUR NAME?"

The feeling that one is not oneself is part of the traditional story of being under the spell of the sirens. But the state is temporary in narratives where the world features only classically ordered things and bodies. Ulysses knows that even though he is an experienced and masterful sailor, he would drive his ships onto the rocks upon hearing their song. Lashed to the mast of his ship, his loyal crew in attendance, he is never really very far from the indubitable compass points of a structured and secure society. Even in a more modern tale of the siren, Orson Welles' *The Lady From Shanghai* (1947), which stands somewhere between the *Odyssey* and *Lost Highway*, the loss of proper identity under the influence of the femme fatale, though it shakes the film's protagonist to his roots, has a limited time frame. The force of female evil is not as potent apparently as the force of destabilization in the modern marketplace. Hero Michael O'Hara (Orson Welles) tells us in a voiceover that he was not in his right mind once he laid eyes on femme fatale Elsa Bannister (Rita Hayworth). Welles's film lays the guilt on Elsa, but ultimately O'Hara finds himself

The Mystery Man in tight focus, which visually reproduces his tyranny of Fred's vision when he roars at him, "WHAT THE FUCK IS YOUR NAME?"

again in a solid, understandable world. *The Lady From Shanghai* is modern enough that Michael has a brief time in the clutches of uncertainty in the famous amusement park funhouse and magic mirror maze, where he is almost killed because of the siren. The funhouse resembles Arthur Eddington's description of a physicist entering a room, as Mike careens helplessly down a series of slides that replicates both the effect Elsa has on him and an untrustworthy material terrain into which he may tumble at any point and gets lost in a hall of mirrors that poetically suggests entangled bodies through their reflections. But O'Hara leaves the funhouse. There are discernible limits to the circumstances in which the material world seems frightening. By contrast, Fred cannot answer the Mystery Man's question. What IS his name? He has been both Fred and Fred/Pete, and now what can he say he should be called?

Perversely led away from the energies that would sustain him, and pushed toward the illusion of sexuality fostered by the marketplace, Fred and his other selves find that identity becomes increasingly precarious— and involvement in a descending cycle of misery, crime, and a pornographic way of experiencing sexuality more inevitable. Misrecognition and the suffering it causes is the rule, not the exception, in *Lost Highway*.

Ironically, it seems, if we do not avail ourselves to the bounty of cosmic opportunity, we will be attacked by the boundless cosmic forms of malevolence that also exist beyond the limits erected by culture.

## THE PORNO KINGS SING SONGS OF DOOM

Unable to see the marvelous in the limitlessness of possibility, Fred becomes the prisoner of the evil aspects of the boundless universe. Lynch has spoken to me of Rakshasas, diabolical beings who populate Vedic stories. Along with many good forces, they emanate from the limitless Cosmos beyond the marketplace, and produce Maya (illusion) in human affairs. In *Lost Highway*, an evil Rakshasa-like character exercises influence over Fred in all his manifestations.

There are no actual Rakshasas in Fred's story, or in any of Lynch's films, but there are figures in *Lost Highway* and several other Lynch second-stage films that exert that kind of influence on events. In *Lost Highway* there is the vitriolic Mystery Man, who is like a Rakshasa, and, although it takes a while for us to see it, it is he who controls and spreads illusion, fear, and violence in Fred's blighted adventures. The Mystery Man's ability to instigate fear keeps Fred from seeing what really is, and as a result Fred seems to be on a course of endless descent into suffering and crime. The Mystery Man is Lynch's emissary from the great beyond of culture that complicates his vision of boundlessness.

At first, the dark influence in Fred's life seems to be Andy, but once Fred has passed through his threshold experience and transformed into Fred/Pete, it becomes clear that Andy is negligible in the grand scheme of things, a factotum controlled by mob boss Mr. Eddy, also known as Dick Laurent. Laurent/Eddy then comes to loom large as the shadow over Fred/Pete's life. Ultimately, however, we can see that Mr. Eddy too is a pawn, a doomed pawn at that, in a much larger game being played by the Mystery Man. There is a destiny in progress from the very beginning of the film; Dick Laurent is dead even before the action begins, although he has yet to be killed, because that is how time works at the most profound levels of the marketplace, beneath the illusion of solidity. It is also Fred's destiny to kill him, although he doesn't know who Laurent is when the story starts, because that too is how time works. It would seem that Dick Laurent is alive for almost all of the film, since we see him in action for a long time before Fred kills him. But then again nothing is what it seems in *Lost Highway*. The Mystery Man seems to be nothing more than a strange peripheral blip on the screen for most of the film, until it is revealed, as we shall discuss in detail below, that he has masterminded the destinies of both Fred and Laurent/Eddy. In fact, it is the Mystery Man, an agent from beyond the marketplace, whose malign, indeed obscene, intent is to keep Fred and everyone else mired in the lies and illusions of the plane of everyday transactions. And he does a pretty effective job of it.

The Mystery Man is never spoken of by name, reflecting his existence beyond the labels of the marketplace—after all, names affirm the kind of finitude that culture wants to believe in. By contrast, Fred, Fred/Pete, the Fred that emerges when Fred/Pete is gone, and Dick Laurent/Mr. Eddy operate in a confusion of labels and motives within the illusory constraints of finitude. Like the ringmaster in a carnival of fools, the Mystery Man is always present to stir up anxiety when, under the pressure of uncertainty, finitude breaks, goes into superposition, or undergoes some other change that contradicts the illusion of a definite, bounded world. He agitates behind the maelstrom of names and identities. He feeds and feeds off of the characters' desperation to maintain the marketplace illusions of solidity.

As *Lost Highway* unfolds, the darkly comic obscenity of the Mystery Man's ability to snap the whip at all the forms of Fred, and the power of the Mystery Man himself, is revealed in ever clearer intensity. No one who seems to be in control actually is. Fred, of course, who wants nothing more than he wants control, has less and less with each scene. But so does the mob boss Laurent/Eddy, the Mystery Man's friend—for most of the film. Laurent/Eddy seems to be portrayed as one of the porno kings in the nightmare-like funhouse in the carnival, but he is simultaneously mocked as a man filled with delusions of grandeur, so we are well-prepared for the final revelation that he is a dupe of the Mystery Man. Laurent/Eddy walks and talks as if he is a victorious general in a conquered country, but his bloated confidence reeks of perverse grandiosity, as we see with particular clarity in his most extreme scenes—for example, in the "tailgating scene" on Mulholland Drive, in which Fred is in Fred/Pete mode.

After Fred/Pete, Laurent/Eddy's favorite car mechanic, makes a small correction on his big, expensive car, Laurent/Eddy takes Fred/Pete for a spin. With his two large thugs occupying the back seat, Laurent/Eddy becomes annoyed with another driver who tailgates his car. Laurent relentlessly forces him off the road. As Laurent/Eddy—and his thugs—beat the man into incoherence, Laurent/Eddy cites chapter and verse from the government-printed driver's manual and statistics about the evils of tailgating. There is a kind of (comic) obscenity in this scene regarding the way he throws his weight around—the quintessential folly of using a baseball bat to catch a flea—when he's "in charge" that characterizes much of his imbecilic authoritarian style. Another notable instance of Laurent/Eddy's dark comedy of mastery is when he interviews Alice "for a job." He keeps her waiting many hours as part of the prerogatives of his power. When she is finally called into a room, ostensibly for an interview, she is confronted by him sitting magisterially in a chair, silently scrutinizing her as one of his thugs holds a gun to her head. Laurent/Eddy says nothing, but Alice clearly gets the message that she is supposed to take her clothes off and kneel before him. The comic excess in the scene is the gun, hardly necessary for the compliant Alice. It is a comedy of bitter incongruity that reveals the pointless force which makes up a part of the twisted erotic pleasures of the marketplace.

When Fred re-emerges as himself post-Fred/Pete outside the Mystery Man's desert cabin, he has descended sufficiently into the marketplace morass to fully assume his place as a fool of its violent and obscene illusions—as a man caught in the grip of the Mystery Man. In a scene punc-

Pointlessly, absurdly, Mr. Eddy's henchman (Lou Slaughter), in the style of power in the marketplace, menaces the compliant, vulnerable Alice (Patricia Arquette) with a gun.

tuated by the blinding flashes of energy whipping through the universe, evidence of how boundless Fred's possibilities really are, this third avatar of Fred Madison has a seminal encounter with the Mystery Man that drives him the furthest away he has yet been from everything he might have become. In this encounter, Lynch displays the dark side of the medium in which he works, the moving image, as a stunning metaphor of modernity's abandonment of life for the illusions of the marketplace.

Whereas Lynch's films—and *Lost Highway* more daringly than ever before—work against Hollywood's replacement of organic being with insubstantial images, the Mystery Man is precisely the opposite of Lynchian cinema. He is the purveyor of the dangerous, deceptive moving image that steals us from connection to living. Stalking Fred with a video camera, the Mystery Man actively reduces him to corrupt digital information within the video finder; an image marred by horizontal black lines, showing matter as the aggregate of particles in motion that it is on its most profound level of reality. In this shattering image, Lynch bares the heart of Fred's situation. The Mystery Man, framed by the limitlessness of the vast desert, presses the video camera to his right eye, an icon of how everything is reduced to nothingness in the marketplace.

Although Fred seems to escape from the Mystery Man at that moment by driving away from him toward the Lost Highway Hotel, he is only moving toward the destiny to which the Mystery Man has led Fred since the arrival of the videotapes on the steps of the Madison house at the beginning of the film. Although Lynch leaves the origin of the tapes uncertain, once we see the Mystery Man with the video camera almost wedged into his face where his right eye should be, we know that the tapes originated with him and that the compression of Fred's life into an illusion has been a diabolical process of his making. In the first instance, a videotape replaced actual experience when Fred was convicted of a phantom murder. Now, as he is captured again in the bad video image characteristic of Mystery Man productions, Fred is ready to kill. The Fred who drives away from the desert cabin is not the first Fred we saw, nor is he the Fred/Pete who emerged after Fred's threshold experience. They were fearful and angry, but they weren't violent; this third form of Fred—whatever his name may be—is savage. And he is not particularly interested anymore in Renee, whom he silently watches sneaking out of a room in the Lost Highway Hotel where she has been having sex with Laurent/Eddy. Fred waits for her to leave and then attacks Laurent/Eddy, shoves him in the trunk of his car, and cuts his throat when he releases Laurent/Eddy from the trunk. The Mystery Man furtively shadows this new form of Fred all through his attack on Laurent/Eddy, placing the knife in Fred's hand for the moment he mortally wounds the older man.

As Laurent/Eddy lies dying, he tries to make bargains with the Mystery Man and with Fred, as if he were still in control, but the Mystery Man mercilessly reveals to him that he is the fool of his own delusions. Laurent/Eddy receives from the Mystery Man a cell phone that plays, in staccato bursts, snippets of orgiastic lesbian sex intended for exhibition. This is not private sex between lovers, but horror images and bloody violence. The Mystery Man shows Laurent/Eddy to himself as a buffoon, the victim of the obscenity he has unleashed on the world. In the images the Mystery Man shows, Laurent/Eddy sees himself and Renee as part of a group of people watching the pornographic montage—some images of Renee herself. Laurent/Eddy and Renee are giddily goaded on to have sex themselves. Mystery Man concludes this demonstration by wordlessly signaling to Laurent/Eddy that his time is up when the montage shuts down with a decisive finality and is replaced by an image of Fred and the Mystery Man standing together.

The Mystery Man is now Fred's friend. Mr. Eddy has been replaced by Mr. Freddy. Laurent/Eddy remains too delusional to know what is happening. With his last breath, he continues to assert himself as king of the mountain, "You and me, mister, we can really out-ugly them sum'bitches. Can't we?" In response, the Mystery Man shoots him dead, and underlines his new affiliation with Fred, by leaning over and whispering something into Fred's ear. The camera comes in for a close-up of this hidden exchange—we never hear the words—and when it pulls back, Fred is alone and the gun is in his hand. With Laurent/Eddy lying moribund in the desert, Fred drives up to his own home in Laurent/Eddy's car and speaks the first words of the film into the intercom, "Dick Laurent is dead," also the last words of the film. Time has moved both backward and forward, backward to the first spoken words in *Lost Highway*, and forward to a new incarnation of Fred.

If the worst possible uncertainty scenario has had its day here, there is one certainty left: Fred has made a deal with a devil. At the end of the film, an aggressive expression has replaced the expression of angst with which Fred began the film. Whatever the Mystery Man says to him when Laurent/Eddy is dead, it will lead Fred toward more violence and obscenity, the only destiny in a life filled with dread of the vast possibilities of the universe. The course Fred is now on also keeps him the target of a society that is still reaching for a certainty it will never find. As Fred finishes speaking his words into the intercom, he sees that Detectives Ed and Al are hot on his trail, and he flees from them. They follow him from the light of day into darkness, and from a Los Angeles street into the desert, multiplying the resources mobilized to catch their man. One car turns into four, and four turn into an uncountable line of police cruisers with their red and blue lights blazing. But the upshot is that if and when they catch him, it won't be him. Fred begins to undergo another threshold experience. Although we will not see where this experience leads, we now know that the larger forces of truth continue to penetrate the house of illusions Fred has built. The last we see of Fred, he is about to undergo another change, all the while yelling, "No." The universe is still giving him another chance and he is still not ready to take it.

*Lost Highway* is a Lynchian "bad-case" parable of modernity, but not one without the possibility of redemption. Armed with a faith in the limitlessness of human possibility, Lynch asks us to find room for hope in Fred Madison's self-generated plight. Blinkered by illusions about materiality, our hero has forced his way into nothingness when everything was possible. The power was always in Fred's hands. His alliance with the Mystery Man is of his own creation. And at the end of the film, there is still an opening for him to go in a better direction, even if he continues to opt for the dark side. However, this is not Lynch's only way of speaking about the way we live now. In his next film, Lynch illuminates the human condition in an entirely different light.

# CHAPTER TWO

# THE STRAIGHT STORY: "AND YOU'LL FIND HAPPY TIMES"

There's a whole theory . . . called decoherence. Which is the business of explaining how classical-looking phenomena arise under the appropriate circumstances from an underlying quantum mechanical set of laws. . . .

DAVID ALBERT, APPENDIX II, "PARTICLES AND HUMAN BEINGS"

. . . the quantum reality is the fundamental one. That's certainly the way quantum mechanics is presented. The Newtonian world is a set of appearances that quantum mechanics can produce under certain circumstances.

DAVID ALBERT, APPENDIX II, "WATCHING *INLAND EMPIRE*"

Wish on the moon
And look for the gold in a rainbow
And you'll find happy times."

"HAPPY TIMES," WRITTEN BY SYLVIA FINE AND JOHNNY GREEN (1949),
PERFORMED BY JO STAFFORD

From certain vantage points in Manhattan, the Empire State Building seems to be directly ahead in a straight line and very close when it is actually significantly east or west of where it seems to be and very far away. This kind of illusion is typical of space as Lynch presents it—usually. But in *The Straight Story*, things are generally exactly where they appear to be. Spatially straightforward in its construction, *The Straight Story* (1999) is a fictional recounting of the trip one Alvin Straight (played in the film by Richard Farnsworth) actually made in 1994 from Laurens, Iowa, to Mt. Zion, Wisconsin, in order to try for a reconciliation with his estranged brother Henry. (In the film, Lynch changed the name of Straight's brother to Lyle.)[1] Where's the Lynchian twist? Well, it isn't that Alvin's brother Lyle (Harry Dean Stanton) has recently suffered a serious stroke and that Alvin fears that if he doesn't act quickly, he and his brother may never have time and space here on Earth to get past their hostility. That's the sort of plot complication that raises the stakes in many an ordinary Hollywood movie. And it isn't that Alvin Straight makes this trip of more than 300 miles on a small John Deere riding mower attached to a primitive trailer he has thrown together out of scrap wood to tote his provisions along with him. What Alvin decides to do in order to get to Lyle is only a matter of common sense. Alvin, who can't walk without the aid of two canes and is legally blind, no longer has a driver's license. There is no bus or train that can get him from Laurens to Mt. Zion, and there is no one to drive him there. So he takes the mechanically improbable yet strategically logical step of using a riding mower—which he can legally drive—for heavy duty transportation, far beyond what it was made to stand. Still, it is all that Alvin has on hand to accomplish his purposes. Eccentric. Implacable. But not really Lynchian, since in his films Lynch has never been a fan of unstoppable determination—or linearity.

The twist here is that Lynch embraces *this* linear story with a passion: Alvin's tale traces a straight line from observable and observed point A to a similarly uncomplicated point B, the story's terminus, exactly where we expected it to be, at Lyle's house. Business as usual in the minds of many, but not Lynch as usual. The clean lines of the journey could not be further from Lynch's typically complex interconnected narrative arcs. Nor could its tale of an old man's last hurrah be more different from Lynch's usual baroque violence and byzantine, convoluted patterns of lurid sexuality. The simple clarity of Alvin's trip seems to be a universe apart from Lynch's hallmark visual and narrative digressions; his reversals of time or his forays into the mysteries of space, which Lynch takes as a constant in human life. But it isn't part of another universe; it is a Lynchian miracle. The lovingly rigid motivation driving Alvin's story constitutes a wonder within the Lynchverse, and this is how Lynch treats it.

For an artist like Lynch who believes that the world is a tangle of uncertainly motivated particles that confound our illusions about stable measures of time and solid objects in space, linearity is miraculous, especially when it is benign. Thus this "straight story" told by an artist who understands the world as part of a boundless universe (curved if we are to believe Albert Einstein) is much more eccentric—from the Lynchian point of view—than the possession of Leland Palmer (Ray Wise) by BOB (Frank Silva) in his *Twin Peaks* cycle or the machinations of the Mystery Man (Robert Blake) in *Lost Highway*. Leland/BOB and the Mystery Man, figures of violence and disturbed sexuality, are utterly comprehensible within the frame of reference that is normative for Lynch. He sees them and the power they have as natural consequences of the illusions culture maintains about the physical and spiritual nature of being. What astonishes and moves Lynch about the story of Alvin Straight is the sweet, quiet, purity of a simple intent systematically realized. Love, to Lynch's delighted amazement, can exist within the illusions of a bounded culture. And Alvin, whose story has roots in reality, is the proof. But you have to squint to see it.

Yes, yes, Lynch affirms, we can speak of solid presence within the landscape of uncertainty, but our ability to look at it must be tightly circumscribed and controlled. Somehow it must be cast in a light that hides the truth about matter in space and time at its most basic level in order to reveal another truth: that people can under certain circumstances willfully assert what is best about human nature. As we know, for Lynch, willful assertion usually masks the truth of an indeterminate marketplace and comes in the toxic forms of a Mr. Eddy and a Mystery Man. Here, on the contrary, willful assertion of purpose is filled with the power of familial love to transform the limited, linear marketplace perspective into a way of channeling love. However, Lynch does not stop being Lynch when he tells Alvin's story; rather, an important part of his tale is to reveal how such an inversion on the usual state of things in the marketplace can exist.

In *The Straight Story*, Alvin's devotion to his quest to mend fences with Lyle is a certainty not easily spoken of by Lynch or simply achieved. But the elements of *this* true story (only slightly altered in Lynch's version) serendipitously permitted Lynch to tell the tale with a focus so narrow that the usual disturbing elements that require Lynch to depict action through superposition, entanglement, and many worlds could be marginalized to the periphery of our vision. And there they linger, present only as a subtle sense of something unspoken, maintaining Lynch's view of the universe as he draws a portrait of a man who for all intents and purposes shatters that view and comes as close to being a conventional hero as Lynch can imagine.

What will concern us here is Lynch's ability to include in his horizon of reality an event that he has often publicly said is very moving to him but which would seem to negate every other statement he has made about the way human beings live. How can a man like Alvin exist in the imagination of David Lynch? As we shall see, there is only one way. Alvin's labor of love needs to be looked at in the moments in which he plans and executes his mission of mercy to his brother, and in those moments alone, so that the cosmic details that usually complicate the Lynchian character are filtered out except for traces of their absence. To celebrate Alvin's deed, which Lynch clearly wishes to do, he must ask us to see it as a privileged horizontal cut of time and space, in which things seem to be certain and determined. To accomplish this, Lynch withholds a great deal of information about Alvin and the people he meets on his way to Lyle's shack in Mt. Zion. In *The Straight Story*, isolated comments by the characters that suggest qualities and situations just beyond the limits of our vision as spectators abound, but find no visual or dramatic elaboration.

For example, in an early scene, Alvin tells a young, unmarried, pregnant girl he encounters, who is running away from home out of guilt and shame, about his own daughter Rose (Sissy Spacek) and the loss of her children. Mentioning that Rose had her children taken away from her by the government because her little boy was badly burned while "someone" else was babysitting for her, Alvin opens up an ellipsis of significant proportions. Who is the tantalizingly vague "someone"? Was it, as Tim Kreider speculates in his review in *Film Quarterly* (Fall 2000), Alvin? Rose is blamed for the incident by the authorities because she is simple-minded, says Alvin, a description of his daughter that he does not endorse. That being the case, did he try to do anything about appealing the official decision? If not, why not? If he did, why didn't he succeed? Of course there is no room in this scene for that kind of exposition. But these uncertainties forever twist in the wind as Alvin moves toward Mt. Zion. And, as we shall see below, these questions are joined by many, many more.

The task of this discussion of *The Straight Story* will not be to flesh out what Lynch leaves only partly evoked, but to note the importance of the tantalizing incompleteness of the picture we get, an incompleteness that by accretion forms a generalized aura of uncertainty that shakes up the minutely detailed images we get of what is immediately in our line of vision as spectators. The film has a two-tiered structure, what is present with a clarity rare in a Lynch film, and what is noticeably absent. *The*

*Straight Story* is a special case of Lynchian reality; so, not unsurprisingly, the visual vocabulary Lynch uses to depict the world of matter comes from the vocabulary of physics that explains why, although at its most profound particle levels matter is indeterminate and uncertain, we see a solid, clearly measurable and finite plane of materiality. The term that would be used in quantum mechanics to describe the situation in which we seem to see the well-defined world of action and reaction described by Isaac Newton is decoherence. As physicist David Z. Albert says, deco-herence is "the business of explaining how classical looking phenomena arise under the appropriate circumstances from an underlying quantum mechanical set of laws."

Decoherence is a theory that quantum physics had to develop in order to explain why quantum theory about matter is so counterintuitive. We don't see what modern physics tells us is the truth about matter. The theory says that under certain conditions—the conditions that form the basis of most of our lives—a macroscopic view is created, either intention-ally or spontaneously, that allows us to believe what we know of the world of matter. Flooding a landscape with light, water, or dense air are three primary ways of creating an impression counter to the microscopic condi-tions created in the physics lab, in which uncertainty reigns and science no longer believes that it is in complete possession of knowledge of where objects are and the moment with which they are moving. Macroscopic conditions occur naturally in sunlight, wind, and rain. Within daylight, we feel we know what we're looking at. Decoherence can also be created in a laboratory, by flooding particles with light and creating the appear-ance that none of the troubling quantum behaviors of particles exist.[2]

Lynch conjures decoherence in *The Straight Story*. He does so to explain (to himself and to us) the story of Alvin Straight as an exception to the world he usually shows in which many worlds, and troubling forms of entanglement and superposition, become visible to his characters when they are shaken or inspired. There is a reality to Alvin's journey, but for us to experience it as real it needs to be flooded with light and seen from a high angle down, a cinematic simulation of the macrovision. The trip on the John Deere mower is so atypical of what is possible in the Lynchian marketplace that it must be viewed in the kind of light that gives it the appearance of reality, a believable and important linear trip that takes place in a world hostile to straight lines and linearity and heroism. The film is composed to gently open our eyes to the immensity of Alvin's production of a straight line. In a Lynch film, a straight line is a noteworthy thing—much more noteworthy than using a riding mower to travel from Iowa to Wisconsin.

The tropes of decoherence that Lynch employs are helped significantly by the fact that he is dealing with sharply limited central characters, unlike those that ordinarily people his work. Alvin and Lyle are fiercely circumscribed by old age and Alvin's daughter Rose by limited mental capacity. It is easier to create an impression of finitude and certainty with characters like these than with the visionary Dale Cooper in the *Twin Peaks* cycle; the young and volatile Sandy (Laura Dern) and Jeffrey in *Blue Velvet*; the young and boisterously visceral Sailor (Nicolas Cage) and Lula (Laura Dern) in *Wild at Heart*; the young and yearning Fred, and the young and sexually complicated Alice/Renee in *Lost Highway*.

Part of the decoherence of *The Straight Story* is created through the visuals, in frame compositions that are aglow with the relationship between light and Alvin's journey. Part of it is the narrative exclusion, within this light, of everything extraneous to Alvin's goal, all of which needs to be held in abeyance for this particular story to come to its conclusion. Released from Lynch's layers of darkness that are infused into his other films, *The Straight Story* takes place only in the light—of the sun and the stars, usually, but sometimes also of lightning. Lynch pointedly allows us to see Alvin and all those he comes in contact with from the perspective of a "big picture" that is not boundless, but flooded with light so that we seem to see a rigidly defined world.

With its happy ending, which will require much discussion before this chapter comes to a close, and its minutely scrutinized linear progress, an illusion is created that the uncertainty principle has been temporarily suspended. *The Straight Story* is the single film in Lynch's filmography in which his protagonist thrives even though he is blocked from moving under or behind the surfaces of the world. But, in fact, its shadows are everywhere on this canvas. Lynch leaves telltale signs of uncertainty that lurk just beyond Alvin's narrowly focused way of living and thinking. This renders Alvin's sunny vistas both a noteworthy avoidance of the characteristic Lynchian plunge into the hidden depths and a deeply emotional celebration of the kind of miraculous human triumph that is only rarely possible within the limits of the marketplace. Alvin's reunion with his brother Lyle (Harry Dean Stanton) is (astonishingly) real and it is moving, but the film lets us know early and often, through the strong sense of absence that Lynch creates, that Alvin's loving quest is part of a much larger, complexly nonlinear picture, invisible to Alvin and the others in his story. At the same time, because of the light of Alvin's miraculous love that fills him within this special moment in time and space, he does not succumb to or even meet the devils that Fred's negativity in *Lost Highway* exposes him to. If we fail to notice Lynch's subtle, delicately drawn chiaroscuro, we defeat his artistry by creating an ersatz, smarmy Alvin in our minds as Lynch never imagined him.

## ALVIN AND THE MACHINE

Lurking behind the well-defined logistics of Alvin's preparation for his trip and his execution of his plans, which take place up front and center of *The Straight Story,* is a deep layer of shadows. The characterization of this 73-year-old man is defined by what is only partially sketched of his biography, but there lingers a palpable sense of missing information. The portrait of Alvin is enigmatic, made equivocal by the part machines play in his story and by the distinct differences in his behavior when he is seen in the context of his town and family and when he is on the road.

There's something tantalizing about Lynch's presentation of machines in this Grandpa-on-the-road saga. In *The Straight Story,* machines, principally Alvin's John Deere riding mower, define the landscape as solid and substantial, as is typical of Hollywood movies. It is this air of clarity that is principally responsible for the perception of *The Straight Story* as un-Lynchian. However, there's an interesting trace of something behind the cut-and-dried machine presence. It's true that they're so metallically complete that the various mowers and farm machines populating *The Straight Story* seem to give the lie to quantum mechanics and all the uncertainty we have already addressed as the primary quality of Lynch's marketplaces. What could be less indeterminate than these serviceable mechanisms of all sizes and colors? And yet everything in the film conspires to show us that these objects only seem to encapsulate the solidity of the world as we would like it to be; their durable integrity is a mirage. Alvin's machines are, in fact, an eloquent revelation of the illusory quality of solidity ordinarily attributed to materiality. So much attention is paid to the mechanics of Alvin's trip. Everyone comments on the mower, the easiest issue to hand in thinking about Alvin's plans, but Lynch uses the sturdy little mechanical body to reveal that the real marvel, the energy that keeps this strange pilgrimage going, is not in the machine, but radiated from something invisible and expansive in Alvin. Machines have a rugged aura, but, as we see early and often in Alvin's story, they are breakable. It is precisely when the machines break, as Alvin struggles toward Lyle, that we discover that there is something in play that is unbreakable. What's left when the machine fails is the invisible something that drives the universe. In this case, it is Alvin's commitment, which is invisible, infinite, and unstoppable. The finite machine is only a fallible vehicle.

The importance of the point-by-point tracing of the logistics of the two mowers that are a part of Alvin's plan, a minute attention to detail that isn't necessary for the linear story, is the way these minutiae disclose slowly the contrast between the seeming importance and solidity of the objects in the marketplace and the real power of the energy of love that comes from somewhere else beyond the marketplace. It can't be visualized but presents itself to the audience as what abides on a terrain where materiality *will* falter, even when seen from the classical point of view as essentially solid. If, in most of his work, Lynch calls on quantum physics for a visual vocabulary that demonstrates that matter is always shifting and transforming, in the special circumstances produced by the patterns of decoherence governing *The Straight Story*, the traces of the profound quantum reality Lynch sees in all our daily endeavors show through the seeming down-to-earth conventional normality of Alvin's life. We see those traces in the inevitability that materiality will degrade through age, rupture under adverse conditions, or merely lapse for no particular reason. Basing one's security on materiality alone is not feasible, even in a life like Alvin's.

For much of his journey, Alvin hums along like clockwork, a small figure mechanically making a straight line in a large landscape seen as the legendary bountiful rolling plains of middle America, a vision of solidity and blissful certainty. There are numerous idyllic scenes of Alvin making progress, like the one just before the Rehds gives out when Alvin glides by a farmhouse, outside of which a mother peacefully hangs the laundry on a clothesline while her son and a pleasant dog stand nearby. It is all very sunny and distant.[3] Alvin waves happily as he moves onward, never speaking to the woman and child. The vista is untroubled at that moment. But the line of blissful motion is ultimately discontinuous, and the dynamics of the discontinuities in his progress take him through roughly four stages. Once he learns of his brother Lyle's stroke and determines to go to see him, the first stage is the formation of the plan to equip his very old Rehds riding mower for the journey; the second stage requires him to cope with the failure of the Rehds to get him past the Grotto, a tourist landmark several miles from his hometown of Laurens, at the beginning of his journey, and the need to get a new mower. The third stage involves making necessary repairs when another breakdown occurs perhaps a bit further than midway in his journey, when one of the belts in the mower's transmission breaks as Alvin is riding down a fairly challenging hill, a terrifying moment in which Alvin is very nearly killed. After resuming his peaceful approach to Mt. Zion where Lyle lives, Alvin is stymied once again when his mower appears to break down only a few hundred yards from Lyle's shack.

Each stage is a material crisis, but not a spiritual one. Alvin so miraculously channels the positive energy Lynch gleans in the cosmos that nothing in the ordinary conditions of the marketplace ever seems like a crisis to him, which is surprising, given his restrictions. If we make a checklist of all of the limitations in Alvin's way as he seeks to get to Lyle, the task seems materially impossible. Alvin can't drive; there is no mass transportation available between his house and Lyle's; he can barely walk and hardly see; and there doesn't appear to be anyone around to drive him. Yet if others are more than dubious about the trip, the material logistics are always no more than a puzzle to Alvin at the outset. His solution takes stock of the raw material at his disposal, and when the Rehds proves undependable, he merely substitutes another mower. The

The rolling plains of mid-America, solid-seeming in the sunlight.

THE STRAIGHT STORY

situation that comes closest to catastrophe is the sudden trauma for Alvin when his mower/trailer contraption goes careening down a steep incline and Alvin's life is in danger. However, when Alvin reaches the bottom of the incline alive, he again treats the situation as a set of logistics, using whatever and whoever is on hand to help him find someone (in this case two) to make repairs so that he can be on his way. The fourth disruption seems to underline the reality of the skeptical point of view about Alvin's plan. Almost at his goal, the mower breaks down again. But this time the breakdown is only apparent. Time passes; an old fellow driving a much larger farm machine comes along and suggests that Alvin try "starting her again." And the mower responds. Alvin's physical journey is a marriage between a never-flagging spirit and fallible machinery that contradicts the sense of security that Americans take in mechanisms. Alvin is a creature of the visible world of machines, but it is always the invisible world of the Vedas—that unity behind an undependable physicality—that holds his journey together.

Traces of quantum uncertainty also show through in Alvin's characterization. He is not constructed along the lines of character consistency that rule Hollywood. Instead, he is portrayed as an indeterminate creature of shifts, but with such delicacy that it is entirely possible to watch the film many times without realizing how enigmatic Lynch has made his down-home protagonist. These shifts are motivated by the differences between being "at home" and being on the road. At home, parameters are pronounced and limitations on the uncertainties of human nature are rigidly in place. On the road, the limits relax and the diversity of human beings finds a great deal more latitude. In response, Alvin shifts his behavior. Within the context of Alvin's family and community life in Laurens he is a rebel, a voice—on his own behalf and no one else's—in opposition to the way things are, but out on the road he is a kind of "lone ranger" of order, taking the large view and pontificating about how people need to behave in families and communities. When we first meet Alvin, we see him as a man exasperated by life within ordinary restrictions, both because it is cramped and because people who live with each other from day to day tend to get tangled up in misunderstanding and cross-purposes. The gently comic tone of Alvin's life in Laurens is rendered by Lynch with a light touch, but it captures the real frustration of his hero, and the uncertainty and indeterminacy of town life—despite all appearances to the contrary. We see this immediately when Alvin's friend, Bud (Joseph A.

69

Carpenter) strolls over to the Straight house from the local bar because Alvin has not shown up to meet his pals when he was expected. As Bud tries to determine what has happened to Alvin, he and Alvin's neighbor Dorothy get their wires crossed and hackles are raised. Dorothy tells Bud she saw Alvin's daughter leave a couple of hours ago. But Bud isn't looking for Rose and he's not happy with Dorothy's pointless interference with his search for his friend. When Bud gets into Alvin's house through the back door and finds him lying on the floor and unable to get up, Dorothy rushes in and noticing Alvin's plight, nervously asks, "What's the phone number for 911?" Alvin, really fed up with the nitpicking fights between Bud and Dorothy, is adamant in his demand that Dorothy not make the call. Then Alvin's daughter Rose abruptly walks in with her shopping cart. Stopping dead in her tracks at the sight that greets her eyes, she asks frantically, "What have you done to my Dad?" Everyone sees only a small fragment of the situation. No one sees the whole thing. Tempers fray. The air is rife with garden-variety miscommunication that is funny for the most part because of its familiarity.

The small conflicts that occur at home and in the town continue when Alvin is pressured to go to the doctor by Rose, where he stonewalls all therapeutic attempts. He rejects medical science wholesale. No tests, no X-rays, no medical advice. He also rejects the limits imposed by his aging body. After Alvin leaves the doctor's office, having heard a list of his medical problems, including emphysema, and after being warned of the necessity to make some lifestyle changes, the first thing we see him do is light up a cigar. The second thing he does is lie to Rose, telling her in effect that the doctor has given him a clean bill of health, when we know that the doctor has warned Alvin of dire consequences if he goes on as he is.

When Alvin goes to the local hardware store to equip himself for the journey, stocking up becomes another trial by constraint for him. The old guys who hang around the hardware store are the buddies he meets with in the local bar, and at least one, Sig, makes claims on Alvin. He wants to know why Alvin's stocking up on gasoline. And when the hardware store owner doesn't want to sell Alvin his grabber, but Alvin makes it his business to pry it out of him, Sig wants to know why he needs a grabber. (A grabber is a stick with a mechanism on the end that makes it possible to get hold of objects stocked too high up to get hold of comfortably.) When Alvin makes his maiden voyage down the main street of Laurens heading out to Lyle, the old men come running out of the hardware store to try to stop him. When they express fears for him. Alvin stonewalls them completely and wordlessly.

There are two people with whom Alvin is comfortable in the initial scenes in the film: Rose, who is portrayed as the source of his stability, such as it is, when Alvin is at home, and Tom (Everett McGill), the proprietor of the John Deere store that is the source of both his old Rehds riding mower and the "new" 1966 secondhand mower with which he completes the trip to Mt. Zion. Significantly, both of these characters are Alvin's link between home and being a traveling man, which is subtly built into the film as Alvin's most natural state. When Alvin tells Rose about his plan to travel to Lyle's house, he tells her he's getting back on the road, one of those enigmatic statements about Alvin's life that opens the door to his past, but only a crack. Yet there is a sense that Alvin's tenure in Laurens has been intermittent, that he has spent his life traveling, that NOT being a part of a settled community is more his usual state. This sense is supported by Alvin's transformation when he sets out on his mower. He's happier, freer, and more comfortable on the open road. No longer chafing against limits, he fluidly moves into the stance of the teacher, a source of wisdom for troubled people. Like Fred Madison, Alvin never purposely changes himself. But as he spontaneously takes on certain qualities born of experience on the road, his character, seemingly so normal and set in a certain mold, dissolves into smoke, since much of his text of counsel and advice concerns stability and the unity of people, a situation with which, as we have already seen, daughter Rose is quite uncomfortable and Alvin cannot actually endure.[4]

## ALVIN UNBOUND

Once Alvin leaves Rose and the town of Laurens, his character undergoes a transformation; the change is not constructed through the apocalyptic cinematic fireworks that mark Fred Madison's metamorphosis in *Lost Highway*, but it is equally significant to Alvin's characterization. The differences between Alvin at home and Alvin on the road are defined by contrasting image and soundtrack designs. *The Straight Story* begins with a familiar Lynchian vista of the stars and moves into a fluid high angle montage of images of the beautiful rolling country and then the town, scored by sweet, very harmonic music. Once the camera drops into Laurens and Alvin's daily life, however, the music (which will resume once

Alvin is on the road), is terminated and the soundtrack is composed of ambient sound, music lacking harmonic sweetness and resolution, and diegetic music coming from local radios. Similarly the sense of freedom, sky, and air temporarily goes on hiatus when we see Alvin in situ in his home town. Most of the frames completely enclose Alvin and the other characters within walls and objects. Sometimes, a freer and larger terrain is visible, but at a distance. Alvin manages with difficulty within these initial circumstances and there is frequently a sense of oppressiveness.

There are two exceptions to the somewhat claustrophobic, limited vistas in the first part of *The Straight Story*. The first occurs when Alvin and Rose luxuriate in the pleasure of a lightning storm that brings a much larger sense of being into their little home. In the second instance, Alvin and Rose are looking up at the stars shortly before Alvin leaves to visit Lyle. The news that Lyle has had a stroke reaches Alvin in the middle of a clap of thunder and flash of lighting, a cinematic stroke that would be corny if it were not made new by the context of this particular film as the eruption into Alvin's uncomfortably circumscribed life of something much larger, and not, as conventionally in horror films, sinister. Rather the lightning brings Alvin back onto the road, moving in freedom toward affirmation. When Alvin announces his decision to travel, the sweet harmonic music recurs briefly in Alvin's home. It occurs again when Rose and Alvin are looking at the sky and Alvin explains to his daughter why he has to go to see Lyle even though, as she says, the rig he has put together is problematic. But that sweet music is continuously characteristic of his time on the road.

Visually, when Alvin is riding along on his mower on the open road, he is photographed to fit into the larger landscape harmoniously. Other characters may find the contraption grotesque, but the point of view of the film does not. There is a beauty and sweetness to watching Alvin move smoothly over the terrain, and when we see the high, wide, and open terrain that Alvin now finds himself in—a rightness to these unbound moments that is echoed in the theme music of the film. This is true both in the first botched attempt that ends with Alvin shooting the old Rehds and buying a reconditioned Deere motor, and when Alvin makes his second try, which will result in success. The point is not Alvin's triumph, but the spirit with which Alvin leaves his hometown confines.

Within that open atmosphere of the road, Alvin positions himself as a wise counselor, creating for some critics an annoying "Ann Landers effect"

Alvin (Richard Farnsworth) oppressively enclosed by the objects in his kitchen; at this moment he is literally immobilized within his familiar environment.

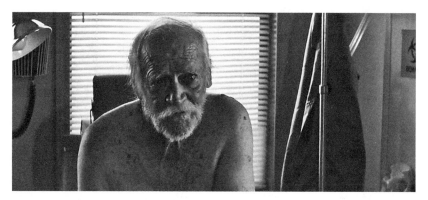

Alvin (Richard Farnsworth), uncomfortably boxed-in within the confines of the doctor's office, as he fights off what he sees as the intrusive nature of the medical profession.

Even in the open air of his own backyard, Alvin (Richard Farnsworth) is fenced in.

as he gives frequent advice to those he meets on his travels. But, in fact, Lynch fills the segment of the film in which Alvin is traveling and dispensing good advice, the largest segment of *The Straight Story*, with as many perforations in Alvin's solid-seeming performance as there were empty spaces in Arthur Eddington's threshold. This is not to say that the film mocks Alvin, because it never does. It always venerates his striving, but at the same time Lynch creates a complex, complicated vision of this beautiful, but uncertain world. The advice that Alvin hands out leaves many questions in its wake. In his first on-the-road encounter, when he meets up with a runaway teenage girl, unmarried and pregnant, he counsels her to return home in tones that reflect a mythic solidity and homogeneous quality to family life. But under the surface of this scene—in which it may be that Alvin has successfully convinced the girl to get off the road and go back to her people—many shadows lurk. We know nothing of what made her run away from home when she found herself pregnant, nor what she will face if she returns. Nor is there anything solidly defined about Alvin's family life that gives substance to his sunny view of "home." Where are the seven children that his now-dead wife Frances gave birth to? (There are no pictures of Alvin's other children or of Frances anywhere within Alvin's home.) Why do we only see a connection between Alvin and Rose? What experience of family has he had that validates the advice he gives her? The story he tells the nameless girl about how the government took Rose's children away from her is no endorsement for family life either.

Alvin gives the teenager only some flimsy details from this heart-wrenching part of his past, details that have led some to question what part Alvin played in Rose's tragedy. Alvin's story leaves us with many unswered questions. Loose ends abound. One of Rose's four children was hurt in a fire when "someone else" was taking care of them and Rose was blamed, ostensibly because she is a bit simpleminded. But what is the full story? Why didn't Alvin petition to have the children returned? Alvin tells his tale as if he is simply a detached observer, but he isn't. He is Rose's father. There is a counterpoint between the elliptical details of what he says to the runaway girl and the sweet music on the soundtrack, which is compatible with Alvin's placid affect but not with what he says. There is something discomforting about this scene that points away from the surface and toward something underneath that we can't see and are being blocked from seeing.[5]

This sense that we don't really know what we are looking at is especially true of the parable of the sticks that Alvin lays on the runaway girl. To prove his point that family is the source of strength, he tells her how he would give his children each a stick and ask them to break it and then demonstrate that they couldn't break a bundle of sticks tied together. That's family, he says. Is it? Alvin's family is broken in several ways. Almost all of his children are not in touch with him (Rose never suggests that any of his other children drive him to Mr. Zion), and Alvin has not spoken to his brother in ten years. At the point that he speaks to the girl, he has no real idea whether Lyle will accept him if and when he reaches his brother, or if he'll be alive by the time Alvin gets there. Moreover, when the girl is gone the next morning and has left a bundle of sticks, we really have no idea what message she is sending him. Is she saying that she's going home? Or that she heard him? Might she think for a moment she will go home and then change her mind? There is no telling. Uncertainty courses through this interlude even as, for just this one bundle of time, there is a sense of certainty and harmony. Once Alvin leaves that time and place during which he speaks with the runaway girl, there is nothing left but the dream of human happiness he dispensed.

Moreover, this interlude characterizes Alvin's dreamlike view of women that is present throughout the film. Certainly, we don't have an image of the unattainable siren at work here, as we did in *Lost Highway*, but we do have a dream of women as the linchpin of "home" that has no real connection with how Alvin treats women when he is at home. While Alvin is happily out of place, on the road, he thinks of women as the ones who hold the fort while he is around and about; he thinks of women as the people who have a rightful place. Alvin is neither affected by nor concerned with women's troubling erotic power, nor is it in evidence in the film. The closest he gets to sex is a busload of lady tourists who get giggly in his presence, but they, like the runaway girl, are all asexual figures to Alvin. The pregnant runaway had sex but we see her as Alvin sees her, as he sees all the women in the film, dressed in clothing that disguises the sexual contours of the feminine form. Similarly, Dorothy, Alvin's plump, cake-munching neighbor, is a parody of female sexuality with her very ugly "beauty parlor"-styled red hair and her unattractively exposed body. Later, when Alvin is in the midst of some young, good-looking girls who are part of a bicycling tour, he doesn't seem to notice them, and talks only to the young men. And when he is thrown back into domesticity for a while, when Danny and Darla

Riordan (James Cada and Sally Wingert) help him out after the transmission on his mower breaks down, Darla is barely on his radar except as a part of Danny Riordan's domestic arrangements. Alvin's wife is remembered by him only in her capacity as a mother of fourteen children, only seven of which survived, and the affection he has for Rose is clean of any erotic aspects of her being. She keeps order. For Alvin's dream of harmony in the world to be true, he must be the one moving about while women safeguard the order of the "normal" world, an order that seems increasingly to exist only in Alvin's illusions.

The closest Alvin comes to confronting the uncertainty around him out on the road is in the interludes when he meets up with a big entourage of bicyclists on a tour; when he meets up with the "deer lady" (a woman who is not staying in a contained place); and when he careens dangerously down a steep hill after the belt on his mower suddenly snaps. When the cyclists intersect with Alvin, they are a whirling mass of moving bodies and machines, whizzing past him dizzyingly. He spends a night with the cyclists, who give him an ovation and enjoy the originality of his vehicle. But when Alvin strikes up an acquaintance with two of the cyclists, it's hard to say whether he's jealous of them, and taunting them as they converse, or whether he's speaking as the voice of wisdom. This is especially true when one boy asks him what the worst thing is about getting old and Alvin replies, "remembering when you was young." The look that passes from Alvin to the young man is baleful, almost a reproachful *memento mori* that cautions the young, handsome, virile boy that this will be his fate too, someday. Yet, we will come to know that Alvin was

Alvin's (Richard Farnsworth) irritable response to a young, virile man's question about old age.

not happy when he was young; he was beset by war, a fiery temper, and alcoholism. If we pay close attention to this film, the tensions between the surfaces and the depths are quite evident. We never go beneath the conversation in this scene, but something disquieting peeks out at us from what we do see.[6]

When the "deer lady" appears, a deer crashes into her car right in front of Alvin, leaving the poor creature's corpse on the road and the woman's car badly damaged. Alvin is reduced to speechlessness before the spectacle of a world that is painfully indeterminate. Unlike in the other scenes on the road, Alvin dispenses no wisdom, but stands back before the furious tirade of this woman who says that she finds herself hitting deer a couple of times a week on a highway she can't avoid traveling on twice a day. Scanning an empty horizon, she asks in despair, "where do they come from?" And indeed, as the camera scans a perfectly flat horizon, without even a stand of trees or a line of bushes behind which the deer might hide, it *is* absolutely unfathomable how they can continue to surprise her. When she leaves, Alvin's response is to cook and eat deer steak. Strangely, as he does so, we see him surrounded by effigies of deer standing in the high weeds in back of him. Where did *they* come from? Alvin looks guiltily at the deer figures, but continues to cook. Their liminal quality, seeming somewhere between possible figures on someone's property where Alvin is camping for the night and images with which Alvin has peopled the landscape, leaves a hole in the tapestry of this seemingly down-to-earth, but actually very uncertain film.[7]

The wide-open vista from which deer emerge to collide with the car of the "deer lady"; the lack of cover on this horizon renders truly mysterious her question, "Where do they come from?"

**77**

At least as challenging to Alvin as the mystery of the deer lady is his ordeal when his mower breaks down as he is descending a dangerous hill in the small town of Clermont, Iowa. Alvin is faced with death again, not only Lyle's possible demise but also his own. And the incident takes place in a strange context. The hill down which Alvin speeds leads to an old, abandoned house burning in the middle of nowhere, seemingly for no reason. But ultimately, the fire is explicable. The old house has purposely been set ablaze by local firemen for practice, and the tear in Alvin's complacent happiness is restored when he is rescued by some friendly locals who have gathered to watch the firemen burning down the house. The shots of Alvin experiencing terror during and even for a few minutes after the out-of-control descent against the background of a burning house are expressive of the world that Alvin really inhabits as opposed to the one he dreams of on the road. However, most of what maintains Alvin's sense of well-being in a world that is increasingly defined for the audience as highly uncertain is his refusal to enter again into a domestic setting. Alvin rigorously refuses even to briefly enter the home of the Riordans, who have let him camp out on their small property. When he wants to make a telephone call, Alvin doggedly insists on using a cordless phone outside, refusing numerous invitations by Danny to come sit inside to talk. Nor will Alvin accept Danny's good-natured offer to drive Alvin to nearby Mt. Zion. Alvin says he wants to finish the trip the way he started, which seems like garden-variety rugged individualism.

Maybe it is in part. But it is an individualism defined as a way of preserving a sense of solidity in a world in which domesticity and too-intimate connection reveal the indeterminacy Alvin does not want to face. Another interesting way in which Lynch defines Alvin's maintenance of his on-the-road sense of a harmonious world is when Danny and Darla Riordan help Alvin set up a tent canopy so that he can camp out in their backyard. It is rendered in a very long shot, for no obvious narrative reason, and their voices, as they speak casually to each other, are extremely muted, emphasizing the distance from which we see them. They chatter about the logistics of putting up the canopy, which are not at all complex or interesting; moreover, nothing at all meaningful for the film's narrative happens in this scene. Yet, this enforced distance places a silent exclamation point over the scene, marking it as Alvin's way. On the occasion in which Lynch lets us into the Riordan home, Alvin's skepticism is justified, or at least it is justified in the sense that illusions of certainty cannot sur-

Alvin's (Richard Farnsworth) one moment of sheer terror in *The Straight Story*, when he loses control of his mower near a burning building on a sharp incline leading into a small town. We see in this moment how unprepared he is for the uncertain universe that lurks behind the sunny appearances of his daily life.

vive being locked into a narrowly fixed set of parameters. As Danny uses Darla as a sounding board to convince himself to offer to drive Alvin the rest of the way on his trip, Darla says, "You're a good man, Danny Riordan. And that's why I married you, despite what my mother said." Why didn't mama approve? What's in Danny's background—or mama's?—that underlies Darla's comment? Or is it just a lightly made in-joke between husband and wife? We won't ever know.

During the Riordan interlude, Alvin reveals more of the darkness in his background and inadvertently makes us realize how little we are able to know about him, even though we barely take our eyes off him during his road trip. One of the Riordans' friends, Verlyn Heller (Wiley Harker), a man of Alvin's age, talks with Alvin about World War II, and they each tell terrible stories about how indeterminate the world is and how death can strike without warning or reason. Clearly Heller will never recover the peace of mind he lost during the war, and Alvin also reveals old war wounds on the soul. Heller and Alvin talk in a bar, where Alvin will not order anything alcoholic because, as we learn, he came back from the war a mean drunk, in response to all the terrible things he saw under fire, and feels that his hard-won sobriety depends on abstinence.

Interestingly, according to Alvin, his return to sobriety was only possible when he could acknowledge that wartime is not the only time that human beings behave badly. Alvin reveals that he only came out of his downward spiral when a clergyman made him see that an important reason for his inordinate drinking is that he couldn't leave the war behind because he saw similar terrible things in the United States when he returned. Murmuring on the soundtrack are sounds from wartime that infiltrate this quiet corner of Iowa, suggesting the uncertainty of time and space—even inside this very ordinary setting. This is another moment when Alvin is confronted by the omnipresence of disjunctions and discontinuities in what he wants to see as a certain world, but at the same time we witness the way even so powerful a rupture in everyday illusion is covered over.

Music floats through a portion of this scene on the soundtrack, mysteriously filling the air in the bar with an old 1940s recording of a song called "Happy Times." Is it playing somewhere on a jukebox? Has it erupted from the men's memories? We never know. It is 1940s feel-good music that appears and disappears in a way that makes it unlikely that it is actually diegetic, adding to the dislocations of time and space effected by the low but palpable war sounds: "Wish on the moon and look for the gold in a rainbow and you'll find happy times," sings Jo Stafford, a very popular chanteuse of the day, in her rich, calming, yet sensual voice, a siren with a difference. She doesn't lure sailors to die on the rocks on which she sits, but rather lures ordinary folks away from the troubles they face in daily life to the comforts of distant paradisal locations. In fact, she enunciates a kind of truth: happy times of the kind she speaks are only to be found on the moon, a place Alvin cannot go, and the gold in a rainbow, an object that does not exist. When the scene ends, Stafford is no longer in the air and the temporary anodyne of popular music has burst like a bubble; in its place, the film supplies the down-home melodies that have characterized the "harmony theme" on the film's soundtrack. But by this point, the theme no longer seems completely happy, but tinged by melancholy, a recognition perhaps of the fragility of the way we paper over the essential darkness of the world in order to keep our spirits up.[8]

Once Alvin's mower has been repaired and he is ready to return to the road, Alvin, the wise traveler, reappears. Confronted by the bickering Olsen twins, Harald (Kevin P. Farley) and Thorvald (John Farley), who fixed the mower, Alvin efficiently takes care of the domestic tangles that remain by shrewdly cutting all the padding off his repair bill—extra hours that he principally ascribes to the time they wasted abusing each other. Here Alvin comes up with more of his illusory images of the "happy family." He reads them the riot act about how brothers should behave. A brother, he tells them, knows you better than anyone else. "A brother is a brother." As with the runaway teenager, the solidity of this scene, when the brothers seem chastened by Alvin, is only in the moment. There are too many ellipses in our knowledge of Alvin's relationship to Lyle, and the relationships among Alvin's sons, to give Alvin's doctrine credence as anything more than a wish. Except that, illusory though his belief in the importance of the fraternal relationship may be, it has positive energy coursing through it, even if it is not connected with a real pattern of historical behavior that is completely created by that energy.

## LOOK UP AT THE SKY, ROSIE

Positive energy abounds in Alvin, even if the marketplace has not permitted Alvin to make a truly happy life. Stuck in constraints all his life, Alvin looks up, and always has. When he tells daughter Rosie to look up at the sky as she is trying to talk him out of making an against-the-odds long-distance trip on his riding mower rig, he is providing a perfect example of his own non-abusive way of transforming an uncertain, unfathomable system of objects and bodies in space. Looking past what surrounds him to the stars was the way he and his brother coped with the terrible Minnesota cold of their youth and the oppression of unending farm chores that nearly killed their parents, as Alvin confides near the end of his journey to a priest he meets just before he finds Lyle. As a result—since, in accordance with Lynch's understanding that the world is what you are, a Lynch film is what the protagonist is—*The Straight Story* is visually composed of high-angle vistas of harmony and radiance that compensate for the frustrations and mysteries of the marketplace of ordinary transactions.

*The Straight Story* counterpoints above and below, beginning and ending with the stars. Along the road, as we have already said, high-angle blissful shots abound of rolling countryside, sunrises and sunsets. At the start of the film, Laurens is seen from the air, so neat and well-ordered that it could be a toy town. Everything looks plotted out clearly on a grid of streets, cross streets, trees, little homes, and businesses. The next lap dissolve brings us in closer, to what looks like Main Street USA, but we are still kept at a pristine distance. Low, neatly arranged brick buildings line the street. Again, there are no people in sight as a truck with complicated farm machinery attachments on it slowly tootles toward the back of the frame. Suddenly, to break the spell of perfection, from out of nowhere, dogs come running across the street, a disorderly cascade of motion. Where *do* they come from? It is only when we drop into the marketplace, the level of materiality on which Alvin lives, that we begin to see the scene as much less well-defined. Throughout the film, Lynch continues to include telltale traces that Alvin's vision is only a small part of an uncertain cosmos.

There are numerous places in the film where Lynch laps images of earth and sky over each other so that the neatness of compass points of up and down disappear. One interesting place is just as Alvin is turning

The street grid of Laurens, Iowa, seen from the air; in the light of day the town appears to be fully ordered by human thinking and controllable, which is how Alvin sees it.

The sudden emergence of exuberant dogs, as Alvin leaves Laurens on his mower. Where do they come from? We never know how they fit into what Alvin sees as an orderly environment.

off a main road onto the street where he will meet the "deer lady," which signals an intersection that greatly challenges Alvin's neat ideas about his circumstances. Another place is just before Alvin meets the cyclists when the clouds and the fertile land are lapped. But even more powerful than this kind of uncertain image is Lynch's depiction of the direction of Alvin's trip. Alvin is traveling east from Iowa to Michigan, which, if it were true to the way we measure and map motion, should show Alvin moving from left to right. Moreover, there is cinematic vocabulary to consider as well. In American movies, everyone driving from right to left is moving westward toward the setting sun, one of the conventions that is particularly true of the western, and Alvin's cowboy hat and resemblance to the long, lean, rangy cowboy stereotype plucks at the generic memory of that genre. So Alvin's progress from right to left resonates against several filmic traditions of representing motion.

Although the soundtrack music conveys harmony and stability as Alvin rides along, the images seriously confuse our sense of direction, so that when the characters speak of which way Alvin is going and where he is coming from, a feeling of disorientation invades the film that collides with all the markers that convey ease and rightness. The confusion is quiet because it is not accompanied by blatant disturbances of the eyeline match—the editing technique that assures audience clarity about the physical construction of a location—but by the destruction of conventions of direction. Alvin's reversed trajectory is comparable to the disturbances of audience orientation in space that Lynch creates in the scenes in the Red Room in the *Twin Peaks* cycle and in Fred Madison's movement through the dark corridors of home in *Lost Highway*.

Nor are the images of Alvin's eastward motion, presented in the conventions of westward movement, the only instance in which Lynch confuses the compass points in *The Straight Story*. A discombobulation occurs every time characters speak of Alvin's eastward trajectory. And when Lynch shows us the placid topography of Alvin's landscape from the air, since he looks as if he is going west, the golden images, smoothly and expertly shot from a helicopter, put us into a kind of trance that is augmented by the traditional American music on the soundtrack. So we do not easily notice that the camera moves through the air in a circular fashion that turns us and turns us again and again until we are not at all certain about the directions from which we are viewing this "blessed land of room enough." A close reading of what Lynch does to direction

In the code of movie space, moving to frame left means moving west, which is the direction Alvin (Richard Farnsworth) seems to take here. But within the narrative of the story, Alvin is moving east. This image is part of a pattern that renders the direction of Alvin's motion indeterminate.

and orientation in space when Alvin is in motion changes what he experiences from a straight line to Zion into a dream of coherence in a landscape in which there is nothing certain. Moreover, the uncertainty of how the area Alvin is traveling through has been mapped increases as Alvin nears his goal.

## ARRIVING IN ZION

Alvin does, however, achieve his goal. He does find Lyle. Whether or not he "lives in a dream," as Lynch has said we all do both in his films and in his public statements, Alvin makes for himself one of the happiest of happy endings in any David Lynch narrative. Lynch plays with the audience when Alvin finally sets foot on Lyle's property and calls out to him. There is no immediate response. But Alvin's anxiety is terminated after a brief period of uncertainty when Lyle answers him. And yet. Like all the interludes along the way, finding Lyle and the encounters Alvin has just before the brotherly reunion with a Catholic priest and a bartender in the Mt. Zion area are also tinged by questions and uncertainties. In the prelude to Alvin's arrival at Lyle's house, in fact, we find a singularly powerful evocation of the uncertain shape of Alvin's journey.

When Alvin is in the vicinity of Mt. Zion, he stops for the night in a country cemetery just a few yards from the home of the Catholic priest who serves the church connected with the cemetery. This, the last of the full-fledged road interludes, very interestingly sums up the inextricably intertwined beauty of Alvin's trip and its illusory nature. The imagery is safe enough, as Alvin sits with the priest underneath the same conventional star-filled sky that beams down on Hollywood's independent souls on the range, near a campfire that casts the familiar shadows and lights on their faces that we have seen in dozens of westerns. And the conversation seems to seal Alvin and the priest into the well-defined parameters of classical time and space as they discuss the history of the graveyard, where some of the members of the famous Marquette party are buried. The story of the Jesuit Priest Jacques's travels in the late seventeenth century to map the waterways of the area in order to find a way to the Pacific Ocean and, if possible, to China, is part of grade-school history.

However, here again, under the veneer of stability evoked by the historical tale of Marquette, depleted of the dangers of exploration by time and repetition, lurks the confusion and uncertainty of all the explorations of that period. Marquette's party laid the foundation for France's political claim to that area, but they never found a way to the Pacific Ocean. And what they did find—the connection between the Mississippi River and the Gulf of Mexico—they never mapped accurately because they were too confused by the pathways on which they were taken by the local Indians who tried to help them. The Marquette story is commemorated richly as a triumph of discovery, but Marquette's experiences were actually quite haphazard. It was never fully clear where he had been, and the site of his death at the very early age of thirty-eight remains controversial. Nor does the priest identify exactly which members of the Marquette party are buried in the land behind them.

Not coincidentally, as the priest asks about Alvin's history, Alvin gives a few details that completely confuse his time line as well. When Alvin tells the priest that he is traveling to reunite with an estranged brother, the priest naturally asks about the cause of the rupture. Alvin cannot remember the exact issue about which they fought, but he does say that it flamed forth as a result of anger, vanity, and liquor, about ten years previously. So, Alvin has been estranged from Lyle for ten years, as a result of some drunken quarrel. It all sounds quite neat and plausible until we, as the audience, ponder what we already know of Alvin's life. When Alvin was in the bar in Clermont with Verlyn Heller, a fellow World War II veteran, we learned that Alvin had become a mean drunk as a result of the war, which places his troubles with the bottle around 1945. We also learned that a priest had been able to get Alvin to quit drinking by helping him understand that it was caused by the connection he made between life at home and some of the terrible things he had seen in wartime Europe. Alvin, by his own word, had nothing alcoholic to drink after working things out with the priest. And yet in 1983, we now learn, Alvin and his brother stopped speaking to each other when a bout of drinking drove them to say "unforgivable" things to each other. Alvin's history suddenly fragments before us.

In the film we have seen, Alvin clearly does not have a drinking problem. Yet he once did. It seems as if the problem had cleared up somewhere in the post-war period, but with the discussion in the graveyard—where members of a rather confused and confusing mapping party are buried—the mapping of Alvin's life also takes on a confusion that the film will never clear up. The next morning, Alvin has his first beer "in a long time"—we now have no way of knowing how long a time—and he very obviously is not moved to overindulge. Nevertheless, Alvin is a mystery, not at all the "nice old man" of popular culture lore. He looks and sounds the part, but beneath the solid-looking surface are indeterminate aspects of his life and personality.

Alvin's meeting with Lyle is no less uncertain. There is no doubt that they are now together. But in this moment, they share very little aside from the stars to which they gaze together as the final act of their reunion. They greet each other almost wordlessly, and without any physical contact whatsoever, and sit on chairs separated by several feet. After a moment of tearstained silence, they move their attention upward, toward the bright, distant stars. The acting depth necessary to carry off a scene this quiet as the climax of the entire film is considerable. And, the muted tones of this ultimate moment, structured by the tensions between fraternally imposed boundaries and fraternal closeness, are crucial to Lynch's purposes. In the thunderous quiet of the final scene, Lynch celebrates the culmination of Alvin's dream journey, but never lets us forget how much has been erased in the lives of Alvin and Lyle Straight in order to have this perfect moment. For all the strong, sweetly melancholy emotion attached to Alvin, his decisions and actions are defined with a particularity that keeps him from being a model for us. Rather, he is a phenomenon of a specific time and place.

Can anything of fraternal love be sustained beyond this culminating moment of the trip and the film? The answer to this question lies beyond

Alvin (Richard Farnsworth) arrives in Zion, but he and Lyle (Harry Dean Stanton) never touch.

the purposes of this film. The final image is what it is. And perhaps what it has always been. As Alvin tells it, the bond between the brothers was always about reaching beyond the unsatisfactory immediate impulses and circumstances, which were painful and full of the suffering of poverty. The beauty of Alvin's hopes and his success are about sustaining illusions, not about engagement in the actual uncertainties of the marketplace of the Straight family's lives. As Alvin reported to the priest, when they were young and life was hard, the brothers used to distract themselves from the terrible Minnesota cold by talking about the stars, whether there was human life on other planets, and faraway lands that they wanted to visit. Age has drained away all the problems caused by the basic chaos of indeterminacy and left them with the illusion of certainty in the stars.[9]

Like Fred Madison's, Alvin's is not a reliable point of view. His trip is a dream. Of straight linear roads. Of brotherly love. Of an orderly material terrain. But Alvin's illusions about earth and humanity are filled with a poignant beauty to them and a responsibility to his brother that touches Lynch. Alvin is of the marketplace, but his illusions miraculously are not those of the enclosed self, like those of Dick Laurent/Mr. Eddy, which repel Lynch. Alvin speaks to Lynch, and to the audience through Lynch, of human illusion at its most lovely and Quixotic bittersweetness.

*The Straight Story* takes decoherence as its motif. That is, it evokes the circumstances that allow us to create the sunny appearances of solidity. A trick of the light, and the conditions of old age, help foster a vision of family life emptied of both its surging blood connections and its trouble, one in which men and women are stripped of both sexual delight and turmoil, as well as the violence of war and warlike situations. Hero Alvin Straight is an equivocal figure, all passion spent in his past, who achieves the smallest modicum of order, void of everything that makes us humans the creative and exasperating rascals that we are. But like the stars, the sunlit hills of Iowa, and those untroubling violin melodies on the soundtrack, Straight inspires in us a melancholy respite from the turmoil of the Laura Palmers, the Sailors and Lulas, the Fred Madisons, and, of course, the pandemonium faced by the girls who flock to Hollywood to be stars on earth, the subject of Lynch's next film.

# CHAPTER THREE

# MULHOLLAND DR.: AN IMPROBABLE GIRL IN A PROBABLE WORLD

We assume that in order for something here to have an effect on something there it needs to be the case that there is some continuous, unbroken chain of mediating subcauses and effects stretching from here to
there in space and time. So, for example, if waving my hand here causes
somebody to be hit over there, it's because light is bouncing off my hand
and traveling and causing a signal. . . . I flip a switch and over there a light
goes on, we know that if we rip up the wall we'll find wires, radio signals.
So the conviction is that things only directly affect other things that are
right next to them. Any effect on anything that is not directly next to
you is necessarily indirect. It occurs through the agency of other things
between you and them. It's this principle that quantum mechanics apparently violates, that entangled particles violates.

**DAVID ALBERT, SEE APPENDIX II**

We live under an assumed identity in a neurotic fairy tale world. . . .
Hypnotized by building, we have raised the houses of our lives on sand.

**SOGYAL RINPOCHE, *THE TIBETAN BOOK OF LIVING AND DYING***

Hey, Betty, Betty Elms (Naomi Watts), you are throwing your life away,
says *Mulholland Dr.* (2001). And she isn't alone. David Lynch reflects both a
dangerously destructive world of mysterious entanglements and a "neurotic fairy tale world" in this second-stage fable of misrecognition in
Hollywood. There's reflexivity in the air, of course, since Lynch himself is
a filmmaker and has a relationship, ambiguous and ambivalent though it
may be, to the Hollywood community, but he's not creating a self-portrait.
He is using his intimate knowledge of Hollywood as a very particular

part of the marketplace that shows with vivid clarity how people get fatally stuck there. What we see in *Mulholland Dr.* is that despite its ostensible existence as a magnet for hope, creativity, and desire, Hollywood is a place in which the free flows of energy that can generate endless possibilities are too often misled, corralled, and replaced by the certainties of degeneration and death. The usual polarities in behind-the-scenes Hollywood films that shape the action are cynicism and idealism; lust for power and creativity; and a craving for money and the desire to express oneself. But in Lynch's film, these psychological characteristics shape nothing; rather they are determined by the cultural habit of imposing illusions of certainty and the cultural fear of the nothingness beyond those illusions.

Using a collage-like narrative technique, Lynch juxtaposes fragments of the careers and personal lives of Betty Elms, a young Canadian girl set to audition for a part in a small, independent film, and Adam Kesher (Justin Theroux), an up-and-coming director at the helm of a big-budget studio extravaganza. Kesher has lost his starring actress and is experiencing unexpected resistance from studio higher-ups as he tries to recast the role. Thrown in for good measure is the plight of a dark-haired beauty (Laura Elena Harring) who loses her memory in a car crash. (Possibly she is the actress who was originally cast in Kesher's film?) Still more fragments reveal the machinations of the entrenched power players in the marketplace around Betty, Adam, and the brunette woman. We also get glimpses of the problems of people going about the strange business of ordinary life on the streets where Adam, Betty, and Rita walk. The reality of *Muholland Dr.* is not a well-defined landscape mapped out by the logically interconnected Story A and Story B typical of Hollywood screenwriting. Instead, Lynch shows us fragments that relate to each other in ways that are reminiscent of the physical processes of superposition (one particle in many places) and entanglement (many particles mysteriously connected with each other) that we have already seen in *Lost Highway* and, minimally, in *The Straight Story*. As a result, Lynch summons his own unique version of Hollywood as a city of dreams.

When Americans talk about dreams, they are generally referring to fleeting mental dramas or images that exist in contrast with an assumed solid, dependable, material, external world. But, as in Lynch's previous second-stage films, what the characters misunderstand as solid materiality *is* the big dream, misperceived as reality: a paradoxical gossamer dream of certainty, a dream that is sometimes momentarily sustaining—as in the case of Alvin Straight—but more often devastating. The task Lynch sets for himself as an American filmmaker is no small one. Most Americans, with their eyes riveted to their possessions and the financial means to acquire them, will not be receptive to the idea that we live in a hopeless dream of material security and stability, and that to wake from that nightmare-like dream would mean inhabiting the real, hopeful boundlessness—our genuine source of security. And yet this is just what Lynch means to show.

Sweet Betty, brash Adam, and the mysterious dark woman are all filled with uncertain potential as the film begins, especially the dark woman whose life is nothing but potential once her memory is wiped out by the car accident that is the initiating event in the narrative. But all the pressures from the people and forces that control moviemaking box them into illusory certainties from which they cannot escape. In this backstage Hollywood film, the movie industry is, as we shall see, the equivalent of a black hole, swallowing up energy and converting life to death. Again, as in *Lost Highway*, an illusory certainty is combined with a rakshasa-like, negative interpretation of boundlessness.

Certainty in the Hollywood marketplace is represented by the combination of the politics of filmmaking and the marketplace depiction of limitlessness in sinister terms. This vision of certainty comes to life in the stage show in an after-hours club on a backstreet in Los Angeles named Club Silencio. The show at Silencio questions Hollywood's illusions all right, but in such a way as to provoke terror, not freedom.[1] The combined terrors of this spectacle of nothingness that Betty and the dark mysterious woman encounter at Silencio, and the nothingness Adam Kesher fears will envelop him if he doesn't do what he's told by the mysterious people who control the studio for which he is making a movie, lead inevitably to a threshold that is like an annihilation, a black hole. The analogy of the black hole is aptly drawn from the phenomenon described by astrophysics in which mass becomes so dense that it draws all light and substance into itself as a total negation of materiality and being. To enter a black hole is to incur some form of decreation from which there is no release. Nothing escapes it, not even light.[2] In the poetic vocabulary of *Mulholland Dr.*, the black hole defines Hollywood's ultimate effects on the lives of Betty, Adam, and the dark woman.

When the characters become so afflicted by Hollywood's ruling twin errors of certainty and fear that possibility dies, Lynch uses the image of the black hole to enable him to talk about how the initially creative energy they brought into the story becomes overtaken by a fatal negativity. Those familiar with the mysterious blue box in *Mulholland Dr.* will correctly assume that it is through this image that Lynch evokes the black hole phenomenon. The use of the enigmatic blue box is but one of an array of images Lynch opts for to speak of certainty and uncertainty; conventional representations are far too evocative of the certainties he questions to be useful to him as a storyteller. Through these visuals, Lynch creates fissures in Hollywood's armored wall of standardized images. His inventions include not only the mysterious blue box and key, but also radical identity shifts and bodies about which it is hard to say whether they are organic life or things.

These strategies take Lynch into an area much more complex than any of the previous celebrated films about making films, for example, Billy Wilder's *Sunset Boulevard* (1950), a favorite of Lynch's to which this film alludes occasionally. Wilder gives the story of Hollywood's sins against reality a psychological and moral twist in his tale of a May-December Hollywood romance between a young man and an aging, narcissistic silent movie actress. In time-honored, sexist, patriarchal fashion, *Sunset Boulevard* represents the way Hollywood clouds the perception of the real through the image of the voracious narcissism and sexuality of the femme fatale.[3] In *Mulholland Dr.*, Lynch puts a new spin on the elements Wilder used. Wilder's hero Joe Gillis dies at the hands of a woman whose personal obsessions require her to eliminate his challenge to her fantasy world. In *Mulholland Dr.* the threat is not personal, and it certainly isn't associated with gender, but with what Lynch understands as a cultural confusion that treats the flow of organic life as if it were a bound and limited thing, commodifies it, and leads us, in a manner of speaking, to die at the hands of the phantom of certainty.

## BETTY, WHERE SHE DANCED

*Mulholland Dr.* has a three-part structure, which begins with a brief but crucial montage that describes for Lynch's audience the nature of the terrain on which the rest of the film's narrative will be played out. At first, the opening montage evokes pure playful energy and possibility through images of teenage dancers who move freely in ways that make them seem as if they are in many places at once (superposition), and connected to each other in mysterious ways (entanglement). This initial joy is soon replaced by the airlessness of a room in which nothing moves. The boundedness that has replaced the limitless flow of energy and shape is claustrophobic and sinister, but the montage provides no details about how and why the mood has shifted.

What first greets our eyes (and ears) in the initial montage is a joyous dance of non-locality. Matter is portrayed in the form of spirited, smiling young people dancing. However, the way the bodies of the dancers occupy the space is nothing like what we would see if we were at a party or club somewhere and looked at our surroundings through the eyes that culture has taught us to see with. Lynch gives us different eyes, first visualizing the dancers as flickering shadows of no density or defined outline against a purple background that makes the dancing space seem infinite. That is to say, Lynch initiates us into the world of *Mulholland Dr.* through a poetic image of what perception might be like before we impose shapes on our exterior circumstances.

Quite quickly these dancers come into focus, but the world we are entering is still a curious spectacle. Although there seems to be a screenful of bodies in motion, actually the same eight people are being doubled, sometimes tripled and quadrupled. These figures also often appear to be out of proportion to each other. Some figures are much smaller or larger than the others, as if landscapes of different physical proportions were inhabiting the same space. At moments in this opening montage, the

The representation of the joyous dancers here evokes a notion of unconfined space in which the unlimited possibilities of the particles evoke no fear.

dancers don't appear to be in their own discrete spaces, but rather they all seem to be occupying the same spaces at the same time. Shadows of the couples flit in and out of the mise-en-scène, sometimes huge, sometimes dark, sometimes like light-colored cutouts of one of the moving forms on the screen.

The spectacle of the doubled and tripled bodies is not in synch with classical physics, but it does reflect the way quantum science speaks about matter at its most basic level. Moreover, the shadows intermingled among the dancers suggest the negative particles that quantum science says accompany all positively charged particles. Perhaps most telling of all, our ability to see their momentum but not their location corresponds to the basic tenet of quantum physics, the uncertainty principle, which asserts that we can never see everything about matter all at once. Under the uncertainty principle, the clearer we are about momentum, the less we can know about position, and vice versa. Although there is nothing about measurement in this sequence, there is a metaphoric incompleteness of information. We get the movement; we don't have the location.

When the mood switches to certainty and locality, the party is over. We have crossed a threshold. What was joyous is now lugubrious. What was wide open is claustrophobic. When the new location comes into focus, we are in a very tight shot of an empty bed covered by rumpled terracotta-colored sheets and a mustard-gold-colored blanket in disarray. While there is palpably heavy breathing on the soundtrack, we cannot identify its source. There is no one visible in the bed. Again, we cannot have full information about the scene. But this time, there is fear involved. Mortality is evoked by the harsh breathing and the dark atmosphere of the bedroom. The camera moves into the empty pillow on this bed until we see nothing on the screen but darkness. The push of the camera into the pillow has signaled to some commentators that Lynch is telling us that what comes next is a dream, Betty's dream to be exact. They distinguish the series of events in which Betty still seems hopeful as a dream from which she awakens at the end of the film as Diane, who is anything but happy.[4] However, that is not the pattern that Lynch lays out for us in this montage.

Just as there is nothing to suggest that Lynch is presenting the original joyousness of the dancers as less real than the subsequent sense of suffering in the bedroom, so there is nothing to suggest that what happens early in the film is less real than what happens after Diane takes

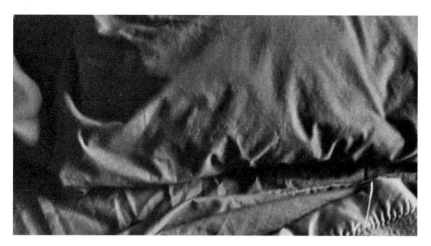

This representation of confined space, accompanied by the sounds of labored, terrified breathing on the soundtrack, evokes the fear inherent in imposed limits on human experience.

Betty's place. Rather, as in the opening montage, Lynch is introducing the threshold transition that shapes the lives of the three main characters, Adam, Betty, and the dark woman, as the narrative of *Mulholland Dr.* plays out. The mystery of how the terrain changes from open possibility to inescapable fear and mortality in the opening montage is a prefiguration of the shape of the narrative of the film, and it offers some insight into the transition.

Because there is no character in the bed when the camera pushes in on the pillow, we have reason to imagine that, if a dream is beginning, it is our dream, the dream of the culture to which Lynch is speaking. The dream that interests Lynch in his second-stage films is the cultural dream that matter is the solid array of shapes that we think we see—which is the case in the misery-filled bed. The culmination of the opening montage, then, shows us the direction of the cultural dream, in which Betty and all the other characters will eventually partake. The sound of mortality in labored breathing on the soundtrack, and the claustrophobic density of the images of the bed, is our introduction to the dream of certainty (and negativity) that buries everyone in this film. Betty, Adam, and the dark woman as well will be destroyed by the cultural dream without ever knowing what hit them. And us? As audience, we are given only enough information to let us know what probably happened. In telling his tale,

Lynch presents information in a way that invokes the uncertainty principle, perhaps asking us to wake up from the nightmare caused by the inhibiting cultural illusions that surround us. We're thus distinguished from the characters, who atrophy into the black hole created by illusions of certainty even as they sleep, so to speak.

## THIS IS YOUR BRAIN ON PROBABILITY

The montage done, the story begins. We are now in Los Angeles, which is, depending on what piece of the city we see, and when, either a dark Mulholland Drive, filled with danger that threatens a beautiful woman being driven by a sinister chauffeur, or an airport flooded with sunshine and resonant with the happy chatter of Betty, a would-be actress arriving at the terminal with two friendly people she met on the plane. Thus the city is immediately evoked for the audience as a fragmented landscape in which what meets the eye is not the whole story. What can we know about the entirety of circumstances if all we can see are pieces of it? On the airplane that brings Betty to Los Angeles to begin her career as a movie star, Betty meets grandmotherly Irene and her chivalrous companion, who sweetly reinforce her daydreams of becoming a star. But there is something Betty does not know about these two. After the pair has left Betty, Lynch allows them to reveal to his audience another aspect of themselves, an enigmatic demonic gleam in their eyes. Similarly, behind the beautiful, frightened amnesiac dark-haired woman, who has just narrowly missed being killed in a car crash, there appears to be a web of intrigue and sinister intentions. Behind a clean, well-lighted fast food restaurant, Winkie's, there is a frightening humanoid figure seemingly made up of an excremental tangle of matter. Behind the glamour and stylish comfort of the apartment Betty's Aunt Ruth is letting her stay in lurks an oppressive studio system ruled by a mindless void at its center that has tentacles reaching everywhere in the city. Later, we discover that, except in the case of very small-time independent productions, the audition process masks with a deceptive veneer of possibility the ironclad decisions already made. And just as we see the characters caught like flies within the web of illusion, we see it stripped away brutally at the Club Silencio where Betty and the dark woman are told that everything is simulated. "It's all tape recorded!"

This is our brains on probability, a central assumption of modern physics that states we can never know all the details of any circumstance with certainty. From the first action of the film, when a limousine moving on Mulholland Drive stops and the driver takes out a gun and points it at his passenger, the dark, unnamed woman, Lynch takes heroic measures to prevent us from being too precipitously certain of what we think we know and what we don't know. The way the dark woman's story is related as the film begins starts teaching us to think in terms of the probable not the certain. The opening sequences show us that we need to get out of the way of the film and let it talk to us; that we need to avoid imposing certainties of our invention on situations that are intentionally sketchily defined. There is little about the danger posed to the dark woman that is clearly identified, and though each new fragment of the collage Lynch assembles for us contains new information, it yields only a probable big picture. If we attempt to force the dark woman into a pattern of certainties, we destroy the relationship between audience and film that Lynch is encouraging. However, if we "let go," we enter into the film Lynch made for us, and leave off imposing alien ideas on it.[5]

This means we must tread lightly as we receive information. We clearly see some joyriders careen around a curve on Mulholland Drive and crash into the dark woman's car, and we clearly see that, the only survivor of this crash, she dazedly leaves the scene of the accident and winds up in the apartment where Betty will live. But there is much that is elliptical about the telephone calls that are subsequently made about a "missing girl." Are they about the dark-haired woman we have just seen? Later we realize that the calls are connected to a film studio, in fact the studio that controls Adam's film. But there's still a lot of fresh air here. What has the dark woman to do with the studio? Why did the driver pull a gun on her, and why is there no identification in her purse, only a very large amount of cash? Is there a connection between her disappearance and Adam Kesher's recast of his leading lady—which we only learn about later? Is the accident in which the dark amnesiac is involved connected to a low-level hit man named Joe Messing (Mark Pellegrino) who later kills a seedy man named Ed (Vincent Castellanos) for an address book in the middle of a conversation about a "strange accident"? Are Joe and Ed speaking about what happened to the dark woman? Why isn't Lynch making these connections explicit, if there *are* connections?

Simply this: Lynch wants his audience to experience the uncertainty of the marketplace behind its vivid appearances. If he made the connections for us, he would support the illusion of certainty. Because he doesn't, he encourages us to experience the tension between the cultural expectation that certainty is the truth and his belief in an open universe of potential. Yet, Lynch is not interested in encouraging a nihilism that insists there are no inherent connections. The tantalizing feeling that there are connections to be made as these fragments are revealed is also part of our experience. Lynch tells this story in a style that allows us to realize ourselves as complex viewers of the world. There is some way in which the dark girl is linked to numerous seemingly disparate people, which we sense even if we cannot nail down those links. The importance of these unseen but meaningful interfaces pops up everywhere in the film. Indeed what seems fragmentary will eventually form a narrative whole, but a whole that irretrievably contains an ongoing mystery about the entanglement of (mysterious connections among) its parts.

Entanglement is present in the early fragments we see in this film not only in the tantalizing sense we have that the amnesiac, dark woman is somehow connected to many strange doings. It's also present in the unseen connections suggested in scenes that seem peripheral, but add much information, as for example in the grotesque, but hilarious conversation in Ed's office. In this scene, in which a never fully understood character named Ed is shown to be the owner of an address book, the importance of which is never made clear, Lynch not only hints at probable sinister connections with the lost dark woman, but also a connection of everything with everything else. When hit man Joe shoots Ed fatally with no warning, Joe thinks that all he has to do is grab the mysteriously important book and run. But life's not like that in the Lynchverse. Joe cannot eliminate Ed's life without disturbing everything around Ed.

Joe cleans off the gun and attempts to make it look like Ed killed himself, thinking he'll be finished with the job in seconds, but things get tangled. Joe forces Ed's dead hand to fire the gun, so that there will be powder burns to make the death look like suicide, but the bullet goes astray and pierces the paper thin wall of Ed's office, hitting a woman in the next office, a hugely obese woman with whom Joe must now contend. She almost extinguishes Joe with the bulk of her body before he can kill her too—a murder which is observed by a cleaner in the building, whom Joe is also now forced to kill, in the process causing the man's vacuum cleaner to come to noisy life. When Joe shoots the offensive vacuum cleaner, he causes a short circuit that sets off the building's alarm system. Joe bolts out of the window in Ed's office onto a fire escape, trapped by the train of events he has set in motion. It's a funny scene, but it also goes some way toward shaping the cosmic realities of *Mulholland Dr.*: though we can only guess, before the fact, at the intricacies of the big picture, there is nothing that exists solely and by itself alone.[6]

By invoking probability as the real state of things, and implying real, though only possible, connections among seeming fragments, Lynch is able to examine the sinister aspects of a mysterious power that permeates this film in contradiction to all Lynch shows and believes about reality. This power is behind Joe's murder of Ed, and behind the story arcs of the main characters; it is a pull toward certainty that comes from culture, not the organic universe, and it is made visible through the action Lynch depicts as a sterile top-down way of imposing form on the world. Lynch probes its power by following Betty's attempts to remove doubts and questions about the identity of the dark girl—who, in her uncertainty about her past, takes the name of Rita from a movie poster advertising Rita Hayworth in *Gilda* (1946)—and by following Adam's power struggle with the studio, which is determined to control the picture he is directing. These two narrative strands seem entirely separate. And yet they are part of a terrible pattern in the world of *Mulholland Dr.* that Lynch wants us to see as the inverse of a life-affirming way of dealing with form and meaning. As Lynch puts us through our paces as spectators, he shows us that running parallel with the force of certainty is an organic force, a bottom-up process by means of which inherent connections can be spontaneously discovered (not imposed) . . . if this process is permitted to play out.

Betty is a crucial focus of the counterpoint between these forces. She is filled with possibilities that show up unexpectedly, particularly in her audition scene. But she also has a need for certainty that makes her the opposite of the Lynchian detectives who populated his first-stage work, for example, Jeffrey Beaumont in *Blue Velvet* and Special Agent Dale Cooper in the *Twin Peaks* cycle. They were boundary-crossers who questioned cultural limits on perception and opened themselves to a bottom-up process of discovery. Betty, conversely, is faced with a woman who has lost all the limits of an established identity and is struggling to restore them. Where Jeffrey and Agent Cooper are fascinated by crossing established boundaries, Betty is characterized by a penchant for living within their limits. Betty exudes an aura of neatness, and she is shown in numerous small acts of carefully making a place for herself without disturbing the established order.

For example, when Catherine "Coco" Lenoix (Ann Miller), the affably precise concierge of the apartment complex Betty's Aunt Ruth (Maya Bond) lives in, expresses irritation with the turds left by one of the tenant's dogs in the building's courtyard, Betty eagerly reassures her that she has no pets and will not upset Coco in any way. Betty also unpacks her suitcase with precision and neatly eases her clothes into the drawers of her aunt's dresser. The trail of clothes Rita has left on the floor as part of her entrance into this orderly, lovely space defines her in opposition to both Betty and Ruth. Similarly, Rita's terrified confusion about who and what she is contrasts sharply with Betty's neat scenarios about what she wants (to be a star, but also a great actress) and how she will behave—taking her script and a cup of coffee out to the courtyard like a real movie star. Betty's unflagging confidence in her illusory grasp of her space and circumstances is demonstrated by her lack of fear about the mess that Rita has brought into her life. Rita does not alarm her. Rather, Rita is, in a manner of speaking, just another blouse to be folded expertly and placed where it belongs. As the film will reveal, Betty's confidence in a world where everything has its proper already-determined place is unwarranted. Fatally unwarranted, as it turns out, since this misperception also leads Betty to foreclose all of the positive possibilities in her life, even though life keeps telling her she is on the wrong path.

As Betty cheerfully proceeds with her "Rita project," she refuses to heed warning signals about this unknown woman. After all, Rita is afraid of the police, and has a purse full of money but no identification. If there is a strange blue key in the purse along with the money, the signs that Rita is on the wrong side of something suggest that what it unlocks may well be dangerous. (Experience will prove that the literal key Rita has brought into Betty's life is also the figurative key to the beginning of the end of everything for Betty.) Moreover, helping Rita betrays the confidence that her Aunt Ruth places in Betty. Aunt Ruth, who clearly has a caring and affectionate relationship with her niece—she goes far out of her way to give her a leg up in Hollywood, and leaves a note on a robe intended for Betty's use that addresses her with what is obviously a childhood pet name, "Bitsy"—does not want this woman in the apartment. Helpless-seeming Rita is setting off everyone's alarm bells but Betty's.

Still, Lynch knows, as do we, that there are times when one must act against common sense, family obligations, and other people's intuitions, so he deals with those possibilities, as part of his exposition of Betty's

Hollywood story, in two scenes related to an audition Aunt Ruth has arranged for Betty. This audition is the central reason for Betty's journey to Los Angeles, and she receives the script in advance and practices it in the kitchen, running lines with Rita. We see her go through the scenes again during her actual audition in the office of a producer named Wally Brown (James Karen). The contrasts between these two readings have numerous significances, and one of them gives us deeper insight into Betty's rapport with Rita.

When Betty is rehearsing with Rita, nothing spontaneous happens. Rita is unable to bring anything to the reading that would ignite any lively response from Betty. We gather from the lines that the scene is between a victim (a young girl) and a victimizer (an older man), and in a sense this is what it is. But we will see when Betty reads for the audition that she has the capacity to discover other elements in the situation, for example the power that the young girl has over the older man, and that there is an attraction/repulsion at work that makes it very difficult for either of them to extract themselves from the vortex of energies in play. The lifeless reading with Rita suggests the tenor of their relationship. There is something hollow in the way they relate, making a mockery of the audition. It is the essence of the vacuousness that results from the top-down imposition of order.[7] The opposite is true when Betty actually auditions for producer Wally Brown, a good friend of Betty's aunt. It is the essence of bottom-up discovery.

Betty's audition for Wally takes place in a small office, and involves absolutely no technology, costumes, or studio bigwigs. It's just people: actor Woody Katz (Chad Everett); Bob Brooker (Wayne Grace), the director; a number of production assistants; and Linney James (Rita Taggart), a high-powered casting agent, as well as Wally's ex-wife and her assistant Nikki, who are just visiting. In many ways, this is not all that different from reading lines in a kitchen, as Betty did with Rita, but something important takes place here. The audition scene takes on a life of its own as, to use David Lynch's words for letting creativity happen, the two actors spontaneously get out of the way of the expansive forces in them. In other words, this moment of mood, energy, and the kind of vital, flowing reality shown in the opening montage is released because neither Betty nor Woody has blocked it with stock responses or learned efforts to be certain.

One of the great things about this amazing scene is how unpropitious everything seems at first. In addition to the simplicity of the room, Wally

Betty's (Naomi Watts) audition with Woody Katz (Chad Everett) in Wally Brown's (James Karen) office lacks devices of mechanistic control that are abundantly visible on the major studio soundstage on which Betty and Adam later glimpse each other but fail to meet.

seems to be little more than a sweet, glad-handing producer. Bob Brooker, the director, muttering what seem like incoherent words, appears to have recently been extricated from the day room of a mental hospital. Woody Katz, a tanned cliché of a leading man, smilingly mouths platitudes about acting being reacting. He makes Betty nervous with little witticisms, like "Tell me where it hurts, baby," and with his smarmy manner that screams of his view of Betty as little more than fresh meat. But, damn, if it all isn't suddenly beside the point. What is crucial is the freedom that exists in this room, the lack of constraint. Suddenly, a whole world of conflicting emotion emerges as the actors exude the kind of mixed feelings endemic to the forbidden affair in the audition pages. With this scene, Lynch accomplishes the unthinkable: an actual demonstration of acting talent in people who are playing actors. So when this stunning display excites everyone in the room, we are as convinced as they that a star is being born. But Betty's audition with Wally represents everything that the movie marketplace as depicted in *Mulholland Dr.* is dedicated to exterminating— and in this film the marketplace will succeed, in stages that lead toward a point of no return for Betty, Rita, and Adam.

The first stage of Adam's defeat in the Hollywood marketplace occurs during the production meeting where we first meet him. It is a meeting with a perfect marketplace tone; nothing spontaneous is possible. Two monosyllabic men, the Castiglione Brothers—Vincenzo (Dan Hedaya) and Luigi (Angelo Badalamenti, Lynch's preferred composer)—produce a photo of a blonde girl (Melissa George) named Camilla Rhodes and tell everyone at the table, "this is the girl," with the monotonous repetition of a simple machine. Period. No discussion. Moreover, the meeting is being surreptitiously listened to by Mr. Roque (Michael J. Anderson), the center of power of the studio, from his inaccessible office—though there is no explanation of how he has organized this surveillance. Between Mr. Roque and Lynch's darkly comic depiction of the Castigliones as stereotypical movie Mafiosi, this is an over-controlled situation. What could be more certain and less reflective of the flow of life than the omnipotent movie power player and the clear-cut Hollywood clichéd gangster? What is more evocative of a marketplace built on certainties than these stereotypes?

Adam is still fighting to make movies his own way when he meets the Castigliones, albeit in a way that predicts failure. He storms out of the meeting, but has no resources at his disposal other than infantile panic. He takes out his anger at the Castigliones on their car, smashing its windows and headlights with a golf club that he affectedly carries around with him, and making a quick getaway. Hardly an effective strategy, as we see as the marketplace closes in on him. His marriage is as conditioned by the marketplace as his job. His wife, Lorraine (Lori Heuring), whom he finds in bed with a very muscular pool man (Billy Ray Cyrus) when he returns home from the production meeting, is more attached to her jewelry box than she is to him. Extramarital sex is obviously a part of her domestic vocabulary; she is hilariously critical of Adam for catching her with the pool man. But her jewelry box is sacrosanct, and Adam instinctively knows this. His riposte to her tantrum is to pour pink paint into it in retaliation. So, home is not a refuge, and there is no place in town where he can escape the marketplace wrath at his rebellion. When he runs to a hideout in a seedy part of the city where he has clearly hidden out before, he discovers that he has been tracked to the broken-down hotel and his bank accounts are emptied and his credit cards cancelled. Moreover, his set has been closed down and all the employees who work on it have been dismissed. He reaches his point of no return in an actual corral, from which there is also no figurative way to escape, when he is pressured to "take a meeting" with a studio enforcer called the Cowboy (Lafayette Montgomery), dressed in oversized western garb. (To add a reflexive joke to the proceedings, Montgomery is a real producer who has produced numerous shows and films for Lynch.)[8]

Adam is corralled by the Cowboy at the dead end of a hidden byway somewhere in Los Angeles.[9] The presentation of the Hollywood Cowboy emissary who breaks Adam's spirit draws on the other primary generic Hollywood cliché of masculinity, this one a symbol of purity and unfailing loyalty to his principles. Although this Cowboy sports a large version of the white hat associated with the western hero, he plays a villainous role in *Mulholland Dr.*, as he herds and binds Adam as if he were cattle. The cowboy catechizes Adam, ironically berating him for not being sincere, when it is not sincerity but utter submission the Cowboy demands in this non-conversation, even more repressive than the non-conversation with the Castigliones. At the production meeting, Adam could choose to yell and leave. Here, Adam has only one part he can play, the acolyte who agrees to the mentor's propositions. The Cowboy speaks of how a man's attitude determines what will happen to him, as if Adam has a choice, but the reality of the situation emerges when the Cowboy makes Adam admit that it is the Cowboy who is driving the buggy, so to speak, and that Adam doesn't get a seat in the buggy unless he chooses to accept Camilla Rhodes, while pretending to audition "many girls." If Adam seems to escape the brute grunts of Vincenzo Castiglione, he is finally penned in—and figuratively hog-tied—by the Cowboy. He takes the proffered metaphorical seat in the figurative buggy, but he pays an inordinately high price for his ticket to ride.

Betty's and Rita's points of no return are complexly entangled with Adam's. Once he no longer believes he has any options, he also dooms Betty during a faux audition for his movie that forecloses the possibility that ought to be at the core of the audition process. The bogus auditions Adam oversees, in the wake of his defeat in the corral, stand in stark contrast to the audition in Wally's office. The room is full of technology, studio bigwigs, and slick costumes and makeup, all a setup to mask a situation in which no choice is possible. Betty has been brought there by Linney James, the high-stakes casting agent permitted to watch Betty's audition by her ex-husband, Wally. She treacherously intends to steal Betty from Wally and wow Adam with Betty's talent. But Linney is not as much of an insider as she thinks she is, since neither Betty nor anyone else other than "the girl," Camilla Rhodes, has any chance of being cast.

Betty's entrance onto Adam's soundstage is the beginning of a love scene manqué. While the pretense of an audition proceeds, although the outcome is already determined, and the candidates for the role (interchangeable except for the color of their hair) parade before Adam, Betty appears, and both she and Adam spontaneously sense a special energy. They turn toward each other, and each fills with visible longing and sadness. We are in the presence of something rich with promise, but something embryonic that will never evolve further. Lynch visually emphasizes the importance of this lost opportunity by moving in for extreme closeups of each of their eyes in turn. It is no coincidence that at this point the Camilla from the photograph thrust at Adam by the Castigliones appears, the studio's terminator of a potentially creative impulse, a product off the same assembly line as the previous girl who auditioned, slickly presented and full of nothing but predictable mannerisms.

And that is the point of this crucial scene. The studio choice, on which the powers that be insist so emphatically, is no choice at all. She is "the girl," because the studio says she is, Hollywood illusory certainty incarnate, since "the girl" has no distinguishing beauty or talent to set her apart from any other auditionee. The pure nature of the marketplace is on display here; it is a barricade against the kind of potential with its uncertain surprises that we saw in Betty's audition for Wally. There is no one but the spectator who sees that that energy is also present, as we watch it connect Betty and Adam through their eyes. Is this a nascent personal possibility that is stillborn? A professional opportunity? Both? Even Lynch cannot tell us. All he can do is bear witness that it was there for a moment. There is a profound melancholy at the impossibility of further discovery when an entire world that might have been born disappears and a number of fates are sealed. It is perhaps the famous "eye of the duck" scene Lynch and I talked about many years ago that must take place in order for the story to end as it does.[10]

The false audition, the essence of how the marketplace works through top-down imposition of illusory form onto organic life, is a negative event. It is constituted of what is not possible and who is not there, specifically the man behind this terrible moment, Mr. Roque. His longdistance power, which is evident from the moment he makes calls about the "missing girl" shortly after Rita escapes the car crash, reigns over this suppression of bottom-up spontaneity of discovery. Such power is always cut off from direct experience, from doing and discovering through doing; accordingly, Roque, the source of the paralysis of the system, is never

Adam (Justin Theroux) registers something powerful and unspoken at seeing Betty (Naomi Watts).

Betty (Naomi Watts) responds strongly but silently to being seen by Adam (Justin Theroux).

Attempting a connection would be futile. Adam (Justin Theroux) experiences regret at being in bondage to the power players at the studio, who have told him which girl he must select. He will need to turn from Betty (Naomi Watts) and toward his own destruction.

As Betty (Naomi Watts) and Rita (Laura Elena Harring) run from the Sierra Bonita apartment, they begin the process of molecule dissolution that will lead to their disappearance in the black hole of the Blue Box.

encounter, it ultimately becomes a relationship that echoes the siren's taunting statement to Pete, in *Lost Highway,* "You'll never have me." Post-coitally, instead of basking in the glow of satisfaction, Betty is wrenched out of any sense of security and fulfillment when Rita wakes her with a terrible fear of nothingness: "there is no band," she says in her sleep; "there is no orchestra." Rita then drags Betty, at two in the morning, to Club Silencio, where a revelation that everything is insubstantial appearance is forcefully thrust at the two women.

Club Silencio takes its name from its existence as a hush-hush after hours boîte, secreted at the end of an alley filled with windblown garbage. But its secret involves more than its location. It is a place in which the illusions that fill Hollywood are revealed by a demonic master of ceremonies. "It's all tape recorded," he mockingly says. It seems a subversive form of resistance to the power of the marketplace, but is it? No. Rather it strengthens the negativity of the marketplace by generating a debilitating fear of a purported empty nothingness that lies beyond "tape recorded" illusions.[12] Musicians who seem to be playing their instruments stop playing, but the sound of music continues. Rebekah Del Rio, a featured singer at the club, to all appearances a full-bodied, sensual, sweating singer, belts out Roy Orbison's "Crying" (in Spanish), and then collapses, revealing that she is nothing but a hollow form, while her powerful voice continues making its way through the song. Lynch's use of a Spanish-speaking singer emphasizes the experience of this unmasking of illusion as something "foreign" or other, the dissolution of the world as Betty has insisted on knowing it. Watching all this from a box above the stage is a woman with bright blue hair who, like Roque, gives the appearance of being both human and thing. Puffs of smoke and fire punctuate the spectacle, creating the look of Hell. And the savage attack on our understanding of the world as a solid, physical place tears into the molecular structure of Betty's and Rita's bodies. The assault takes its strongest toll on Betty.

How fearsome these revelations are to her becomes clear when Betty is wracked by violent tremors and tears as she watches the show. The result of her bone-rattling terror is annihilation. Betty is impelled to open her purse in which she discovers something new: a blue box that matches the key they found in Rita's purse along with the mysterious stack of paper money the day Rita stumbled into Aunt Ruth's beautiful apartment. The women rush home, planning to open the box with the key, but before they can, Betty disappears, leaving only Rita. Rita is soon to disappear too.

We have already witnessed the fatal shock of moving from dream to reality early in a film, in the strange scene in a fast food chain restaurant, Winkie's, just before Betty arrives in Los Angeles. It's a sign of things to come, as it turns out. The scene features a conversation between two characters who play no further narrative role in the film, in which an ordinary fellow named Dan (Patrick Fischler) tells his similarly ordinary

The blue-haired woman in Club Silencio (Corri Glazer). Like Mr. Roque, she is neither fully alive nor fully dead.

friend Herb (Michael Cooke) about his dream that something terrifying lurks behind the restaurant they are sitting in. Winkie's is obviously a chain restaurant, standardized in every way to reassure patrons that they can be certain of what they are going to find there. Yet even here there may be something evil behind the picture of safety it presents, or so Dan's dream has told him. Dan, with gut-wrenching trepidation, has come to see if his dream is true. He insists on making his inspection even though he says, in a cold sweat, "I hope that I never see that face ever outside of a dream." When Dan and Herb look behind Winkie's, the monster of Dan's dream—a humanoid shape larded with excremental matter—does appear, and Dan drops to the ground, dead, while Herb is completely unaffected. Revelations are not the same for everyone, but Lynch makes clear even before Betty arrives that the fear of what is behind appearances is fatal. That is to say, being stuck in the marketplace, whether at Winkie's, Aunt Ruth's, the Cowboy's corral, a studio soundstage, the Sierra Bonita apartments, or Club Silencio, is not just about being inveigled by appearances; it is also about having no way out of them. Illusions: these characters—even those not directly connected with Hollywood—can't live with 'em; can't live without 'em.[13]

Yet, looking at the Club Silencio experience from the perspective of the mysticism at the core of Lynch's worldview, the revelation of nothing-

Dan (Patrick Fischler) dies behind Winkie's as the monster in his dream turns out to have dimensional, physical life. But Herb (Michael Cooke) is unaffected. It is not his time to glimpse the truth that exists past the perplexing threshold.

ness need not deal a death blow. What lurks behind Winkie's and on the stage of Club Silencio, which triggers moments of collapse and traumatic despair, might, in another world, have been a moment of potential liberation. As in the Bardo moment of Tibetan tradition, these incidents could have become what I have called threshold experiences. In the mystic tradition, the Bardo moment can occur either before, during, or after death, in which the lesson of the empty world is being presented. Lynch's cinema tends toward threshold moments that take place for living people.[14] Both Lynch and the Tibetan masters know that a person entering a Bardo moment can collapse into fear and still evolve positively toward more wisdom. Moving toward evolution manifests humor and elation, the opposite of what happens behind Winkie's and in Club Silencio. The mystic wisdom of Tibetan masters goes something like this: "Seeing emptiness, have compassion. . . . Contemplation of the dreamlike quality of reality need not in any way make us cold, hopeless, or embittered. On the contrary, it can open up in us a warm humor, a soft, strong compassion we hardly knew we possessed, and so more generosity toward all things and beings."[15] In fact, Hollywood itself has had moments when it laughs at its own illusions in a comic light, for example in *Road to Morocco* (Dir. David Butler, 1942) when, as Bob Hope, Bing Crosby, and Dorothy Lamour sing, their voices become interchangeable, and Dorothy Lamour is surprised to find she is singing with Crosby's voice, as Crosby discovers that the voice coming out of his throat is Bob Hope's, and Hope realizes that his voice belongs to Dorothy Lamour. The light whimsy of this scene in which the fact that "It's all recorded" is played for fun is hardly the demeanor of Silencio's master of ceremonies, which suggests that the world is a horror show of emptiness—an attitude in keeping with the fear that lies at the heart of some perspectives on quantum mechanics and also at the heart of the cultural nihilism of those who have seen that social systems are relative in form. But this is not what Lynch sees.

He sees the Bardo moment (or its equivalent) when enlightenment might be the result of the perception of emptiness. He sees that those who misunderstand emptiness drop into a lower level of existence. Betty's misprision, cultivated in her by the floor show at Club Silencio, does indeed lead to the radical decay of the tone and substance of her, Rita's, and Adam's lives. However if the characters are stuck in the downward descent into death fostered by the marketplace, we are not. We retain the possibility of spontaneously bearing witness to other possibilities.

## THROUGH A BLUE BOX DARKLY

The encompassing negativity, shown to be inevitable within the circumstances of this film, is metaphorically physicalized by the events involving the blue box. The mystery of the blue box arrives with the mysterious dark woman and finds its full expression of marketplace decreation when it meets the blue key that appears while Betty and Rita are at Club Silencio. At this point, the audience is propelled imaginatively into the black hole toward which Betty, Adam, and Rita have been heading since the beginning of the film. The pattern of shots that Lynch offers after the blue box is opened by the blue key is an extensively detailed threshold between what Betty and Rita, and Adam too, were at the beginning of the film and what they have become under the pressure of the Hollywood dream and its thrust toward non-being. It turns out that we have been witnesses to a fully detailed map of the steps by which the marketplace relentlessly extinguishes openness and possibility.[16]

Astonishingly, Lynch does not merely indicate that a transition takes place, he brings us moment by moment through the transition, evoking the fluidity of time and space with such originality that he makes his audience live the shattering of Hollywood's construction of certainties at the same time that he shows the path by which Hollywood has led the central characters of the film to destruction. In my interview with Lynch on March 18, 2010, he spoke of the images of doorways and corridors, which for him could be transition points not only between rooms, but between different worlds. He uses that kind of image pattern to evoke the changed worlds of Betty and Rita once they have encountered the space of life as a black hole. Moving us through corridors that denote mysterious dislocations of time and space, Lynch allows us to undergo what the characters have undergone as they materially change from what they were at the beginning of the film. Betty's dark awakening as Diane is no waking from a dream, as many critics have liked to imagine it. It is a threshold experience in the continuum of movement from lively desires and hopes to the death of creativity in this Hollywood tale.

That is to say that at this point, Lynch takes us through the physical events of Betty's and Rita's disappearances from the landscape of the film in their original forms and their reappearances in a much-degenerated space of fear and death. This space is also Hollywood, but Hollywood as it exists when its illusions have fully transformed life into a black hole.

After Betty's and Rita's terrified flight from Silencio, they return to Aunt Ruth's apartment where, after Betty disappears, Rita opens the blue box with the newly acquired blue key and then vanishes too. The camera pans to the doorway of the bedroom in which Betty and Rita were last seen, and Aunt Ruth appears briefly wearing the same clothes she wore when we saw her earlier leave her apartment for the airport before Betty arrived. She seems surprised to find no one and nothing out of the ordinary in the bedroom as the camera imitates her gaze surveying the room. We see that neither Betty, Rita, or the blue box is there. Then Ruth moves somewhere else in her apartment. We are no longer able to orient ourselves in time and space.

Aunt Ruth is not in Canada, where, in the initial world of the film, she had gone, leaving her place for Betty to use. It is impossible to tell whether she has returned from her trip or never went to Canada at all. It is also impossible to know whether Betty and Rita were ever in this space. Is this part of the parallel world to which we will soon be introduced? We move again to the frame of the bedroom door and shift suddenly into a corridor, but not one in Ruth's apartment. A low rumble on the soundtrack accompanies this shift. We briefly shift back to Ruth's bedroom doorway, and then back again to the corridor of another space. We are in the corridor of the apartment in the Sierra Bonita apartment complex in which, in the pre-black-hole world, Diane Selwyn died, and the shot is the same one used when Betty and Rita traced a path to the bedroom where Diane Selwyn's corpse lay on her bed. Time and space are shifting, moving backward, but also grinding to a halt, as we shall see, in the black hole manufactured by the marketplace.

In this black hole space, the stories of Rita, Adam, and Betty continue but as degenerated forms of what they once were. Lynch signals to us that this change for the worse is the routine direction of the Hollywood marketplace story. We are returning to the Sierra Bonita apartments, as if we were continuing from there, but with a new "blonde in the bed," positioned as the old one was, wearing the same lingerie, and lying in identically colored bedclothing to take the last leg of the trip from illusion into putrefaction. At first, we cannot see the face of this "blonde in the bed," but we can observe that this body is not (yet) desiccated and faintly putrefied as was the corpse that Betty and Rita found. We don't know (for certain) what happened to that dead blonde, but once we see this part of *Mulholland Dr.*, a probability emerges that she too took the path on which an unaware Betty was headed. It is a fate that the powers that administer the marketplace press on its inhabitants, but will not own up to, no matter how deeply involved they are in it. After the sound of a door opening, we see the Cowboy standing at the threshold. Smiling affably, he says, "Hey, pretty girl. Time to wake up." We cut back to the body in the bed, which now is desiccated and faintly putrefied, making a mockery of his cheery phrase, "pretty girl." A reaction shot of the Cowboy shows that his expression has changed to one of subtle dismay. But, as part of the world of illusion, he dismisses what he has seen and closes the door. We don't. Later in the film, at the tension-filled party at Adam Kesher's house, he also avoids the ugly aspects of the marketplace on display by walking quickly through the room, his back turned.[17]

When the body stirs and rises to a sitting position, we see she looks like Betty. But it isn't the Betty we first saw. She has a new name and a new attitude. A neighbor who arrives at this woman's door calls her, "Diane," and she is surly and difficult unlike the sweet, accommodating Betty. For the audience, she is now Betty/Diane, since she is a new form of the woman we have seen before, living in a strange, new form of a once-familiar world. The pre- and post-blue-box form of *Mulholland Dr.* is a way of talking about what happens when we get caught in the marketplace. Lynch does not show Betty's change as it would literally look—although people's names do change in Hollywood, they don't change this way—but as it is from a larger, more imaginative perspective. We will soon see a new form of Rita with a new name, Camilla Rhodes, a Rita/Camilla. And a new form of Adam, who has gone through a radical alteration even though his name remains unchanged. This transformation echoes Lynch's sense of transitions (corridors between doors) that result in new worlds—that are not fantasies but complex aspects of experience.

In the black hole world, with its mix-up of bodies and names, we move poetically from here to here. We see Hollywood again through new eyes. Those who have mistakenly divided *Mulholland Dr.* into an initial segment of the film that they interpret as Betty's happy dream and a final part that they interpret as Betty's miserable reality have not allowed themselves to come to grips with the fact that there is no reason to believe that either part of the film is more real than the other. If anything, in the post-black-hole parallel world, time, and space are more chaotic and out of sync with ordinary norms of materiality than in the pre-black-hole action. In this black hole space, time is a maelstrom that bends and turns back on

"The Cowboy" (Monty Montgomery), a crucial studio regulator who enforces the illusion of physical determinacy, smiles as he arrives to wake up . . .

. . . the blonde in the bed (either Lyssie Powell or Naomi Watts), who is a putrefied sight. The indeterminacy of who plays the figure in the bed is part of the reality Lynch is evoking for his audience. However, because the uncertainty of the physical world is something this regulator cannot abide, he . . .

. . . registers displeasure before he turns his back on what he (Monty Montgomery) would rather not see.

itself. Here, Lynch takes for *Mulholland Dr.* his final metaphor from modern physics for the process of decreation that has been imposed by the marketplace on Betty, Adam, and Rita. They are reduced to inert, dead matter in a temporal and spatial maelstrom that echoes the "you'll never have me" refrain from *Lost Highway* in its depiction of the ramifications of the Hollywood dream.

The denouement of the film plays out the impossibility of connection, pleasure, and relationship in a world dominated by the Hollywood dream of certainty. As the story ends, Adam and Rita/Camilla are linked romantically, but their romance, as we shall see, has a sinister overtone. Betty/Diane and Rita/Camilla are also linked romantically, but their relationship too has a sinister and painful cast to it. The deterioration of the world of Betty, Adam, and Rita—instigated by the traumas of illusory certainties—is marked by its disintegration into a negative form of doubleness, a kind of superposition in which the parallel existences cancel each other. In her rage at being the other woman to Adam and Camilla, Betty arranges to have Camilla killed. At this point a second blue key comes into the story. Just as the appearance of the first blue key marked the descent into the black hole space of Hollywood, the appearance of the second key marks the final termination of all life within that space.

Emotional bankruptcy, impossibility, temporal and spatial confusion, and death reign over the third and final segment of *Mulholland Dr.*, which is, appropriately, painted completely in desaturated tones. Adam, Betty/Diane, and Rita/Camilla have all become entangled in a state of non-being that quickly turns to death. There is what seems to be an engagement party for Adam and Rita/Camilla in which Adam is supposed to speak about the connection between the two of them, but he can't get the words out of his mouth. Laughing mockingly, he says, "Camilla and I are going to be . . ." The impossibility of completing this sentence, and the nervous laughter tinged with derision, speaks volumes. They will never "be." There is nothing but an approach to non-being here, with death as the next step, as is made clear in the scene when Betty/Diane meets with a hit man in Winkie's to arrange for him to kill Rita/Camilla. As she hands him the picture of Camilla Rhodes, the woman he is intended to kill, she says, "this is the girl," exactly the words Adam was instructed to say when he selected Camilla Rhodes for his film. In both cases, the phrase leads to a negation. We hear the echoes of negation again when the hit man hands Diane the film's second blue key and tells her that when "it's finished," she'll find it "where I told you." When Betty/Diane asks what the key opens, he only laughs jeeringly. But we will see that the blue key that appears signifying Rita/Camilla's death is about closure, not opening: the closure of Betty/Diane's life—and of the film.

The mockery says it all both in the engagement announcement and in the planned murder. Betty has traveled a long way downhill from hopeful actress to killer. Now Betty/Diane is confronted by the horror of what she has become by the return in very changed form of the people that once seemed to bless her voyage of discovery. In the airport, Irene and her companion were gracious and warmly positive about Betty's future. When they show up at Betty/Diane's apartment, they too have emerged from the black hole as the degradation of those hopes.

Irene and her friend re-enter the film just after the hit man laughs at Betty/Diane's question about the key, "What does it open?" They return to the story unexpectedly near the retaining wall in back of Winkie's where Dan saw the monster that killed him at first glance. Sure enough, the monster is still there. But now it is sad and not at all frightening, warming itself by a trash fire and holding the blue cube. In fact, it is now clear that it is Dan's negative interpretation of the scene behind Winkie's that killed

The twisted emotion that infuses the marketplace success of Adam (Justin Theroux) and the dark woman (Laura Elena Harring) is manifest on their faces in this party scene as Adam announces that they are "going to be" without ever being able to name what form of being they will take. As Lynch believes that being is never purely in the future but is always already there, this aborted announcement of their engagement is an evocation of a hallucinatory state of being.

him. Without the terror that his dream imposed on the creature behind the wall, it is now recognizable as everything that has been excluded from the marketplace's illusions of solidity: the trash piled up out of sight of the Winkie's patrons; the scrawl on the walls where the trash is kept; the excremental monster. (In the credits this figure is referred to as "a bum," but that is also a way of talking about exclusion.) Sadly, curiously, the monster puts the blue cube in a dirty brown paper bag and throws the bag to the ground, linking the black hole with garbage. Tiny figures of Irene and her friend emerge from the bag, small enough to creep under Betty/Diane's door in the space where it doesn't quite meet the threshold. They are the final negativization of Betty's original positive energy, and, as they invade Betty/Diane's house and literally attack her with their jeering reminders of what she has been and what she has become, Betty/Diane completes the job of self destruction that has been in the works for some time now. She shoots herself.

As the shot rings out, her bedroom returns to smoke and particles and the possibility the marketplace would not allow emerges in a cloud of bright light, and we see an alternate Betty and Rita come into sight, enjoying the world, rather than dying of illusions about it. This is a possibility about which Hollywood will remain quiet, for from this vision the film cuts to an almost deserted Club Silencio. Almost deserted. There are no patrons, and no devilish Master of Ceremonies, garishly creating fear. But there is the blue-haired woman, who whispers to no one in particular, "Silencio." A creature neither fully dead, nor fully alive, she has no comment about another possible alternate world in which the joy of a limitless universe can be experienced.

## WHO'S DRIVING THE BUGGY?

What is the upshot of *Mulholland Dr.*? Lynch like all great artists speaks not to what we should or shouldn't do, but to the question of how we understand our lives. He speaks in this case of the dire consequences of mistaking certainty for security and uncertainty for danger. In a figurative way, *Mulholland Dr.* shows us that we deplete our creative energy to keep pointless illusions alive.

When I interviewed David Lynch over a period of four days in 1993, I knew little about him; so to sound him out on his basic attitudes I repeated to him Plato's parable of the chariot, by means of which Plato described the rightful organization of human faculties. In Plato's meta-phor, the driver of the chariot is reason and the horses he rules over are emotion and instinct, which from the Platonic point of view require the stewardship of reason. When I asked Lynch what he thought of that anal-ogy, he responded, "What if no one is driving the chariot?"[18] Years later, I now know that he was talking about possibility, not chaos. And even David Lynch is not driving the buggy for the audience of *Mulholland Dr.*; he disclaims full knowledge of why he has used certain images, identifying his reception of their effects with ours. The images are not those enforced by power but are there to stimulate the moment.[19]

It's not that Lynch disclaims the importance or value of culture; that would be ridiculous, especially for a man so cultivated in the ways of the arts and the practical crafts. The portrait that Lynch paints in *Mulholland Dr.* is of a malignant imbalance. The Cowboy's boast that he is the driver of the buggy, or the person who calls the shots, invokes his disproportion-ate sense of his power. He, Roque, and the Castigliones are the anti-Lynch in Hollywood. Once in the figurative buggy, we are cut off from the posi-tive forces in the universe, whether we are winners or losers from the Cowboy's point of view, and we entangle others, who are connected with us whether we know it or not—in the spirit of non-locality in physics. Adam is in and Betty/Diane is out, but they are both in the same black hole, as we see when they are all together at Adam Kesher's ostensible engagement party. At this gathering, both Vincenzo Castiglione and the Cowboy stamp the occasion with their authorizing presences. The world has been reduced to what Roque and his minions have made it. Whatever was possible that we saw in Wally's office and on Adam's soundstage is absolutely absent from this mean-spirited party. And this is true not only for the ostensibly successful Adam, but also for the defeated Betty/Diane and the perennial object of desire, "the girl," Camilla Rhodes, on this occasion.

When Alice moved through her mirror she saw Wonderland, a revela-tion of the meaninglessness and absurdity of Victorian society. When we move through the black hole, we see the meaninglessness and absurdity of Roque and company. But even though they can foreclose possibility in the lives of Betty, Rita, and Adam, for Lynch there are other potential lev-els of the real in which it remains. As the Tibetan mystic tradition might phrase it, "what happens at the moment of death is that the ordinary mind and its delusions die and in that gap the boundless skylike nature

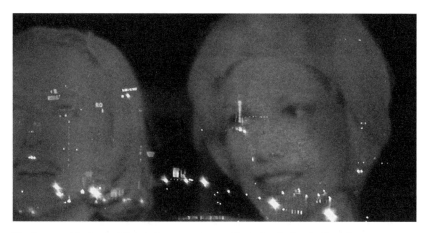

The image of Betty and the dark woman in a radiant cloud after both of them are dead in the narrative suggests the simultaneous presence of other universes/worlds. This happy possibility was never realized in *Mulholland Dr.*, but perhaps in another co-present time/space continuum it already is.

of our mind is uncovered."[20] At the moment of Betty/Diane's death, she is released from Roque's tyranny. We see her with Rita in a radiant cloud of light as the two look with delight at the world. There is a quality of peace, freedom, and happiness that accompanies this vision of a better place beyond the marketplace: the two women awakened from the "city of dreams." Perhaps in the next life.

Nevertheless, Club Silencio endures. It still lives too, and it has the final word in this film through the lady with the blue hair. She like Mr. Roque is a hybrid of thing and being that confuses the two, the hallmark of an artificial culture, commodified into silence. The lady with the blue hair and Mr. Roque, both terrible forms of rigor mortis, have succumbed entirely to the illusion of certainty that confuses dead images with animate life. As she murmurs, "silencio," she is the enduring negation—for now. But Lynch has unmasked the negativity of the marketplace in *Mulholland Dr.*, whatever the blue-haired lady may whisper. And, as we shall see in *Inland Empire*, the Hollywood marketplace need not have the final word.

# CHAPTER FOUR

# INLAND EMPIRE:
# THE BEGINNINGS OF
# GREAT THINGS

> But many primal atoms in many ways moving through infinite time
>     up to the present,
> Clashing among themselves and carried by their own weight
> Have come together every possible way,
> Tried every combination that could be made
> And so advancing through vast lengths of time,
> Exploring every union and motion,
> At length, those of them came together
> Which by a sudden conjunction interfuse
> Often became *the beginnings of great things*—[italics mine]
> Of earth and sea and sky and living creations.

**LUCRETIUS, *ON THE NATURE OF THE UNIVERSE*,**

**TRANSLATED BY SIR RONALD MELVILLE**

[A]t every occasion where a quantum event has more than one outcome (e.g., when an electron may strike one atom or another), the universe splits. We have one universe where the electron hits atom A, another where it hits atom B, and so on for all of the possible outcomes. . . . a new universe for each and every potential outcome. This is the Many Worlds (MW) interpretation. From the MW viewpoint, the universe is like a tree that branches and re-branches into myriads of new sub-branches with every passing picosecond. And each of these new branch universes has a slightly different sub-atomic "history." Because an observer happens to have followed one particular path through the diverging branches of this Universe-Tree, he never perceives the splitting. Instead he interprets the resolution of the myriad of possibilities into one particular outcome as a Copenhagen-style collapse [decreation]. . . . There should be a MW universe in which every physically possible event has happened. There should be MW universes where the dinosaurs dominate the planet . . . Even as you read this sentence your universe may be fragmenting into a number of branches too large to count.

## APPENDIX II

Actress Nikki Grace (Laura Dern) isn't sure what's going on or even who she is. She has the role she's been hoping for in a new film, *On High in Blue Tomorrows*, yet at the same time, she's more confused and frightened than she has ever been. But is that a bad thing? The director of *Blue Tomorrows*, Kingsley Stewart (Jeremy Irons) is certain of what he's doing, as he begins to tackle a script blueprint, for which he sees himself as a kind of construction boss who faces the task of building the film from script specifications with the help of a crew of actors and technical personnel. Just like in the "making of. . . ." featurettes so prevalent on DVDs. But is that a good thing? In Lynch's portrayal of the Hollywood marketplace in *Inland Empire*, Lynchian confusion trumps certainty. Nikki complicates Stewart's plans—for the better. Inside the bound horizons of Stewart's busy marketplace activity, when Nikki finds that something boundless is breaking into her life as an actress and a woman, the ensuing uncertainty changes everything on the studio soundstage, inexorably flooding *Blue Tomorrows* with a depth and power beyond Stewart's wildest expectations.

A counterforce on the limitations of Stewart's working style, Nikki imports into the production of *Blue Tomorrows* a spontaneous and uncertain process resembling the spectacle of atoms described above in the quotation from Lucretius, a Roman scientific philosopher who lived roughly between 99 and 55 BC. Lucretius was an early exponent—without benefit of modern laboratory equipment and the knowledge accumulated in the intervening history of scientific thought—of the uncertainty principle. In his masterwork, *On The Nature of the Universe,* he essentially described an uncertain cosmos in which, at unpredictable times in unpredictable places, "things swerve." This framework of thought was eclipsed for many centuries by the absolute ideas of Newtonian physics, but the tide has now turned. The philosophical leap from Lucretius to Heisenberg is not a big one, so the parallel I draw here between Lucretius and what happens to Nikki in *Inland Empire* is continuous with my argument that Lynch has drawn on intuitions resembling those of modern physics for his portrayal of matter in his second-stage films. Lynch has not read Lucretius recently, if at all. Nevertheless, as we shall see below, Lucretius, as an ancestor of present-day quantum physicists, is helpful for illuminating the very complex (and, to many, elusive) narrative structure of *Inland Empire*.

Director Kingsley Stewart has a marketplace approach to filmmaking that resembles assembling prefabricated furniture—and Newton's ideas about how time and space work. Not much of a story. The narrative gets its juice when Nikki Grace, a faded though still young Hollywood star and at first a compliant member of his team, separates herself from the marketplace that Stewart represents. In the words of Lucretius, she is buffeted by the "many primal atoms" of her situation that "clash among themselves." They "by a sudden conjunction interfuse" and become "the beginnings of great things." Her story is like the films we have just discussed in that it plays with uncertainty, but it is unlike the tales of Fred Madison in *Lost Highway* and Betty Elms in *Mulholland Dr.*, because it does not culminate in lives drained of joy and love by the power of the marketplace. Nor, although it has a harmonious conclusion like *The Straight Story*, is it like that film. Alvin imposes the form of his journey. Nikki's more extensive narrative is not under her control. Instead, the marketplace becomes a possible launch pad for the "beginnings of great things" because Nikki Grace allows herself to benefit from the energies that sweep her up and move her past the Hollywood culture that Stewart has bought into. Through Nikki's story, Lynch revitalizes the film-about-making-films genre as he invents numerous ways of depicting with vivacity and intensity why and how filmmaking at its best is the marriage of Hollywood technology and the energies of uncertainty.

When Nikki, her co-star Devon Berk (Justin Theroux), and Stewart begin to work, the image of the script they are about to bring to life fills the screen, conveying a sense of its dominance. But it is a false sense. The paper script turns out to be as apocryphal as its author, one Lawrence Ashton, a ghostlike fiction who never appears. (Nor does anyone ever speak of him.) Rather, *Blue Tomorrows* evolves dynamically in ways that are beyond the conscious will of the creative team, as material hidden in the depths of its story churns up to the surface. Of all the people involved with the film-within-the-film, it is Nikki Grace who most fully rides the wave of the story's evolution. In fact, Lynch would not use the word evolution because that implies a linear process of change endemic to the marketplace. What happens to Nikki is much more non-local. Lynch would be more likely to describe her experience as a revelation of what *Blue Tomorrows* always was, though initially blocked by false appearances. However, as stunning as Nikki's unexpected triumph is in her role in *Blue Tomorrows*, the more central issue for *Inland Empire* is her growth as a human being. With the freedom that Nikki gains from her creative process comes not only artistic liberation from the shallowness that *Blue Tomorrows* manifested when Kingsley Stewart began shooting the film, but also a release from the constraints of a stifling marriage to a domineering husband, and the petty and nasty influences of the industry around her. And there is more: freedom also brings a responsibility to others and a capacity for helping them. Nikki's story is the opposite of Fred Madison's. As he becomes less and less free, he becomes less and less his brother's keeper; a murderer in fact. Nikki's freedom, by contrast, enables her to help a needy character known as the Lost Girl (Karolina Gruszka) and lifts her into a generous, ascending cycle of being.

Of course, Lynch is not just talking about filmmaking. Filmmaking is one of the aspects of human endeavor that he knows best and he focuses on it, but he believes that all work participates equally in the same process by which art is created, and he accordingly uses the specifics of the creation of *Blue Tomorrows* to talk about the enterprise of doing and living, what it means to be fully and vibrantly alive.[1] As he shows us the way that Nikki, for reasons that can never be fully known, surrenders to the larger forces around her, he makes her experience a model for letting go of the narrow limits set by the most constricting aspects of our society that foreclose our full potential as people. I make a distinction here between society as a whole and its most constricting aspects because, after all, Lynch is also part of our society, the part that moves toward openness and hope. Moreover, his Hollywood *in this film* is a place of opportunity for those who can avail themselves of it. Meaningful stories can be told in the marketplace, if the Stewarts of the mass culture industry do not have their way completely. Meaningful life can be lived if, like Nikki, we have the courage to let it happen.

Non-locality permeates Lynch's vocabulary for depicting Nikki's brave journey; it is a concept we have discussed before, but for easier application of the non-local phenomenon of entanglement to *Inland Empire*, I will review its definition here. Entanglement literally occurs when physicists observe particles involved with each other without being in direct (or even indirect) relation to each other in a single time/space frame. Lynch's figurative use of this quantum paradigm allows him to portray creation in art and life as a mysterious, large confluence of multiple time/space frames permitting processes of influence and counterinfluence unrestricted by any of the specifications of the usual chains of causality.[2] And that process allows Lynch to dramatize Nikki's "risk taking" in a way that reveals the hard struggles of the creative life and how they require her to brave the fears of uncertainty, as if she were thrown hither and yon into and out of unfamiliar and strange worlds. Thus the process is not presented in *Inland Empire* as a dance of a few dreamworlds that are purely imaginative. That would be too tame a way of depicting the considerable and necessary turmoil Nikki must endure. Nikki's confusing but rewarding experience is metaphorically set forth as a disorienting encounter with numerous possible worlds that are unsettlingly endowed with time/space realities of their own. There is nothing easy about Nikki's encounters with possible worlds that are the particles or molecules of the "great things" in store for her.

In fact, everything is particles/molecules (that is, potential) when *Inland Empire* begins. There are molecules of what will become the finished form of *Blue Tomorrows*.[3] And there are molecules of what will become the new emotional shape of Nikki's life. The collisions of the many basic versions of *Blue Tomorrows* with the particles of emotional states that stimulate Nikki's renewal as a person are remarkably reminiscent of Lucretius's picture of the collisions of moving atoms in the process of creating matter. Indeed, in this story of growth and regeneration nonlocality is a useful metaphor for invoking the multitude of time/space frames necessary for the creative changes in Nikki's life. In Lynch's words, the nature of the infinite cosmos is composed of many universes, some of which become permanent, and "take hold and grow." Some last only brief seconds.[4] Creative possibilities manifest themselves for Lynch as entire worlds that may come and go like bubbles. In *Inland Empire*, the characters must fully experience numerous metaphorical bubble worlds—whether or not these worlds "take hold and grow"—in order to realize the final form of *Blue Tomorrows*. The process is very non-local. But, in Lynch's eyes, this is authentic, energy-filled nature, an example of how life fully lived unfolds and how we generate the most exciting form of storytelling as well.[5]

The main title of *Inland Empire* begins (appropriately) with a Lynchian image of creation, which is followed by a banquet of non-local particles, all ready to entangle with each other. The first thing we see is a beam of light piercing opaque blackness and revealing the words *Inland Empire*, accompanied by vibrating sound. This montage has rough similarities to the Vedic creation story, as Lynch told it to me. This ancient myth describes the emergence of material life out of the unified field at the core of the universe through the spontaneous eruption of words that become matter. The beam of light that explodes into darkness and reveals the form of language through the title of the film places us within a space carved out of the enormity of limitlessness. We are now in the marketplace.

From the general idea of creation, Lynch then segues to a particular particle that will be part of Nikki's journey, the radio play *AXXON N.*, one of the fragments of what will become *Blue Tomorrows*. *AXXON N.* is visualized as a mixture of details and ellipses, as if it were the molecules of a story that has yet to cohere. We see the mise-en-scène, and yet we don't see it. We learn a detail or two about the characters that leave many questions unanswered. It is but a fragment, and Lynch's story will be, as in *Mulholland Dr.*, derived from numerous entangled fragments. The bigger picture will be an aggregate of what is known combined with the gaps between the pieces displayed for us—bits of information and the void between these bits. It recalls Arthur Eddington's particle-by-particle description at the beginning of the book of how a physicist might imagine entering a room. However, there are nothing but particles at this point.

The parallel process by means of which Nikki's life is transformed will involve still more particles, visualized as worlds, worlds that are molecules of the states of emotion that Nikki will metaphorically inhabit on her journey and at journey's end. It is unorthodox to think of emotional states of being as places we can enter, which Lynch does here. Lynch also challenges the way we usually think about time by locating these "feeling places"—bubble worlds—in a future that is already present when the film begins, way before Nikki finds these worlds. But Lynch's ideas about how life and art come into being include a belief that everything that will be, already is. Nikki's future encounters with faith, negativity, and the responsibility she has to all people are present even before she enters the narrative, and those worlds are made manifest for us in a prologue to her first appearance.

Faith, metaphorically pictured as a world Nikki will eventually enter, takes shape as a stage set populated by actors in rabbit suits. The negative energy she will conquer lurks in the form of an abusive figure called the Phantom (Krzysztof Majchrzak), present in a world of anger set in a charming period room. The world of human suffering for which Nikki will eventually take responsibility is embodied by the Lost Girl. Only their common humanity connects the Lost Girl and Nikki: the Girl needs help, and Nikki's need to provide that help will become an interesting debt that she carries with her. This is the "unpaid bill" that Nikki and her character Susan Blue are so enigmatically told they owe.

Lynch's vision of faith reveals itself rather unusually in a patently theatrical set of a working class apartment where three actors wearing rabbit suits wait for understanding in a state of Pinteresque/Beckettian confusion. I will call this world the Rabbit Room. The world of human need, the Lost Girl's Room, provocatively combines an elaborately appointed but realistic looking hotel room with a magic mirror shaped like an ordinary television.[6] The world of rage, which I will call the Rage Room, piques our visual interest by placing two men, one of whom is filled with violent, negative energy, in a beautiful, traditional, gilt-covered European salon. These worlds are part and parcel of the "something" that is happening— that will require Nikki and the spectator to expand our limits and let the Rabbit Room, the Lost Girl's Room, and the Rage Room speak to us. The "happening" that involves moving through these worlds is enunciated by a lyrical, melodic song called "Polish Poem," written by Lynch

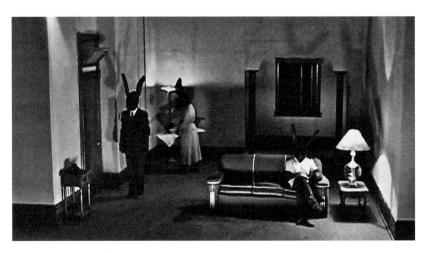

The world of faith; this frame evokes, through the three actors in rabbit disguise (Scott Coffey, Naomi Watts, and Laura Elena Harring), a strange amalgam of simplicity, theatricality, material poverty, and imaginative richness, and above all, patience.

The world of human need; this frame evokes in the sobbing woman (Karolina Gruszka) impotent suffering and a state of being cut off from the flow of events.

and Chrysta Bell. The song wafts onto the soundtrack when these worlds are being revealed, signifying something redemptive that will fulfill "the dream of an innocent child." Since Lynch believes that we are all innocent before we are distracted by the marketplace, Nikki's innocence is being redeemed because she courageously breaks free of the marketplace by opening herself up to many possibilities, despite the confusion and fear provoked by the uncertainty of this process.

At the outset, let us understand that all of the many worlds in Lynch's film reveal themselves as thresholds through which Nikki moves *without thinking*, propelled by a force more potent than rational thought. Although the process begins consciously when Nikki willingly agrees to be in Stewart's film, it quickly becomes one in which she temporarily and spontaneously loses the boundaries of her distinct ego, a process that is part of diving beneath the surface of the world, with its neat borders and definitive structures. Ultimately, as we shall see, Lynch illuminates Nikki's ride on the roller coaster of a "becoming" energy, which already has a destination when Nikki begins—even if she (and we) don't know what it is while she (and we) are in the throes of the process.[7]

The magic of the narrative is that Nikki, because of her artistic daring, is both becoming something new and is already someone new. The three worlds of faith, rage, and altruism are the future/present of Nikki's story. In presenting us first with these many bubble worlds that will emerge,

The world of rage; this frame evokes through the two men (Jan Hencz and Krzysztof Majchrzak) material affluence, imaginative aggression, and above all, raging assertion.

shimmer for a while, and then disappear, Lynch begins *Inland Empire* with a tantalizing display of non-locality in which the personal and the professional entangle and the future and the past are now.

## THREE RABBITS, ONE PHANTOM, ONE LOST GIRL, AND A VISITOR

Nikki's voyage to a happier and more expansive personhood, which begins with some freewheeling creativity as an actress, is the narrative subject of *Inland Empire*. On the road to "the palace," Lynch's name for the state of enlightenment—which Nikki will finally achieve—a thrilling process takes place through which Nikki will create the character Susan Blue in the film *On High in Blue Tomorrows*. At the same time, immersion in her artistry will instill in Nikki the ability to acquire faith, fight negativity, and assume responsibility for helping others. That said, we need to consider the complex way the film makes the excitingly unusual and imaginative, extremely expressive shapes of the molecules of faith, negativity, and human connection manifest.

The Rabbit Room is envisioned through the image of a room that is obviously fictional—a place, a world of theatrical disguise and performance. Yet while it is fanciful, it is also thuddingly mundane. Actors in rabbit suits occupy a theatrical representation of a working class home.

Suzie Rabbit (voiced by Naomi Watts), a motherly figure, stands at an ironing board, and two young rabbits, Jack Rabbit (Scott Coffey) and Jane Rabbit (Laura Harring), sit in front of her, doing nothing in particular. There is high fantasy here in the midst of banality, a tantalizing metaphor for the combination of the embroidering imagination and the effortless calm and patience needed to face the uncertainty of the marketplace. The discussion in the Rabbit Room is a tissue of unanswered questions that provokes inappropriate laughter and applause from the audience, one more representation by Lynch of the woeful state of public discourse. But despite everything, the three rabbits remain icons of faith. (The parenthetical descriptions in italics below are mine.)

> JANE RABBIT: I am going to find out some day. When will you tell it?
> JACK RABBIT: Who could have known?
> JANE RABBIT: What time is it? *[Big incomprehensible laugh from the invisible audience]*
> JACK RABBIT: I have a secret.
> (Cut to the Lost Girl crying, and then back to the Rabbit stage set)
> JANE RABBIT: There have been no calls today. *[Big incomprehensible laugh from the invisible audience]*

When we consider the destructive consequences of the misguided public pressures in both *Lost Highway* and *Mulholland Dr.*—even in *The Straight Story* there is a negative slant to much of what those around Alvin have to say about his trip—we can see how crucial the Rabbits' patient endurance is as they are beset by the unknown and surrounded by the absurdity of public discourse. Jane Rabbit establishes herself as a keeper of the faith when she asserts her calm, simple belief that she will "find out one day." Nikki will eventually reach this place.

The metaphorical magic of the Rage Room conjures a different but entangled world. (Jack Rabbit is able to enter this world from the Rabbit Room in a magical way.) The Rage Room seems to exist within real, historical time, not fiction. But though beautiful and golden, it is paradoxically the space associated with the Phantom, a profoundly negative character who will eventually be revealed as the prime force seeking to block Nikki. This world, the gorgeously appointed space of tradition, is also the space of the obstacle, the adversary, the rage for control and legibility that has destroyed or at least frustrated so many previous Lynch protagonists. The antagonist, reminiscent of the troublemaking Rakshasas in the Vedic

131

stories that Lynch spoke to me about, pollutes ordinary life as he fulminates with abusive energy among the delicate artifacts of culture.

IMPASSIVE MAN [Later known as Janek (Jan Hench)]: You are looking for something?
RAGING MAN [Later known as the Phantom]: Yes . . .
IMPASSIVE MAN: Are you looking to go in?
RAGING MAN: Yes.
IMPASSIVE MAN: An opening?
RAGING MAN: I look for an opening. Do you understand?
IMPASSIVE MAN: Yes, I understand.

(NOTE: In the film, these characters are unnamed.) Raging Man is abusive in his determination to "go in." As the essence of invasive negativity, he is the quintessential Lynchian villain and throughout the film and the film-within-a-film he savagely attempts to contaminate Nikki's imaginative and real worlds. We have seen this kind of figure before in Lynch's work. The Phantom's growling determination to go in, articulated above, is reminiscent of both BOB in the *Twin Peaks* saga and the Mystery Man in *Lost Highway*.[8] Unstoppable in his previous appearances in the Lynch cannon, this Lynchian figure of evil finally, in Nikki, meets his match.

The world of the weeping Lost Girl, a third "feeling space," is also connected to the other two in a magical way. This world is the space of an emotionally paralyzed sufferer who sees what is happening but cannot do anything about what she knows. Her sorrow will be alleviated by Nikki, who will rescue her. Once Nikki has slain the Phantom, and is enveloped by faith, a generosity spontaneously wells up in her that propels her to give to others. Lynch uses these spaces to prefigure Nikki's destiny, which is a far cry from what seemed possible initially.

Nikki does not look like any kind of heroine when we first meet her in her luxurious but mausoleum-like mansion. She is rigid with security and physical comforts, almost completely lacking in vitality. There is a kind of beauty in her palatial home, forged by the sturdy, classical understanding of the shape and importance of symmetrically crafted and placed material objects and bodies; in its gorgeous luxury, it's reminiscent of the Rage Room. But all its stately proportions and solid walls will not isolate Nikki from the deeper, indeterminate realities of the physical world for long. Into this monument to spiritless boredom comes a Visitor (Grace

Zabriskie), who rocks Nikki's world by acting as the catalyst for permitting her to see the future in the now.

The Visitor is a messenger from beyond the limits of Nikki's ordinary life, a life that we will learn over and over again is too small for Nikki. Why The Visitor appears to Nikki is never explained. The making of *Blue Tomorrows* is simply Nikki's time to grow and learn, and the Visitor, who exhibits knowledge of the film-within-the-film, not as Nikki knows it now, but as it will eventually be, is clearly connected to an energy that will transform Nikki completely. The Visitor is Nikki's (and our) portal to non-locality, a creature of the past, future, and present, in no particular order. Sitting in Nikki's ornate living room, she already inhabits the future. She knows that Nikki will be cast as the star of *Blue Tomorrows* before the casting decision has been reached, and she knows what the eventual story of the film will be, while Nikki, who has read the script, is restricted to knowing only what it is in embryonic form.

The Visitor begins the process of Nikki's release from her golden cage by disrupting Nikki's sense of time and space—much as Lynch breaks us out of our golden cages by disrupting ours. And just as Lynch speaks to us in metaphor, the language of truth, so the Visitor speaks to Nikki in metaphor to begin her journey: a pair of folktales that the Visitor recites to Nikki, apropos of nothing. One concerns a little boy who causes a reflection when he crosses the threshold of his home as he goes out to play. "Evil was born," says the Visitor enigmatically, "and followed the boy." The other concerns a little girl who gets lost in the marketplace, "as if half-born." "Then," says the Visitor, "not through the marketplace—you see that don't you?—but through the alley behind the marketplace. This is the way to the palace."

The evil of the reflection, the marketplace and the alley behind it, being only half-born, and the palace are all images that introduce Nikki, through the vehicle of the stories told by the Visitor, to a new way of perceiving what she has seen every day, even though she doesn't understand at first. It would be ideal for her and for us as an audience to face with Rabbitlike poise and assurance our lack of comprehension of what Lynch means by these images and this vocabulary. However, as most of us cannot master the Rabbits' innocence and lack of irritability in the face of uncertainty, some discussion here of the special meaning of the Visitor's words is needed to help us fully enter and grasp Lynch's beautiful film. That discussion is initiated here with a hope and trust that it will only

Visitor #1 (Grace Zabriskie) is patently physically odd, as if the molecules of her being were always threatening to break away from conventional human shape. Since she is a benign messenger from the uncertain beyond that exists past the limits of the standardized marketplace, this appearance is appropriate.

aid the reader's innocent—in the Lynchian sense of unobstructed receptivity—appreciation of Lynch's larger goals of spontaneity.

Previous chapters have already addressed Lynch's oblique references to Maharishi Mahesh Yogi—the spiritual leader who greatly influenced Lynch—and his teachings about the shallowness of confusing surface appearances with the totality of reality. But in his earlier second-stage films Lynch referenced Maharishi without using his vocabulary; in *Inland Empire*, Lynch puts that vocabulary explicitly into the Visitor's mouth as she speaks to Nikki in parables about the marketplace and the palace. New terms are also introduced. If the little girl in the Visitor's story is lost in the marketplace, she can only find her way out through "the alley" behind it. This alludes to Maharishi's term for a shortcut out of the bottom-line culture, since moving through the marketplace will only leave us trapped by false values and false perceptions. The function of the reflection caused by the little boy is to remind us of the fragmentation we experience in the marketplace even as children at play, and the inevitable fraught relationships between dark and light forces in the aggregate of fragments. The little girl's destination in the Visitor's story, the palace, is interesting since, in marketplace terms, Nikki is already in a kind of palace, but it is not yet the great good place of wholeness it will become after her journey.

The Visitor also speaks of an "unpaid bill" that Nikki owes, which confuses her no end. This also is a figurative, poetic term, but, as far as I can determine, not one used by Maharishi. It is, rather, Lynch's own ironic creation of a marketplace-like analogy for the debts that we all owe to others who may need our help, not for the marketplace motivations of profit and loss, but simply because being fully human involves helping. The unpaid bill the Visitor references is the opposite of what is understood as obligation within the marketplace, and Nikki will understand it one day.

Nikki begins in the marketplace of Hollywood in confusion and with some trepidation, carrying an unpaid human debt. Her voyage into the alley behind the marketplace will plunge her temporarily into the deepest levels of materiality and consciousness, but ultimately the journey will dispel confusion and fear and allow her to pay her debt—a karmic debt in the language of Lynch's Vedic visionary understanding. Initially, the Visitor and the prospects she suggests startle and repel Nikki, but although she wants to get rid of the perturbing Visitor, she cannot help feeling that, as the "Polish Poem" says, "something is happening." ("Is happening," not "will happen.")

It would be a mistake to read the Visitor as either all-powerful or all-good. But it is necessary to read her through Lynch's mystical understanding of moments when life offers us opportunities to free ourselves from the (much too narrow) limits of our perceptions. As Nikki's first taste of non-locality, the Visitor shows herself as a disquieting jumble because making sense of the opportunity cannot be explained beforehand. Full comprehension of this moment requires doing, not just talking. It requires experience. It is only as Nikki avails herself of the opportunity to create Susan Blue in *Blue Tomorrows* that the Visitor's mysterious words about time, evil, "the alley behind the marketplace," and "an unpaid bill" will become meaningful and transformational.

This shock of non-locality administered by the Visitor turns into Nikki's way out of a Hollywood that does not offer much in the way of buoyant creativity and love. There is Devon Berk (Justin Theroux), a notorious womanizer, who casually attempts to seduce Nikki. There is Marilyn Levens (Diane Ladd), a television gossip who trivializes Nikki's work by using it as a pretext for inventing a sex scandal she can expose. Kingsley Stewart (Jeremy Irons) presents Nikki with another form of trivialization when he frames *Blue Tomorrows* only in terms of industry rewards and prestige. His assistant, Freddie Howard (Harry Dean Stanton), a (hilarious) parasite, construes the making of a film as an opportunity to "get over," slavishly fawning on Stewart and scrounging shamelessly for handouts among the cast and crew of the film-within-a-film. In the airless physical splendor of her palatial home, Nikki is also suffocated. Her husband Piotrek Król (Peter J. Lukas) is possessive and devious. Never together with Nikki in any kind of intimacy, he is intent always on establishing his property rights over her, as we see when he warns Devon that there will be consequences if Devon makes free with his exclusive property.

Hollywood's impoverished view of creativity emerges from the contrasts among the actual history of the movie that Nikki, Devon, and Kingsley Stewart are working on; the lurid way it is presented to and by them; and the liberating evolution of the film-within-a-film during the production.[9] Kingsley Stewart speaks of the history of *Blue Tomorrows* in hushed tones, hinting that it has had a shady and perhaps dangerous past, the details of which were initially withheld from him. He reluctantly reveals to Nikki and Devon that their film is a "remake" of a previous project titled *Vier Sieben* (in English, *Four Seven*). According to Stewart, this information was kept hush-hush because the first attempt to make the film was terminated abruptly after the two stars were murdered in mid-production. Shock! They are all apprehensive.

But *Inland Empire* suggests that this "shady past" is the loam from which narrative grows. It is only when the story's past incarnations assert themselves in the creative process that depth is possible. The alternative to that struggle is cliché, which is what would have emerged from the script written by the invisible Lawrence Ashton. The elusive Ashton's *Blue Tomorrows* that we see when Stewart, Nikki, and Devon begin to work is a lifeless, pastel melodrama that takes place in Hollywood's stereotypical version of the American South. The Ashton story takes a superficial look at the attempt of wealthy Billy Side (Devon Berk's role), who lives in a plantation-style mansion, to seduce Susan Blue (Nikki), his employee—doing what is not clear. But while Stewart and his crew play with lights and sound cues, because of Nikki's process the earlier, grittier, mostly forgotten script of *Vier Sieben* becomes one of the many molecules that intersect with the story of Susan Blue and Billy Side, as does its antecedent, a completely forgotten radio play known as *AXXON N.*, "the longest-running radio play in history, tonight continuing in the Baltic region, a grey winter day in an old hotel." Nikki's surrender to larger forces unperceived by her oblivious colleagues make the movie they are working on richer

The image of the phantom script looms large, but along with its purported never-seen author Lawrence Ashton, whose name evokes old Hollywood's anglophile renaming of its personnel, it has little to no effect on the making of *On High in Blue Tomorrows*.

and deeper than it would have been if Stewart's mechanical Hollywood approach to filmmaking had prevailed.

Nikki's emotional and creative breakthroughs originate with her growing experience of a strangeness entering the physicality of her life, a sense of the uncanny that only begins with her Visitor. Subsequently, strangeness on the set blossoms too, almost immediately when Nikki, Devon, Stewart, and Freddie sit down on soundstage 4 for a first reading of scene 35 of *Blue Tomorrows*. Nikki begins to feel something about the set of Smithy's house on that soundstage, a feeling she cannot express in words. (Smithy's house is where Susan Blue lives—with Smithy, a man whose relationship to her is never strictly defined for us.) That there is an unexpected material as well as emotional aura that permeates the set for Smithy's house becomes clear when footsteps from the back of the soundstage suggest that someone is hiding in its depths. Although there is no exit through which the intruder can escape, an attempt to find who is lurking here yields nothing. When we discover that it was Nikki herself hidden in the dark depths of the set, while she was at the same time sitting with Stewart and Devon, we realize there's a breakdown in the boundaries of Nikki's narrowly defined self. However, "breakdown" is not the final destination here as it was in *Lost Highway* and *Mulholland Dr.* In *Inland Empire*, we will see that the non-local metaphors from quantum physics provide Lynch with an invaluable language for depicting more positive breakdowns of the barriers between life and art. Indeed, without those metaphors, how would Lynch dramatize that process? They let us see that her actions across ordinary limits and borders will have consequences; in fact, Lynch's special cinematic vocabulary permits us to see that they already do.

## ACTIONS DO HAVE (NON-LINEAR) CONSEQUENCES

We have already noted that part of Lynch's innovative treatment of narrative time in all his second-stage films takes the form of a future that is both yet to be and already "here" when the story begins. Within this context we find the Lynchian paradox that actions already have consequences. Fred's dark future is already present in *Lost Highway* in the opening frame when he hears that "Dick Laurent is dead." The disintegration of Betty's bright hopes is already there in the claustrophobic section of the opening montage of *Mulholland Dr.*, with its empty bed and heavy breathing. And Alvin's reunion with his brother is already present in the opening vision of the stars. But in *Inland Empire*, Lynch is much more insistent on confronting the audience with information before we are prepared to use it and images before we have any association with them. Running parallel with the literature of modern physics that entertains the possibility that we might have access to both past and future in the present, *Inland Empire* anchors its story about Nikki's creative journey in a non-local process that evokes a future that is always already there in order to dramatize the way omnipresent good and omnipresent evil manifest themselves within the linear action of the marketplace.

Nikki Grace starts out securely within the ordinary linear sequences of daily activity. But almost immediately Visitor #1 alerts us to another type of relationship between human behavior and time because the way she speaks of actions and consequences contrasts with what Nikki's husband, Piotrek, means when he uses the same words. Piotrek conventionally warns Devon of the consequences if he doesn't keep his hands off Nikki. From his lips, the words "actions have consequences" mean that they will have them. Nikki's Visitor #1 speaks of an unpaid debt and consequences within an unorthodox context of time that is an eternal present. The words "actions have consequences," from her lips, means they already have them. Dizzy as Visitor #1 sounds and compelling as Piotrek seems, it is the Visitor and not Nikki's husband whose idea of time has the most force in Nikki's narrative. We are constantly confronted by the paradox that although we as spectators must wait for the arrival of future consequences, they are, in important ways, already present before they happen. Once Nikki is on her creative path, the consequences of actions we may or may not know about burst into view in fragments that are out of linear sequence, fragments that become visible as if the present were a palimpsest scraped momentarily so that we can see it as a layer of events on top of not only the past but also the future.

After Visitor #1 sounds the first notes of a coexisting past, present, and future, we are administered a series of shocks relative to the making of *Blue Tomorrows* that place us inside that very non-linear time. One of the most fascinating and evocative of Lynch's rearrangements of narrative temporality in Nikki's story occurs when, early in the film, one minute we are in Nikki's luxurious home as she explains to some Polish friends of her husband that she doesn't speak Polish and the next minute we are confronted with an already present consequence. Suddenly, we are in a grimy police station. While Nikki's house is real, the police station, as we will "learn someday"—to quote the rabbits again—is not. It is a fictional room in which we are to meet Doris Side (Julia Ormond), a character we will later know as the wife of Billy Side, Susan Blue's employer in the film-within-the-film. We are thus introduced to a curved time that makes everything present in the moment: fiction, reality, then, now, will be. In other words, time simultaneously contains the present in Nikki's elegant house and the future in a fictional police station that will one day exist in *Blue Tomorrows*. (We know this scene must exist in a "someday soon" time frame because Nikki has already mentioned that the script she has read does not concern murder, and this is a scene in which a murder is announced.)

Doris, scruffy in jean shorts and a t-shirt, desperately tells a sweating, bemused policeman that she is going to kill someone, but that she doesn't know who, why, or where. Moreover, she distractedly informs the policeman that she is not motivated by her own will. She has been hypnotized by a peculiar man who did "something funny with his hands," and told her that when the time comes to commit murder, she will know it. (We will eventually identify the man with the peculiarly moving hands as the Phantom.) The murder weapon, a screwdriver, is already painfully lodged in Doris's midsection under a cloth bandage. Doris is a victim before the fact as well as a future perpetrator. This gritty, troublesome scene tells us that there already exists a very different *Blue Tomorrows* from the one we initially see Kingsley Stewart shooting, which entails nicely dressed characters lolling about a southern mansion, while lush, romantic B-film music plays.

This sudden invasion of *Inland Empire* by a scene from a future (but paradoxically already existing) form of *Blue Tomorrows* is as non-local as any particle events that quantum physicists have ever observed. What the film-within-the-film will be someday is already here, a state of affairs very difficult for his marketplace audience to grasp. This fragment of future revealed also establishes the presence of the evil force that will kill Susan Blue, the main character in *Blue Tomorrows*, and educate Nikki, although it has not yet manifested itself in the linear time of the present that is all that Nikki, at this point in the story, knows. This different conception of time permits Lynch not only to invite us to see the final gritty form of *Blue Tomorrows* before anyone knows what shape the film-within-the-film will take, but also to give us an authentic experience of how his own second-stage films operate.[10] They do not develop methodically from a well-defined situation, but rather bombard us with small, fragmentary insights into the final destiny of the characters already in place, but not yet manifest, until we are privy to all the fragments combined. Like discombobulated Doris, who is tormented by her partial knowledge of a murder in the offing, in the seemingly disconnected scene in the police station, we receive only partial, tantalizing, troubling, and vivid information that we can't yet use, prompting questions about which aspects we're watching will ultimately reveal a "here" we did not see at first.[11] Such a prefiguration is difficult to deal with and requires the innocent view of the Rabbits, a view that believes, "I am going to find out someday."

By contrast, the linearity of the Hollywood machine seems much more comprehensible as we see cameras roll. Lights are adjusted; parasitic Freddie goes about gouging the cast and crew for money; Nikki and Devon flirt as they wait to be called to work. If linearity continued to dominate Stewart's production, we would be immersed in the farcical boredom of Stewart whipping his crew into shape, as when he has to deal with the confusions of lighting man Bucky J. (David Lynch, voice only, uncredited), who can't follow Stewart's simple instructions on how to adjust a light. The film-within-a-film would be a melodrama about Susan's adultery with Billy. And if Lynch spoke through Stewart's point of view, in the real world of *Inland Empire*, we would watch a melodrama about Nikki's infidelity to

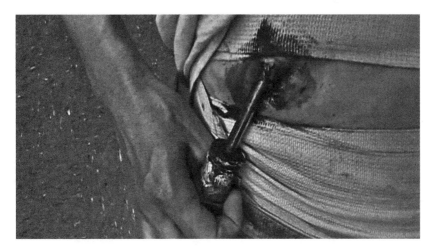

Doris Side (Julia Ormond) is in the police station, a scene that was not yet in the script read by Nikki Grace, and yet already exists, given the uncertain nature of time and space in Lynch's second-stage films. Doris knows that she will kill someone, but in this frame we see that her knowledge is already also an assault on herself. In the Lynchverse, what you do to others, you do to yourself as well.

Piotrek. But that is not the case. We leave behind Bucky J., Stewart, Billy's fictional extramarital shenanigans, and Devon Berk's wild, wild ways. Instead we go on a pilgrimage to greater things. There is in *Inland Empire* a counterpoint between linear time and the idea of consequences that comes from it and non-locality and its very different concept of consequences. In the long run, non-local time becomes the film's overtone and linear time the undertone.

The seminal shock when the film begins to veer off more fully into non-locality and its consequences occurs when Nikki first encounters an *AXXON N.* door in the alley behind the marketplace. *AXXON N.*, which we already know is the earliest ancestor of *Blue Tomorrows*, is the door that Nikki must enter for the new film to reveal what is already there, in its core. This is non-locality. And it is the process by means of which Nikki's experience as an actress in the film opens up for us. The *AXXON N.* door will eventually supplant in importance Devon Berk and the crew members on the soundstage, like Bucky J., and it will relegate Kingsley Stewart to the periphery of Nikki's experience working on *Blue Tomorrows*.

But at first, Berk, Stewart, and Bucky J. seem very significant, particularly Berk, as there appears to be some kind of sexual liaison developing as Nikki and Devon act the parts of lovers Susan Blue and Billy Side. However, all this byplay seems to be the center of the action only as long as there is a clear distinction between stories and life and we know exactly where the characters end and Nikki and Devon begin. Suddenly, when a sex scene erupts onto the screen in which no such clarity is possible, we have a problem critically identifying boundaries. We simply don't know whether they are playing their characters having sex, or whether they are actually having an adulterous sexual interlude. It is no coincidence that this scene, which breaks down Nikki's orientation in local time and space (and ours too), is also about her first encounter with the *AXXON N.* door.

During the sex scene, Nikki tries to tell Devon about the *AXXON N.* door at the same time as Susan tries to tell Billy about it. For us, the characters in Nikki's and Susan's worlds suddenly coexist simultaneously, so that we can neither separate the actress from her role nor discount one as a fiction. What was once just Nikki is now Nikki/Susan and this entangled compound woman is terrified. She begins to harangue Devon/Billy—screaming for him to look at her and recognize who she is. However, definitive identification is now impossible and we see the confusion of this inescapable conflation registering on Devon/Billy's face as Nikki/Susan tells him about the *AXXON N.* door. She speaks both as Susan in a scene in the film-within-a-film and as Nikki describing a scene she was filming. "It's a story that happened yesterday, but I know it's tomorrow," says Nikki/Susan, as time opens up into a loop. Devon/Billy listens to and speaks with Nikki/Susan with the same doubled reality. Here is a moment completely suffused with the uncertainty principle, as no one—not the actors, the characters, or the film's spectators—can precisely identify the borderline between fiction and reality. Some might call it madness. Lynch defines it as a necessary part of creativity and he presents it using a kind of doubling that recalls the phenomenon of superposition noted by quantum physics.[12]

Here, in *Inland Empire*, superposition becomes a metaphor for a stage in the creative process. This moment occurs on the set of Smithy's house—which also has two identities: as the purely fictional set of rooms located on a soundstage and as a physical location independently existing in time and space. As Nikki/Susan and Devon/Billy have sex, Piotrek appears to be skulking around spying on her, alerting us that the sex is real, not part of a movie scene. But, since the same actor who plays Smithy also plays

Susan's husband, this is another moment in the imagery of quantum superposition. Are we looking at Smithy or Piotrek?

Nikki's progress toward freedom from the superficiality of the original written script requires that she cease being merely one person who sometimes acts like Susan Blue. She must at this point begin a creative fusion with the character-in-progress, embracing the myriad possibilities of what Susan might be and engaging the many worlds enclosed in multiple time loops. The eruption of Nikki/Susan during the sex scene with Devon/Billy propels us into the alley behind the marketplace, where Nikki/Susan speaks in her frenzy at discovering herself in superposition. Nikki/Susan, by her very nature, cannot exist in ordinary time and space, and as we watch, time and space undergo major transformation as Nikki becomes more than one person but not quite fully two. This is what finally produces the highly successful act of character creation that Stewart acknowledges when he has finished shooting his picture. The complicated nature of time revealed in this process replaces our ordinary sense of a linear moving from here to there with a different shape. Nikki is moving from here to a deeper, non-linear here.

When *Inland Empire* cuts to the alley behind the marketplace, we see that the fused actress/character is impelled to go through a mysterious door marked with the name of the old radio play. The *AXXON N.* door is a portal into non-locality where yesterday and tomorrow are part of an uncertain time loop, since once over the threshold, Nikki/Susan finds herself on soundstage 4, days previously, during the first reading of scene 35. We now learn that it is Nikki/Susan who is the intruder in the darkness at the back of the set, even though there was no Nikki/Susan when that event took place, and even though the present of the film is now several days later than the scene on soundstage 4. Now we watch Nikki/Susan for a moment or two watching Nikki sitting with Stewart, Devon, and Freddie. Perhaps Nikki also gets a glimpse of the Nikki/Susan she will become.

Lynch tells us—and with much art—that our experiences of "doing" can be only as rich as our capacity for going willy-nilly among the many possible pathways, experiencing them as fully as if we were immersed in numerous worlds. If we want to live life to the fullest, we must necessarily take a journey into the multiple lives we all lead, if the truth were known. In some figurative ways we are all always in more than one place at the same time as we grow and change, so long as we don't allow fear of this strange phenomenon to stop us. Moving through Nikki's journey

What the fictional character Susan Blue, played by Nikki Grace (Laura Dern), sees of the table reading at which director Kingsley Stewart (Jeremy Irons), Devon Berk (Justin Theroux), Nikki, and Freddie Howard (Harry Dean Stanton) are present. The reading has been interrupted by Freddie's awareness that someone else is present in the darkness of the soundstage. This is an eerie moment given our commonsense understanding of the plane of material events. Nikki/Susan, who is fictional and played by Nikki Grace who sits at the table as Nikki/Susan observes her, is an onlooker days after the table reading took place. But that is the nature of time and space in Lynch's second-stage films.

and experiencing both the fear and the revelations of the uncertainty principle gives us the unique opportunity to ponder the successful maturation process.

Because the evolution of the film-within-a-film toward its fullest articulation is a matter of passages through many material worlds and time frames in an organic process that defies linear narrative, we are never in possession of what is usually thought of as "the story" of *Blue Tomorrows*. Rather, it is as if we were inside a script relentlessly coming into clearer focus, rather than being detached observers at a distance. As we watch, we get that most important of rewards, information, but not in the trivialized form imagined by the mass media, the lurid gossip it is for Marilyn Levens, and the commodity and adjunct to power that it is for Kingsley Stewart, scavenged by hyena-like Freddie Howard who can hold his liquor while drawing secrets from people whose lips are loosened by liquor. The point of view of the film is that true information is gained in the upheavals of experience and doing, for example, when a movie is made, or, for that matter, actively watched.

*Inland Empire* drives this proposition into new territory through imagery derived from quantum theory, as Lynch melds the lives of strangers from different parts of this world, from different time frames, and even from both fictional and real worlds, in ways that multiply the possibilities exponentially. A metaphor Lynch used when speaking to me that envisions many possible worlds as bubbles from a freshly opened can of Seven-Up nicely sums up the structure of the extended central portion of *Inland Empire* that contains neither Nikki nor Susan as separate entities, but only Nikki/Susan. Nikki/Susan spontaneously takes on numerous shapes in numerous bubble worlds, many of which burst into nothingness. But there is one that endures and becomes the medium by which the character of Susan Blue and the film-within-the-film achieve final form. Language struggles to catch up with this process, lacking words that express a state of being in which something or someone is both present and yet not fully incarnated in the usual sense of the word. Lynch prefers to rely on metaphoric images, which more easily contain all the contradictions at the core of Nikki's voyage.

This is why Lynch chooses to dramatize Nikki/Susan's next metamorphosis in terms of her involvement with a group of women who are both present and at the same time inhabitants of bubble worlds into which Nikki/Susan enters and from which she exits fluidly. They suddenly materialize in the living room of Smithy's house, linking Nikki/Susan, without explanation, to a much grittier set of circumstances than she originally had as a character. These women—a sisterhood that is sexually abject and in which each one defines herself primarily by her ability to evoke sexual desire in men—baffles Nikki/Susan by their abrupt emergence, and their evocations of time and space in which the future is already under the surface of the present. "Look at us and tell us if you have known us before," one of them says to Nikki/Susan, connecting her to a past so that the always-present future may better be revealed. This abject sisterhood links Nikki/Susan to another potential world connected with *Blue Tomorrows*, a wintry street in Poland that is fused with the image of the record in the main title that first alluded to *AXXON N.* The tearful Lost Girl also is entangled with Nikki/Susan at this point, explaining to her how she can "see"—meaning into other worlds—if she wants to. Why these women? Why now? Because this view of creation is based on a belief—a la Lucretius—in the unfathomable combination of parts, in every possible configuration, until some sustainable form is reached.

The unfathomability of how the parts combine is visually and meta-phorically represented by the magical method by which Nikki/Susan is instructed to move among these many worlds. (The Visitor did inform Nikki that magic is a factor in what will happen to her, and Lynch's metaphors have projected the presence of magic since the beginning of the film.) Nikki/Susan is instructed that if she wears a particular watch and burns a hole into a piece of silk with a cigarette, she "will see." This magical ritual emphasizes through images of time and space—the watch and the altered silk material that forms a portal into other spaces and times—the non-locality of what Nikki/Susan is about. Making the ritual overtly magical forecloses ideas of linearity of motion in Nikki/Susan's real/fictional life, but it also poses a risk that the audience will cease to take Lynch seriously. Yet we should credit him with seriousness. We have all had experiences of déja vu; we have all been moved by intu-ition. Ought we to despair of representing these feelings except in the language of the horror and fantasy genres that deny their reality? Lynch doesn't think so. He shows us in this evocation of magic that he believes that it is better to opt for the poetry of representing those feelings, which are quite real, by giving them, in Shakespeare's words, "a local habitation and a name."

Another part of the magic is that the various worlds are peopled by characters we already know in different circumstances that bring out different characteristics. Deploying his actors in numerous roles, Lynch populates *Inland Empire* with identical-looking characters in different time frames and stories; thus we are often placed in the position of be-ing unable to say with certainty who we are observing. Men who look like Nikki's husband Piotrek move through all the narrative worlds in the story, sometimes pathetic, sometimes threatening. As the film ends, this same figure turns up as the missing, loving husband of the Lost Girl, whose separation from him is ostensibly the cause of her constant tears. And the Lost Girl doubles as the abused woman in the *AXXON N.* play. But, of course, the most important multiple doublings are the women who look like Nikki, who circulate through the film as the numerous incarna-tions of Susan Blue.

One of the most important of these is a horribly abused and defen-sively violent woman who trudges up a long flight of stairs to the dingy office of a man identified in the credits as Mr. K. (Erik Crary). Nikki/Susan talks almost nonstop to this almost silent man, outlining the abusive

treatment she has received at the hands of men, and her grotesquely violent retaliations. This unnamed woman is the penultimate step for Nikki/
Susan before she takes final form as a downtrodden whore on a street in
Hollywood. Every step of the way, Nikki/Susan continues to meet again
and again the abject sisterhood in slightly altered shape, but always the
sisterhood to which she has been destined to belong, who become witnesses to her death. When Nikki/Susan finds herself among these street-
walkers in Hollywood, the importance of that moment is marked by the
kind of explosion of light and sound that we saw during the transformation of Fred to Pete in *Lost Highway*. Gone is the coy Susan of the original
script who kept Billy Side's advances at a distance. We are now watching
the film predicted by Nikki's Visitor #1, about marriage and "brutal, fuck-
ing murder," featuring a character who can no longer be named. Time is
moving deeply into the "here" toward a moment of transparent clarity.

## MY PHANTOM, MYSELF

The driving negativity that dooms Nikki/Susan in *Blue Tomorrows* radi-
ates from the Rakshasa-like Phantom. The Phantom is already within the
molecules of Nikki's story when he first appears in the Rage Room, but
we only gradually learn what he is about. He is certainly sinister when
he appears as the instigator of a murder that Doris Side knows she will
commit. But even at that point, we have no way of knowing what to make
of his malign influence within the context of this film. We begin to see
him as Nikki/Susan's nemesis when Doris understands that it is Nikki/
Susan that she will kill—a result of her jealousy of the sexual relationship
between her husband and Nikki/Susan. Nevertheless, when Doris does
murder Nikki/Susan, the terrible influence of the Phantom seems like
little more than something fictional from *Blue Tomorrows*.

But the Phantom is not contained within the film-within-the-film. His
power extends to Nikki's life outside of *Blue Tomorrows*. And we see this in
another challenging moment when Lynch reveals that the future is now.
Just before Nikki/Susan meets her fated doom in *Blue Tomorrows*, the image of an extremely grotesque woman who resembles Nikki (Laura Dern)
bursts into view. As with the scene in the police station that alerts us to
a future already in place in the plot of *Blue Tomorrows*, the appearance
of this grotesque image of Nikki is a non-local moment that reveals the
traces of a future already in place in Nikki Grace's life.

The grotesque woman bursts onto the screen as a ghoulish, menacing presence, seemingly out of nowhere. Unexpectedly, a circus poster of a sweetly smiling clown appears onscreen. Slowly, the radiantly illuminated image of the branch structure of a tree and a woman's lap dissolves into view over the center of this poster until the poster disappears and we are in a rural setting in which the woman, at first in very long shot, moves stealthily toward us. As she comes close enough for us to see her face, it is visibly in a state of extreme muscular tension. The woman projects a demonic menace, but also seems to be experiencing some internal state of terror. A brilliant golden light illuminates this face as it fills the film frame, accompanied by a high-volume rumbling and clanging that jars not only the audience, but also Nikki/Susan, to whom the film cuts as she sits in Smithy's house, startled. Is this another prophecy of doom? Actually, it is a prefiguration of self-realization for Nikki. Nikki/Susan, a fictional character, is doomed by the malign influence of the Phantom, and has been since the get-go, but, as we shall see, Nikki Grace has been blessed with the power to eradicate negativity, both outside of her (the Phantom) and inside of her (this desperately demonic image of her most fearsome aspect).

## MY PHANTOM, MYSELF

Nikki/Susan dies in *Blue Tomorrows* from a fatal stabbing at the hands of Doris Side, while she is under the control of the Phantom. Her final moments connect his negative energy with the nonsense of Hollywood mythologies. The Walk of Fame, near the corner of Hollywood and Vine, the fabled place created by the local Chamber of Commerce as the origins of movie magic, is where Nikki/Susan will die. Here it does not take its usual shape as a glitzy monument to fame. Rather it is permeated by the dark influence of the Phantom as a location of death. Yet, at the same time, there is another reality: the dispossessed and homeless people who use these streets as a refuge, and who despite being destitute exhibit a capacity for human connection that links them together and that joins them also to the dying Nikki/Susan, whom they do not know. As Nikki/Susan is in her last moments, they ramble on about the bus to Pomona and an ailing woman who cannot afford the necessary medical care and is spending her final days with a cherished monkey companion, but they nevertheless demonstrate a deep feeling for Nikki/Susan's situation. One

A circus poster, located in a highly indeterminate time and space frame, from within which a strange female presence (Laura Dern) begins to emerge.

The revelation of the demonic nature of that female presence (Laura Dern). Like the scene in the police station, this too tells us that what normally we think of as a future event is already present.

of them, a black woman, uses her cigarette lighter to guide Nikki/Susan out of this life. "No more blue tomorrows," she says to her, as if giving her a benediction.

Nikki/Susan has been disposed of by the negative power of the Phantom in the fictional universe of *Blue Tomorrows*, but the image of light and connection that fills the frame as Nikki's character leaves life reflects the existence of the positive energy that persists despite the negativity that has prevailed. This positive energy will reign supreme in Nikki's life outside the studio soundstage where she discovers a power to confront her own interior negativity with a strength she never suspected she had. In short, there are consequences to Nikki's creation of a powerful artistic experience that go beyond the moment when Kingsley Stewart, stunned into almost speechless admiration as he calls his final, "Cut it—and print it!" recognizes the magnificence of her achievement and how little he had to do with it. How peripheral he is to her accomplishment is impressed upon him when Nikki ignores him as he tries to offer his congratulations. She is no longer the Nikki "lost in the marketplace as if half-born," who grinned happily when Stewart told her the film could be a star-maker. Neither is she Nikki/Susan. Susan has just died in the film-within-the-film. Nikki is now in a position to complete the process of her own birth.[13] This is not to say that she will be "born again" in a way that takes her from the world toward some conception of an immaterial deity, but rather that she will be born more fully into the universe. Fully born, she will rid herself of the phantom of compulsive negativity by finding the Phantom within herself and dissolving it—possibly an allusion of sorts to a moment in one of Lynch's favorite films, when Dorothy (Judy Garland) in *The Wizard of Oz* (Dir. Victor Fleming, 1939) dissolves the Wicked Witch of the West (Margaret Hamilton).[14]

Nikki's confrontation with the Phantom is the next step in her creative journey. Walking off the set of *Blue Tomorrows*, she dazedly makes her way into and through the entangled worlds so that the revelation of the inner, true story of the film-within-a-film can take place: Smithy's house, with its corridors and the *AXXON N.* door leading to it; the seedy room upstairs in which a new form of Nikki/Susan confided in an impassive man who ultimately betrayed her confidences; the Rabbit Room (which turns out to be number 47, the name of the first draft of *Blue Tomorrows*), so deeply entangled in the revelation of the final form of Nikki's performance; and finally, the dark room in which the Lost Girl has been weeping, now flooded with sunlight. As Nikki travels through these entangled worlds, we see that her journey does not end with the final shot of the film.

Not at all in command of her actions, Nikki takes possession of the gun that Piotrek/Smithy received in the scene in Poland so that he could kill the unnamed Phantom, a gun he never used, and she completes

Smithy's mission. Gun in hand, Nikki encounters the Phantom outside of the Rabbit Room, which we now see has a door marked 47 (*Vier Sieben*), and kills him, after which she liberates the Lost Girl. With her dissolution of negative force, her full identification with faith, and her humanizing payment of the bill of fellow feeling that we all owe to each other, the cycle of creativity is completed.

This denouement turns the future embodied in the ghoulish version of Nikki into the present. The Phantom has found his way to the *Vier Sieben* door with the express intention of attacking her. But when Nikki responds to his hostile presence, a response that is not conscious but rather spontaneous, we see that this is both an external and an internal event. Nikki, in a state akin to sleepwalking, shoots the Phantom, and it turns out that her gun emits light rather than bullets. The changes in the Phantom's body as she shoots reveal that the two of them are entangled. As the beams of light dissolve the Phantom's face, something material-izes from within and comes to the surface: the image of Nikki/Susan's grimacing, contorted face that first materialized through the poster of the smiling clown. Nikki has met the enemy and it is both beyond and in her. The enemy is always to some degree entangled with us, as is visibly the case when Doris Side speaks to the policeman about the murder she will commit. Nikki, in dissolving the dark layers of the Phantom with her weapon of light, is able to enter the *Vier Sieben* door. Lo and behold, it is the door to the Rabbit Room. Art and life meet here. Within the Rabbit Room, also the *Vier Sieben* room, Nikki, having dispelled the darkness of the Phantom, becomes one with the world of faith.

With the dissolution of the Phantom, all the dark worlds that have been evoked become filled with light. What was bound is now liberated, and the Lost Girl stops crying. In a burst of non-locality, Nikki crosses a threshold from the world of the Rabbit Room into the world of need in which the Lost Girl has been incarcerated, gives her a tender kiss of release from her situation, and we discover that the Lost Girl's Room has changed. With Nikki's freedom has come a larger sense of human responsibility that has nothing to do with her own benefit; it is collat-eral healing, to coin a phrase. Once back in her palatial home, she is at ease and relaxed as we have never seen her before. She is at home, not merely a moving fixture in a well-appointed house. Traveling the route of limitlessness, she has gone from "here" to "here," from her home as mausoleum-palace to her home as a palace of abundant life. Reminiscent

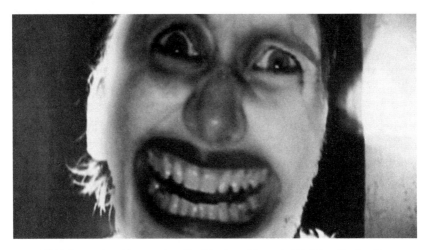

When Nikki (Laura Dern) encounters the Phantom (Krzysztof Majchrzak), she discovers that he is not only an external attacker, but also an internalized rage within her. Transmuting him into light also frees her internally.

of the scene at the end of Federico Fellini's *8½*, when Guido (Marcello Mastroianni) finds harmonious closure in the dance of all figures living and dead, real and imagined, Nikki is the center of such a dance of life, literally and figuratively.[15]

The intertwining of fiction and reality that marks this closure highlights the complexity of *Inland Empire*. Nikki is now relaxed in her sumptuous home when she had formerly been tense and guarded among its treasures; at the same time, she continues to interact with the many worlds to which her art has given her access. She's still surrounded by figures connected with the street people among whom Nikki/Susan died, as well as by Laura Harring, minus her rabbit suit, and the chorus of sexually abject women. There are even characters we have never seen before, generated by Nikki's experience, that are perhaps the seeds of future creative processes. Among these new characters are a group of black women who exuberantly dance and sing to the music of "Sinner Man." In the midst of all this, Nikki sits glowing, quiet, and radiant. The final word of the film, as the credits roll, is the exclamation, by the lead dancer, "POWER!" A new form of power now permeates Nikki's life.[16] And it replaces the regime identified with the false values of Hollywood; her abusive, distant, and possessive husband; her shallow director; and her womanizing co-star, all of whom marked her relationships in the external world at her point of origin into *Blue Tomorrows*. Nikki has not yet found a partner in the external world who reflects her new openness, but Lynch believes that change begins within.[17] And that has happened for Nikki.

## LONG NIGHT'S JOURNEY INTO DAY

Just as Nikki/Susan was already dead, so to speak, in a future already present when we saw the scene in the police station out of linear order, so a large positivity was already in play before Nikki Grace ever walked onto the set to work on *Blue Tomorrows*. She was already free, and the Lost Girl was already found, because of a special light that shines on the terrain of *Inland Empire*. This light suggests that there is a higher power of love and positive energy in operation that is always there even in the midst of negativity and unhappiness.[18] Lynch dots *Inland Empire* with a literal path of lights, starbursts of illumination that can be considered the closest he can get, for now at least, to visually representing the energy beyond the barriers our culture has erected against a limitless cosmos.[19] The images of light can also be considered a kind of benediction from beyond at crucial moments in Nikki's perilous journey. Finally, the "guiding lights" may also signify the infusion of love and positive energy into a world that has seriously misconstrued the face of love. The first starburst appears just before we see the Lost Girl for the first time, as she weeps in front of a screen on which she sees the many worlds of *Inland Empire*. Next we see it radiating energy over soundstage 4, on which Nikki and Devon do a first reading of scene 35 from *Blue Tomorrows* and Nikki gets her first inkling that Smithy's house, the set that is now standing on stage 4, has a special significance to her.

The last three appearances of the signature starburst of the cosmos take place as Nikki's liberation is in progress near the end of the film. The first of these signals the initial phase of the liberation as it pierces the gloom of the dark corridors. It causes two women in the strange sisterhood, formerly mired in bondage sexuality, to run down the newly sunlit hallway and floods the Lost Girl's formerly dark room with light. Right after the Lost Girl is reunited with her husband and son, a second starburst explodes with such force that it washes out the entire screen in light, returning to perceived shape and form only as Nikki appears in its center. Finally, the last starburst occurs right after Nikki receives tumultuous applause in the Rabbit Room, and serves as a transition to a montage that suggests the bill mentioned by Visitor #1 has been paid: we see again the Lost Girl embracing the family that Nikki has freed her to rejoin; the face of Visitor #1; and Nikki, now calm and serene, no longer tense or confused.[20]

These starbursts of illumination light a more meaningful radiance than that attached to the "Walk of Fame," where Nikki/Susan died. The illumination from above is not about fame or money but about the redemption of love, the spread of compassion and joy where previously there was only abandonment, abuse, and sadism. In making this transition from dead stars to stars pulsating with energy, *Inland Empire* reveals itself to be Lynch's most powerful statement of hope yet. It leads us away from the false forms of sexuality and compelled possession that has passed for love, and carries us across the spectrum of worlds that had to collide in order for creation, liberation, and peace to come into being. The film begins with the fear and danger associated with opening up oneself to creativity, and continues to explore the process, during which Nikki copes with her husband's and co-star's sense of masculine entitlement, and is threatened, in her Nikki/Susan form, by the male acquaintances of the fictional Susan Blue as well as Doris Side's homicidal violence. It turns out that, as Visitor #1 asserted, *On High in Blue Tommorrows* is indeed a story about marriage, exploring its deadly qualities when the husband or wife is fatally possessive—which is the case in the *AXXON N.* story that preceded *Blue Tomorrows*, in the triangle of Doris and Billy Side and Susan in the film-within-a-film, and in Nikki's own marriage.

In ways Nikki never imagined at first, her work on *Blue Tomorrows* allows her to face up to her abusive marriage to Piotrek as well as her marriage to a power structure that is all too vulnerable to the negative, destructive energies of the Phantom. As a consequence, Nikki becomes more expansive as the script of *Blue Tomorrows* contracts Susan's possibilities, and the making of this film promotes in Nikki a deep, non-verbal understanding of objectification and abandonment in a loveless world of commodified sex. (Although Nikki glows with well-being in the final frame of *Inland Empire*, she does not utter a single word from the time her character, Susan, is murdered to the last moment we see her in Lynch's film.)

What passes for love in the macrocosmic world of familiar life only looks attractive in conventional Hollywood films. Underneath the Hollywood surfaces we encounter a shock of recognition about the ugliness of the reduction of love to nothing but sex. If we look thoughtfully at the sex fantasies that circulate in *Inland Empire*, we see how reductive and destructive they are in the smut that Marilyn Levens peddles, and in the self-images of the abject sisterhood of women, who lounge about like a pride of cats, obsessing about their breasts and behinds. They speak about themselves in the coarsest terms, as "tits and ass," and talk about nothing but finding and keeping the love of men. And what a degraded idea of love they have, as expressed in the superficially perky ode to the sexualized gyration that defines them: "Locomotion." As Nikki/Susan sinks ever deeper into their frame of mind and tone of existence, she outdoes them, moving beyond coarseness to violence. In Mr. K's office, Nikki/Susan speaks of gouging out the eye of a man attempting to rape her, and coping with an attack from the man she lives with (husband? or not?) after she returns home, perhaps from "screwing for drinks, no big deal." When Doris Side attacks Nikki/Susan with the screwdriver, and immediately is consumed by horror at what she has done, we see that the existence of this "proper wife" is no pleasure either. Women subject to the illusions about love propagated in the marketplace do not lead happy, fulfilling, or generous lives.

The abject sisterhood spontaneously breaks into song and dance to the tune of "The Locomotion." Their affect seems playful, but unlike the liberatory effect of rock music on American culture when it broke onto the cultural scene, this gyrating is more ambiguous. Nikki is the audience for this dance and she is highly perturbed by it. Moreover, the dance is contextualized by a previous conversation in which these women over-emphasize and over-sexualize their bodies. The "cute" tone of the dance masks the suffering and delusion in which they are lost with respect to their roles as women.

In this frame we see an obviously physically abused Nikki/Susan (Laura Dern), the character Nikki Grace creates in *On High in Blue Tomorrows*, as she sits in Mr. K's (Erik Crary) office—who and what he is is never explicitly identified for us—speaking of her own feelings of rage. Not at all the charming girl she appeared when shooting began on the film, Nikki/Susan is now revealing spontaneously a darker layer of herself, one that prefigures her violent death at the hands of Doris Side toward which she is headed.

In counterpoint, as Nikki separates from both the drama created by her husband's treatment of her as his personal property worth killing for and the melodramas of adultery and revenge in *Blue Tomorrows*, she becomes identified with a universal form of love that may be, but isn't necessarily, about sex. Nikki's embrace of the Lost Girl is a blessing rather than a sexual advance. Similarly, as Nikki—still in the guise of the bedraggled, dirty Susan who defeated the Phantom—receives acclaim from an audience, she is anything but an enticing bit of "tits and ass." She is a woman whose dissolution of the negativity inside herself has consequences in the outside world.

The altered Rabbit Room audience is united in a post-Phantom moment through the kind of faith that we initially saw in the rabbit-suited actors; a final fanfare to the importance of art, specifically movies, that saturates Lynch's chronicle of Nikki's journey. This audience is a realization of Lynch's ideal of unity in diversity, and Lynch identifies cinema as a potential vehicle for transformation for us benighted human beings. The love that engenders creativity has a liberating and enlivening power that is the inverse of the perverse forms of love involved in "locomotion" sexuality; of shallow, mechanical filmmaking; and of murderous, willful turf battles. This love is a relationship to the universe, which, as Nikki demonstrates, does not require anything but itself for fulfillment and a sense of belonging. The details of Nikki's domestic and professional life at the end of the film are unknown to us, as is her Hollywood situation. Lynch has freed us from thinking of personhood and reality in terms of status and possessions; there is something more basic, more crucial. When *Inland Empire* ends, the dynamic glowing radiance of receptiveness to life and the imagination is Nikki's enormous illuminated reality—and ours. The enclosures of systems, status, and possessions are just marketplace stories.

In telling Nikki's tale, Lynch evokes paradoxes that unquestionably boggle his marketplace audience with visions of change in a world of changelessness, of a world in which everything is already good, if only we were in a position to know it. To some this may amount to a form of mystification and fatalism, but that kind of predetermination is generally associated with deep pessimism while, in *Inland Empire*, Nikki's already-present future speaks of a natural state of human perfection and happiness that is possible once we've eliminated the obstacles in our way. Here,

A relaxed and peaceful Nikki Grace (Laura Dern), now revealed in all her light-filled contentment, after her creative journey as the actress who created Susan Blue. What has happened during that journey has released her from the confines of the marketplace. Although she appears to be in the same place in which she started, her conventionally palatial house, Nikki's spiritual transformation has changed it from a place of constraint into a true Palace in the Lynchian sense, a place of enlightenment and freedom.

Lynch presents a highly optimistic vision of an experience anyone can have, though the time may not be of one's own choosing.

The upshot of Lynch's cinematic magic in telling his story in this way? He endows us with an expansive visualization of the events of human life as, in their most meaningful form, affirmative elements in a dance of primal power and positive exhilaration.

# AFTERWORD

# A SUMMARY: LIVING LARGE AMONG THE PARTICLES

Therefore we see that human nature's needs
Are small indeed; things that take pain away,
And such as simple pleasures can supply."

**LUCRETIUS, BOOK TWO, *ON THE NATURE OF THE UNIVERSE*,
TRANSLATED BY RONALD MELVILLE (P. 36)**

Lynch began in darkness, where seeds sprout. In his first cinematic work, *Six Men Getting Sick* (1967), a sculpture designed to work with a film loop. (The name of this sculpture has since been changed to *Six Figures Getting Sick*, but I will stay with the original title.) In this sculpture, Lynch called into play a disturbing vision of blurred borders between inside and outside. As insides were regurgitated unceasingly over a series of unchanging molded heads through the nonstop loop, the work seemed to declare an uneasy, diseased, but inevitable interplay between human surfaces and "what lies beneath," an unsettling depiction of human existence as inescapably confusing and wrenching. Living small.

Lynch's other early works also display a dark sense of the shifting line between interiority and exteriority. In *The Alphabet* (1967), Lynch turns a child's first experience of the alphabet into a horror story about an invasion of the human body, and in *The Grandmother* (1970), he depicts one child's highly traumatic experience of family. The young boy's desire to grow a comforting grandmother from a seed he plants himself, at first successful, leads to his tortuous physical paroxysm, as though something inside him was forcing its way out. But these early works were created before Lynch's exposure to the light-filled teachings of the Maharishi Mahesh Yogi, which occurred while he was making *Eraserhead* (1976).

159

Lynch's increasing involvement with the Transcendental Meditation movement, along with the direct personal influence of Maharishi, did not lighten his portrayal of the strange relationships among the many levels of inside and outside in ordinary life. But it did add another layer to his films, a larger, more positive range of possibilities offered by a "beyondness" that provided a new context for inside and outside. Although Lynch's earliest work offered little wiggling room for characters living on a constricted and conflicted plane of existence, Lynch soon took a turn toward stories that allowed for contact with a boundless abundance of potential. A non-marketplace version of living large. In all cases, Lynch's cinema has never been realistic in a reductionist sense; it has always sought the real through the poetic, utilizing images in metaphoric ways to speak of what metaphors speak of: those liminal and complex aspects of our lives that cannot be directly named. But the Lynchian portrait of our expansive possibilities, as we have seen in the previous chapters in this study, has altered greatly since the time he first began to develop his filmmaking métier.

*Eraserhead* was full-throttle cinematic poetry. From *The Elephant Man* to *Twin Peaks: Fire Walk with Me*, Lynch played with the counterpoint between the conventions of traditionally realistic film and those expressive images and sounds he was developing to say obliquely what cannot be directly said. However, the films from *Eraserhead* to *Fire Walk with Me* constitute a first stage in Lynch's cinema because in all of these works the emphasis is on the visionary capabilities of the film's protagonist, his or her ability to receive images and signs that penetrate a highly sensitive subconscious, momentarily revealing what exists beyond the entrenched ordinary limits of cultural linguistic and social structures. In Lynch's second-stage films, beginning with *Lost Highway*, those ordinary limits no longer occupy a privileged, stabilizing (albeit somewhat inauthentic) place within the Lynchverse, and the fear that suffuses modern, no-tradition-is-sacrosanct life took on an enlarged significance for Lynch's characters. Where the development of Henry Spencer, Paul Atreides, Jeffrey Beaumont, Agent Cooper, Sailor Ripley, and to some extent, Laura Palmer, was a positive trajectory toward an affirmative visionary capability within a tightly bound quotidian reality, Lynch's second-stage films offer a much more questioning and figurative exploration of human action and a depiction of ordinary life in the marketplace as always highly unstable. The protagonists of second-stage Lynch narratives have a dubious trajectory; Lynch builds suspense about whether or not they will interpret their experience of energies from beyond in a negative or positive fashion. A mysterious receptiveness or lack thereof to their perceptions of the inherent insta- bility of the marketplace plays a huge role in the protagonists' choices. This new characterization of the marketplace and the capacity of the Lynch protagonist marks a crucial difference between Lynch's first- and second-stage films.

Lynch's Vedic faith in a harmonious, meaningful universe has been a constant in his filmaking since *Eraserhead*. However, his characterization of the marketplace has changed considerably. In his second-stage films, Lynch has audaciously been willing to give a central place to the depiction of matter as our most advanced scientists now understand it. From *Lost Highway* to *Inland Empire*, Lynch courageously reveals that the "rock solid" reality of the marketplace is nowhere near as rock solid and defined as his characters want it to be; the marketplace is, rather, as modern physics would have it, the ceaseless flow of motile particles capable of any and all manifestations. This is a groundbreaking move for an American filmmak- er, since what interest there has previously been in physics in Hollywood film and in the American media in general has been relatively superficial.

Popular film (and television) has tended to use physics to vary its design concepts and turn the same old plots into something relatively familiar with a new twist. All too often, integration of physics into enter- tainment has simply involved variation of the old conflicts and suspense, evoked as cowboys struggling to get the cattle to market by a certain date. In updated plots, intrepid space adventurers struggle to get the dilithium crystals to a space station before it runs out of energy. Critics who have explored connections between physics and cinema—and there have been very few of them—have principally been physicists and engineers who have focused on the scientific accuracy of mass media fictions involving technology and material phenomena. These critics want to know if, when astronauts fly intergalactically, or robots appear, the films convey a real- istic understanding of the science of the machines involved. Examples of this kind of book are *Insultingly Stupid Movie Physics: Hollywood's Best Mistakes, Goofs, and Flat-Out Destructions of the Basics Laws of the Universe*, by engineer Tom Rogers (Sourcebooks Hysteria, 2007) and *The Science of Star Wars: An Astrophysicist's Independent Examination of Space Travel, Aliens, Planets, and Robots as Portrayed in the* Star Wars *Films and Books*, by Jeanne Cavelos (St. Martin's Griffin, 2000).

I am not aware of any other film criticism that has explored, as *David Lynch Swerves* does, the figurative uses of the uncertainty principle of modern physics, or the phenomena of particle entanglement and superposition as potential metaphors for portraying modern angst and the choices of ordinary modern men and women. This is not surprising as most students of the arts don't know enough about physics to recognize its presence in a film unless that presence concerns some kind of futuristic mechanical object. Physics is not often enough taught from a philosophical perspective on an undergraduate university level. Taught philosophically, modern physics, which teaches that there is no absolute objective perspective, can stimulate the imagination with questions that bear on fictional points of view, the kind that have been asked in this study. As modern physics also rejects the absolute nature of the physical object, it also, as we have noted in discussing Lynch's films, bears on questions pertaining to objects as commodities, and the objectification of people, which leads naturally to consideration of cultural values, another seminal concern of film studies. Possibly a rapprochement between the disciplines of physics and the disciplines of all the arts in higher education is in the offing. If not, it should be.

In this study, using physics as a point of reference, I have been able to clarify the cosmology of Lynch's visionary cinematic poetry, particularly in his second-stage films. In Lynch's cosmology, it is not that the universe is uncertain; it's that its certainty is not the one fabricated by the marketplace. Instead, Lynch invokes a stability inherent in a universal cosmic unity that we can only encounter if we accept the instability of the cultural transaction of day-to-day business. Physics becomes a frame of reference for Lynch's work not because it gives him a way to tell us how technology operates in the marketplace, or even because it explains in an intellectually acute way the operations of matter, but because it gives him images that enable him to conjure a modern discovery of limitlessness as the central event of human destiny.

Limitlessness is an old preoccupation of the poetic imagination. Writing over 2000 years ago, especially in Books I and II of *On the Nature of Things*, Lucretius ruminated on the unpredictable flashes of limitlessness in the universe that accounted for creativity, although he also contemplated the kind of boundaries to the operation of matter and void that made possible identifiable and stable forms of life. The eighteenth-century Christian mysticism of British poet William Blake also trumpeted the saving grace of limitlessness. His lyrical and ecstatic visions of the biggest (the infinite) in the smallest (the smallest unit of matter he knew about)—"eternity in a grain of sand"—was a proof of the persistence of the divine in the human and a lever by means of which he pried open the closed systems of the British industrial revolution. American poet Edgar Allan Poe, a precursor of existentialism, was not so sanguine when, in opposition to the materialism of the American industrial revolution, he visualized limitlessness in grains of sand (matter): "How few! Yet how they creep/Through my fingers to the deep,/While I weep—while I weep." Poe saw boundlessness in a morose light; the metaphoric sands that eluded his anxious grasp. For him, they were proof of our human tragedy. Lynch's Vedic perspective inclines him toward triumph, and his quantum mechanics-flavored understanding of matter allows him to turn his camera on marketplace scenes of everyday life in order to tell stories that are simultaneously about bounded cultural events and windows onto eternity.[1]

The importance of how limitlessness can be visualized for the camera cannot be overstated as a factor in understanding Lynch's films. The way physics-like intuitions stimulate his imagination has freed him of the conventional Hollywood solutions to this problem. Typically, Hollywood has mined the conventional vocabulary for talking about the energies of the beyond that have been in play since the beginning of film as an entertainment medium, in the genres of horror, science fiction, and fantasy. However, although these genres have served numerous excitingly creative artists well, their generic vocabularies are not options for Lynch because they lead away from *his* vision of reality. The genres of horror, fantasy, and science fiction are dependent on violations of ordinary expectations, but not in the Lynchian sense. In the Lynchverse, the marketplace blocks experience of the larger energies of the real in the name of a fictitious normality. In horror, science fiction, and fantasy, the larger energies are violations of a highly valued normality conceived of as the real. In the Lynchverse, normality is questioned; in horror, science fiction, and dream/fantasy, it has traditionally been defended.

In the bulk of films that populate established genres of beyondness, dreams, monsters, future worlds, and people and animals with strange powers bifurcate the world of their fictions into real normality and deviant "something else." There are, of course, exceptions, like *Psycho* and *The Birds*, but by and large, in these genres, vampires, werewolves, talking donkeys, X-Men—and the like—invade a bracketed ordinary reality that is *temporarily* disturbed by them. Hitchcock's masterpieces admittedly change our view of normality permanently, but generally "beyond" genres showcase paranormal beings and events that highlight the ordinary world as a context of stability and safety that must be protected. The extraordinary must be exterminated. More recently, extraordinary beings might be called on to give their lives; or they might be necessarily expelled from ordinary life by the forces of good; or perhaps they will nobly choose exile as sacrificial victims to a golden normality. In any case, in conventional mass market fiction, the limitlessness of the monster, and the unusual event, are exceptions that prove the rule. They shore up a belief in the sanctity and truth of a limited world.[2]

By mining metaphors derived from modern physics to support his Vedic mysticism, Lynch turns his back on Hollywood's relegation of amazing energies to a place outside the gates of normal reality and cinematically opens wide our conceptions about the boundaries of the real. Conventional normality does not appear in Lynch's films as a stable contrast to an infinity alien to the human, but as an aleatory illusion that much too frequently filters and blocks human access to a limitlessness that is ours by right, ours by necessity if culture is to be vital. At the same time, the disappearance of the traditional standard of normality is never, in itself, an obstacle to human happiness. Only if the collapse of the normal marketplace illusion is viewed with fear is the lack of normality a source of anguish. It is because Lynch turns the context of commercial film inside out in this way that his films convey not just a thought, an image, or a nod to boundlessness, but an experience of something powerfully moving from beyond what we expect to be the limits of the material world—and of our consciousness of it.

Imagining what would happen if Lynch had used conventional Hollywood visual vocabulary reveals just how important Lynch's discovery of the images of modern physics is to his creation of a very special and specific experience of cinema. Thus, if a fantasy or horror vocabulary were the basis of *Lost Highway*; if Fred Madison were dreaming about his transition into Pete Dayton or the Mystery Man were a vampire or conventional monster; or if the whole story were an illusion—at least as most films employ these tropes—then *Lost Highway* would be a very different film. If Lynch had created a dream or a vampire to bracket Fred's (and the audience's) experience of events that go beyond normality, it would establish the world of the police, the courts, the jails, and domestic spaces as Fred's natural and real habitation. But that is not what Lynch did. Limitlessness, in the form of the Mystery Man and Fred's merge with Pete—both which replicate in poetic form new material realities discussed by quantum physics—establish what passes for normality as a shrunken, deprived context that leads Fred to many misperceptions, the worst of which is a volcanically stubborn determination to hold on to a woman who can't love him.

As Lynch has created Fred's story, we gain insight into the pointlessness of Fred's disintegration. As Fred drifts ever further from an affirmative view of life and enters into a pattern of hopeless desire, we see him succumb to the violence and perversion-producing negativity of the Mystery Man: he's a victim of his own inability—and that of the people around him—to perceive in a positive light the miracles that rock his life. It is the language of physics that liberates this voyage into the heart of darkness from the control of conventional and ordinary limits that would make it impossible for Lynch to ask us to seriously entertain the reality of the beyond. Without Lynch's version of the vocabulary of physics, it would be impossible for him to create that sense of awe we experience as we watch a Lynch film that is, in fact, a moment of communion between his film and that aspect of us that naturally intuits what lies beyond. Unless we witness the extraordinary entanglement of Fred and Pete, during the night on the lawn, Fred's experience becomes reduced to a fantasy on the level of a dream from which we can awaken. What could be further from the sense of cosmic grandeur that Lynch aspires to communicate to us?

By contrast, Alvin Straight, in *The Straight Story*, makes the same point from the opposite direction, as he parlays the culturally imposed rock-ribbed limits that he has learned to accept as absolute boundaries into channels for a limitless love for his brother. Lynch has spoken of the emotional power *The Straight Story* exerts over him. By this, I believe, he means that Alvin is a miracle that inspires him. But we could not see that miracle if the film accepted as finite the world as Alvin sees it; we would not experience the miraculous, moving power of what infuses Alvin that comes from beyond what he misperceives as his limits. After a life of unhappiness in which poverty, war, and alcoholism have turned Alvin away from the joy that Lynch believes is the birthright of human beings, despite a sour feeling about the losses imposed by the effects of aging, Alvin wrests from this darkness a final moment of bliss that he earns by transmuting the kind of implacable willpower that Lynch usually shows as the source of destruction and abuse into a vehicle of positive energy. Although Lynch uses a conventional poetic image when he shows how Alvin forces from a manufactured machine an achievement beyond its industrially intended capacity, he also uses images from physics that make it possible to tell his tale. It is Alvin's screening out of the multiple possibilities we don't see, lurking just out of sight in his story, that accounts for his ability to succeed. The decreation that rules Alvin's mechanically neat world, revealed to us by Lynch from time to time, particularly in Alvin's encounter with the "deer lady," magically inflected by his continuing aspirations to the stars, makes possible our understanding of how he managed to accomplish a previously unimaginable deed. Alvin's is an unusually happy instance of dogged rejection of limitlessness in the marketplace. That one possibility, Alvin's small-town life, becomes translucent as the film proceeds, so that we can look through the surface appearance of absolute normality to find a uniquely flavored cinematic poetry.

In *Mulholland Dr.*, Lynch presents us with a very different film about making films than would be possible if he resorted to using the conventional "beyond" language of dreams that many have mistakenly read into it. By dint of images inflected by modern physics, Lynch avoids the stereotypical image of Hollywood as a town in which business-minded power players corrupt and destroy the dreams of the creative people who come there to work. Instead, the focus is on serious consequences to the creative process caused by the misunderstanding of the construction of the world. In depicting the devastating results of the extreme dependence of his characters, for their sense of security, on illusions of solidity and certainty concerning bodies and things, Lynch creates a powerful analogy. Curtailing human possibility is like worshipping a mail-order catalogue of objects. Using an inverted form of the mystery story, which conventionally exists to return misplaced bodies to their rightful places and correctly identify bodies that have gone astray, Lynch creates a tale in which such an insistence is fruitless, since the actual limitlessness of materiality renders obsessions with location of bodies and objects absurd. As Lynch tells the tale, the combination of Betty's compulsion to find out who Rita is and return her to her place, and the non-negotiable power-player determination to put "the girl" into a particular role, block creativity—indeed, the ability to exist at all. Faith divorced from an appreciation of the immensity of potentiality and wedded to a dependence on the marketplace can lead only to fear, despair, and a black hole in which all matter and consciousness putrefies.

In *Inland Empire*, Lynch discovers a possible balance between the marketplace and the beyond. But to achieve that balance, Lynch needs to abandon the usual language of Hollywood cinema about the objectification of achievement in the form of awards that emphasizes how important control is to gaining material honors. Lynch needs the vocabulary of images made possible by modern physics to assert that the best form of creative process in Hollywood involves losing control, letting go, and embracing the larger forces beyond marketplace ideas of success—and possibly our own ideas of success as well. Dissolving the solidity of technology and the printed script before our eyes, Lynch moves his heroine and his audience away from the uncertain marketplace by connecting Nikki and us to what he conceives of as a stability beyond fleeting stardom: a connection with an infinite, but secure, cosmic source of being.

The visual vocabulary that Lynch has evolved through his interface with modern physics is not just a way for him to express his ideas about freedom; it also facilitates his expression of ideas about human responsibility. I have previously noted that Lynch's passion in his cinema has always been a liberatory one, but what I did not focus on sufficiently in *The Passion of David Lynch* is that it is also warmly inflected by a sense of duty, a sense that we are all our brothers' keepers. While the perception of uncertainty in the marketplace has led other artists to a profound sense of isolation, it has led Lynch to a profound sense of connection. What Lynch sees, and what he shows us by way of his images channeled from physics, is that when people live imprisoned within marketplace parameters, the "you'll never have me" syndrome is attached to an "I'll never help you" abdication of full interconnection. The marketplace is a place in which self-involvement replaces the obligation to give back to the world.

In Lynch's first-stage work, *Twin Peaks*, he shows this to us in a simple way. Enclosure within the marketplace makes of Laura Palmer, against her will, an object that can awaken desire but never satisfy it; it leads to the selfish chicanery of Ben and Jerry Horn and the descent of Leland Palmer into a perverted engagement with larger energies that fill him with the demon BOB. Palmer, an early version of Fred Madison, violates and murders his own child. It is only Agent Cooper, associated with images that challenge ordinary ways of seeing matter and eager to engage larger energies, who has the power and the desire to unselfishly aid others—

although he is not fully enough anchored in the beyond, as are Alvin and Nikki, to avoid collapsing into a destructive way of living. Among the first symptoms Cooper manifests after he has sold out to BOB, in a desperate attempt to save the woman he loves, Annie (Heather Graham), is an uncaring attitude toward Annie. As we see that his image in the mirror is the demon BOB, we also hear him saying, "How's Annie?" in tones that viciously parody the concern that question might ordinarily convey. Similarly, in *Lost Highway* and *Mulholland Dr.*, persistent rejection of the possibilities offered by larger energies is accompanied by an increasing capacity for doing harm to other people and a decreasing responsibility to others. The reverse is true in *Inland Empire*, in which an expanded concern for others—Nikki's rescue of the Lost Girl, which allows her to make good on the unpaid bill of brotherhood that each of us owes to the other—accompanies her refusal to be stuck in the marketplace.

But Lynch weds physics to his cinema not only as part of his vision, but also as part of the sheer metaphoric pleasure of the filmic experience that is its most intense manifestation as entertainment. When Fred transforms into Pete "that night on the lawn," Lynch achieves a breathtaking painter's imagistic metaphor for a state in which a person is himself and not himself. Similarly, in *Mulholland Dr.*, the damage that Hollywood does to creativity is physicalized in the form of the tantalizing blue box and the black hole it represents. In *Inland Empire*, the molecules of life and art are visualized in a series of compelling images as worlds, like a "rain of diamonds in the mind" to quote another poet, May Swenson. There is pleasure attached to Lynch's version of the cinematic metaphor—a la modern physics—the images that elate and delight us as only a few filmmakers can. If this is so, why has Lynch earned a reputation as being a shockmeister, a purveyor of the gruesome and the perverse?

The reason is that Lynch's representations of marketplace illusions also involve undeniable "unpleasure," moments that are painful and grotesque. Two that are filled with almost unbearable pain are the death of Johnnie Farragut (Harry Dean Stanton) in *Wild at Heart* and the murder of Laura Palmer (Sheryl Lee) in *Fire Walk with Me*. Then there are the strikingly grotesque images in Lynch's films, which while compelling can be at the same time repellant, for example the scenes in the after-hours Club Silencio and the office of Mr. Roque in *Mulholland Dr.* Moments like these, in the short run, take hold of the popular imagination more powerfully than those in Lynch's films and television that give pleasure, because they are so unique. Although a comparatively larger number of filmmakers have crafted deliriously beautiful cinematic images, as Lynch does, few have dared to visually sink into the depths of suffering that he has pioneered. In the long run, there will come a time when the balance between the two will be more obvious to filmgoers, scholars, and critics.

The depths of "unpleasure" into which Lynch sometimes plunges his audience are inextricably bound with the heights of ecstasy to which he raises us. There is no way to tell his stories of the terrors of the marketplace without making us feel them vividly, so that the urgency of release is completely present to the spectator. There may be some kind of dark pleasure attached to some of these experiences; for example, many men say that there are patent attractions to the masochism of Dorothy Valens (Isabella Rossellini) in *Blue Velvet*. But Lynch makes even those frissons so uncomfortable that they ultimately conjure a longing for liberation. The beauty of light, as when Laura sees her angel in *Fire Walk with Me*, or when Nikki becomes an instrument of liberation in *Inland Empire*, is only truly comprehensible if we have felt the torment that preceded them; that contrast is crucial to Lynch's message of hope. Refusing to soften for the audience the deep pain that can be part of life in the marketplace, Lynch makes himself credible as a messenger of the hope for a greater power beyond it, not a media glad hand offering false assurances that "everything is all right."

"Joy!" is the cry of *rara avis* David Lynch, but it is not a spurious squawk. Believing that happiness is the natural human state, he makes films that answer our longings for excitement and beauty and offer an expansive optimism about larger values in a way that does not condescend to us with absurdly "happy endings." To grasp what he is about, we must credit his work as coming from the perspective of a man who is honest and unfaltering in his understanding that, as he has said to me many times, "There's a lot of suffering out there." There is a special Lynchian courage at work in all his films, but especially his second-stage cinema, that can enable us to confront the suffering and the darkness, and turn on the light, the light being a kind of educated innocence. Such innocence answers T. S. Eliot's question, "After such knowledge, what forgiveness?" To show with the power that Lynch musters that the worst terrors of human existence are a direct consequence of a polluting misrecognition of the marketplace as the ultimate reality—whether or not we conceptualize the larger reality in religious terms—is to mount a potent assault on the power over us of its false faith and its unrelenting foreclosures of possibility. By means of the Lynchian cracks in the facade of marketplace certainty, false certainty loses its paralyzingly fearful aspects and the cracks become the places that let the light shine in.

APPENDICES

*IN THEIR OWN WORDS*

# FRAGMENTS FROM MY
# MARCH 18, 2010, INTERVIEW
# WITH DAVID LYNCH

*Lynch and I spoke at his compound in the Hollywood Hills, a hive of buildings dotting a terraced slope. At the lowest level, is his workshop. North of the workshop, but also at road level is the "Lost Highway House," used as Fred Madison's home in the film, which no longer looks like a place where people live. It now comprises a conference room and art gallery, as well as a stainless steel kitchen where Lynch's assistant Michael brews delicious, dark, rich David Lynch Signature Cup Coffee. The walls of the "Lost Highway House" are covered with a wonderful material that looks like, but is not, cracked gray/white marble. Maybe it is a surface that is usually used for flooring, Michael said. The building in which Lynch and I met, further up the slope, is the place where Lynch gives his daily weathercasts for DavidLynch.com and where he tapes his introductions for the Interview Project interviews, an online documentary series conceived by Lynch's son Austin and a member of the Lynch retinue known as Jason S., who decided to travel around rural America, interviewing people they met by chance. In honor of the weathercast tradition: Blue skies on March 18, 2010, some fleecy white clouds; the sun pouring through the large office windows. Outside a strong, almost intoxicating scent of honeysuckle, which somehow does not find its way inside.*

*These are fragments from our conversation.*

## FRAGMENT I

"You fall in love with it because you love the idea itself. And then you love what cinema can do with that idea."

D: It's [the *Interview Project*] America along the roadside, but they didn't go into big cities, big buildings and talk to—You know they didn't go into any kind of real—They didn't go everywhere. They went along the road. And they found these people along the road. And it's fantastic to meet them.

M: I found them scary. What about you?

D: Sure. It's a—but you get a feel for a lot of things. You know, all kinds of things of the human condition. Right along the road.

M: In my America everybody is ambitious, and everybody wants education, and everybody pursues dreams. I'm a little apprehensive when I see so many people who reach for nothing outside of their immediate circumstances.

D: Uh-huh. Well, everybody's different. There's many, many road trips. You know the dust bowl when they came to California during the Depression. So many people were out on the road and stories came out of that. Great stories and great songs. And you get a great feel for what's happening. And it does have repercussions. All these people have dreams and some of these people are educated.

M: Not many.

D: But these are the people Austin and Jason met, and you can still get a feel for the country from this.

M: It's true. It's a deep layer of the country and it seems like I should know about it. Do you know what I mean?

D: Yeah.

M: For me, it's invisible America, but it's powerful and it's there. There are a lot of invisible people out there.

D: Exactly.

M: Speaking about fear and ordinary life, at least some kinds of it, the reason that I read that passage to you before by the critic who thinks that Bacon and Caravaggio both wanted to possess the image—to lose mutability by going into art—is because I was reading some interviews—not a conversation you and I had, but interviews you had with other people—and I think you said something like that. Do you remember?

D: [Laughs] No.

M: You expressed a, well, fear of the mutability of the world and said you liked being inside the world of the film.

D: Yeah, yeah, yeah. I love being inside the world of the film, and you know, well, there's all kind of things to talk about; you could say there's many, many, many worlds within worlds. You get ideas. And suddenly in the flow of ideas there's a world coming to you. And you can go in there. And it's totally real. And characters are there and a mood is there. All the things, and you experience that and write that down. It doesn't happen all at once for me. It happens in stages and then you translate those ideas and all those feelings. And you try to get that in cinema.

M: Now, I know this. You've said it to other people. You've said it to me, and it's almost obvious when I look at your movies that that's the case. I guess what I'm asking is whether being in the world of a film is a form of protection for you. In any way. I don't mean necessarily in obvious ways.

D: Well, I don't know. I don't think about it that way one bit. It's thrilling to discover a new world. And I always say the same thing. I love when an idea comes along. You know, there's ideas for everything. You don't do anything without an idea. The thought comes first. I'm going to go to the store and get a loaf of bread. Where did that come from? It bobbed up. It's kind of a desire and a thinking at the same time. And you're off to the store. You go down the aisle and you see the bread. There's a lot of different kinds of bread. Boom! This is the one you want and you get it. You follow through on that idea and you get that loaf of bread. So the same thing happens when you get an idea for cinema and you know it's for cinema. You fall in love with it because you love the idea itself. And then you love what cinema can do with that idea. And it's like there are some ideas that—they're not bad, but they don't feel like things you want to use cinema for.

M: Are you saying to me that a cinematic idea for you is a natural extension of the way you live anyway? You have an idea and you get a loaf of bread. And you have an idea and you build a film world. So, art and shopping are parallel ideas?

D: For everybody, not just for me. If some guy is working in an electronics company, he wants to get ideas in that vein, the electronic vein. And he's thinking all the time about whatever is there so far. He knows what's there so far. And he knows how all the things work. But he's thinking all the time and daydreaming even. Thinking, daydreaming, thinking, daydreaming. And boom! "What if I did this instead of that? And brought in this thing that Frank was telling me about. That could do it." And so he's in there going to work.

M: So as an artist you feel you have a kinship to anybody.

D: All human beings.

M: You're not a different sort of person.

D: No.

M: You're a person who does with film what other people do with baking cakes.

D: Exactly right. Great chefs, they're thinking all the time. They understand all their utensils. They understand all these different ingredients that everybody knows about. They know about it and they are thinking. And they're tasting. And action and reaction. What if I put a little of this in there? And boom! Another whole taste. And it thrills the people. It's like incredible. But they couldn't come up with that unless they're catching ideas based on all the stuff they know. And it kind of builds all the time. Evolution.

M: Okay, so I want to bring this around to what I asked before about possessing the image. And you said, no, that's not striking a chord.

D: I don't know what possessing an image means.

M: OK. When he [the critic in the Galleria Borghese catalogue] says that, that doesn't resonate with you.

D: Not really. If you put it into a different way of saying it, it might resonate.

M: It's OK. Just curious. It might not have resonated with Bacon either.

## FRAGMENT II

"But, looking at the things I shot, I thought there's something going on in this and it's something more than what this is."

M: OK. I want to move from that to something I saw in Lynch I and Lynch II that really surprised me. While you were making Inland Empire, there is videotape of you in the front seat of a moving car. I think you're clutching something. Or maybe you're just crossing your arms in front of you. And you're saying that you're terrified and this is not how you've ever worked before. You don't know what you're doing. Do you remember this?

D: Sort of. Yeah. [Laughs]

M: Why that made me sit up and take notice is that in our conversations you've always spoken about the will to lose your will. You told me that ninety percent of the time you don't know what you're doing. You just stand back and get out of the way and let the thing take over. So that you're not controlling it except in the execution of it. And I was just wondering. Why was this time different when you didn't know what you were doing? Why were you afraid?

[Lynch usually completes his scripts well before he shoots a film, but Inland Empire was written as it was being shot, which means that all the anxiety about developing a script that usually gets expressed before he is in production was floating through the production stage of Inland Empire, while he was working with his cast and crew. In his own words:]

D: It's the same thing. In Inland Empire there's a thing called a script. All those things like those moments sitting in the front of the car and worrying or whatever, normally those things happen during the times you're building the script. You've caught three or four ideas and you're writing them down. But you're a long way from a script. And then you're in this place with these three or four ideas and it's a vacuum for a while. And you wonder what in the world you're doing. What is this going to lead to if anything? And you're looking for more ideas. But you're not as worried as what you saw because you're building a script.

M: And nobody else is involved; nobody's depending on you.

D: Nobody's depending on anything. But you have these times when you're thinking and the next thing isn't coming. And so it may come tomorrow. But you don't know that. And it may come this afternoon. But you don't know that.

M: So you go out and build a table.

D: Or you do something. Or, you're just mulling it over. And you wait and see if by thinking about things something will pop out. And what you saw there—*Inland Empire* started in a very strange way. I wrote a bunch of things, and I shot what I wrote, not thinking about a feature film. But, looking at the things I shot, I thought there's something going on in this and it's something more than what this is. It indicates something more. So then I'm thinking about that and what I thought was a stand-alone thing, I don't want it to stand alone. I want it to be part of something. Then, lo and behold, I get another idea. And it is definitely not part of this; not in a million years. And I go out and shoot that as a stand-alone. And then I'm thinking. . . .

M: Can you tell me what the second thing was? I know the first was Laura Dern as the lady upstairs.

D: Well, we'll go into that later. Then I get another idea and I write that down and it's definitely not part of this one or two. It's three. And then maybe there's a fourth one. And then somewhere along in there it comes together, because, strangely, everything is unified on one level.

M: Are you talking about the unified field?

D: The unified field. So these things suddenly found a way to unite in my brain. And I said, "Whoa, is that a beautiful thing!" It was enough to see a way to unite them, and it was real interesting to me. And it was thrilling. And so that flowered a whole other thing. And so there was many, many pages of script [that] came out of that uniting of those three and what that meant, and it showed much more.

M: Can I ask you a question?

D: Sure.

M: Were the rabbits one of those original segments?

D: Yes . . . That fit in—

M: I mean was it one of the original bits that seemed to be a stand-alone project but then turned out to be connected to *Inland Empire*?

D: That was way before this. "Rabbits" was before—

M: Oh really? So, way before the Laura Dern—

D: Yes. So, it was really the first.

M: OH! So, "someday I will know" and "I've got a secret," all that came first. And the rabbit suits. And the strange, spare almost sitcom *Honeymooners* set. That came before Laura Dern. And at some point you said, "Oh that goes with this."

D: Yeah.

M: That was maybe while you were still working on *Mulholland Dr.*, because the people in those suits were from *Mulholland Dr.* . . .

D: That was right after *Mulholland Dr.*

M: After you mixed it, or after you shot it?

D: After it was finished.

> *[I knew that "Rabbits" was a feature on davidlynch.com in 2003 but for* Inland Empire, *he re-shot the "Rabbits" visuals after having had the set rebuilt, but used the same spoken lines from the original series.]*

## FRAGMENT III

"There's these things called laws of nature."

M: Okay, here's your second surprise. *[The first was a Bacon/Carvaggio catalogue from an exhibit at the Galleria Borghese in Rome that I gave him.]* I've been studying physics.

D: Wow!

M: Wow!

D: Wow!

M: You've been saying "physics" to me for almost twenty years, but, like all of the rest of the people who have written seriously about your movies, I've been saying "consciousness." And consciousness *is* important to you, but so is physics.

D: It's tied together.

M: Yes, that's what I'm thinking now. And what I want to do is share some things with you and just see what happens.

D: Sure. Okay.

M: Now, this is something I'm pretty sure you've never seen. It's from a book by an early quantum physicist in 1927. So just read it to yourself and then let's talk.

> *[I handed him a copy of the following passage from* The Nature of the Physical World *by Arthur Eddington and he read it:]*

D: "I am standing on the threshold about to enter a room. It is a complicated business. In the first place I must shove against an atmosphere pressing with a force of fourteen pounds on every square inch of my body. I must make sure of landing on a plank traveling at twenty miles a second round the sun—a fraction of a second too early or too late, the plank would be miles away. I must do this whilst hanging from a round planet headed outward into space, and with a wind of aether blowing at no one knows how many miles a second through ever interstice of my body. The plank has no solidity of substance to step on it is like stepping on a swarm of flies. Shall I not slip through? No, if I make the venture one of the flies hits me and gives me a boost up again; I fall again and am knocked upwards by another fly; and so on. I may hope that the net result will be that I remain about steady; but if unfortunately I should slip through the floor or be boosted too violently up to the ceiling, the occurrence would be, not a violation of the laws of Nature, but a rare coincidence. These are some of the minor difficulties. I ought really to look at the problem four-dimensionally as concerning the intersection of my world line with that of the plank. Then again it is necessary to determine in which direction the entropy of the world is increasing in order to make sure that my passage over the threshold is an entrance, not an exit.

Verily, it is easier for a camel to pass through the eye of a needle than for a scientific man to pass through a door" (p. 342).

D: Well, you know, it's like they say. There's these things called laws of nature. And the more you know, the more you see how things are. But the laws of nature work so that you can pass through the door. They work on this plane of physical existence. But it's true that beneath that surface there's molecules—

M: And beneath the molecules—

D: There's atoms.

M: And beneath the atoms—

D: There's smaller and smaller particles.

M: Strings.

D: Down near the very base there's these strings.

M: You believe in them?

D: Yes, at the base of everything is unity. Self-referral consciousness: Self-referral means it knows itself completely.

M: Okay, wait a second. As I understand string theory, at the bottom of everything are these one-dimensional strings that vibrate.

D: I think at the bottom of everything is the super-string. Un-manifest, self-referral consciousness. The unified field. That, they say, is perfect symmetry. When spontaneous sequential symmetry breaking starts, the little strings appear. Forces come from this symmetry breaking and act upon the particles. The whole thing starts to grow and change. But really it's all consciousness.

M: The source of time and space is consciousness?

D: Yes, the source of everything.

M: I hear you.

## FRAGMENT IV

"I love thinking about these things, but you know, the nuts and bolts of it would, you know—kill me. I barely made it out of high school."

M: I want to give you another few words from quantum physics. Do you know the word superposition?

D: Superposition? No.

M: OK. Superposition is really important in quantum physics. It's the opposite of entanglement. Entanglement is that two particles act as if they were one. It totally defies the way we think. To say two are the same—

D: And going beyond that to say that everything is the same.

M; Yes, and entanglement is believed to be the state of matter when it first started. Everything was entangled. And then time and tide changed that. You can create entanglement in a lab. They've done that. And it can happen spontaneously. But they believe that at the beginning of creation—

D: Everything was entangled.

M: It was many, but it wasn't many.

D: There is unity and diversity. And out of unity comes diversity. But diversity ultimately is unity.

M: Exactly.

D: So it is that way.

M: So we're looking at two different ways of talking about something at least similar. In addition to entanglement there's also superposition. Superposition is about one particle that's more than one particle. A situation can be created in a laboratory in which one particle is in two different places at the same time. Exactly what we think is impossible. Newtonian physics says it is. You know, entanglement and the whole question of the illusion of space makes me think of folding space in *Dune*.

D: [Lynch steers the conversation toward his way of looking at the universe.] "The path to enlightenment is not from here to there, but from here to here." Same thing. And "Far, far away the indweller of the house sees the self reverberating." That means there is no distance. It is, here, there, and everywhere. And not only that. It's bigger than the biggest and smaller than the smallest.

M: It's very interesting to me that so many of the things you're interested in through Maharishi you could also have gotten to through Western quantum physics, but you didn't choose that.

D: I am a painter. I like painting. And to get to where a quantum physicist gets to, he has to go through so many steps that would have killed me. You see what I mean?

M: I do.

D: I love thinking about these things, but you know, the nuts and bolts of it would, you know—kill me. I barely made it out of high school, but I do love thinking about what the quantum physicists come up with. It's the results that the quantum physicists come up with that I love thinking about.

M: Well, can I continue talking just a little more about the concepts of physics that seem to connect with your films? For example, loops of time. Do you know what this is?

D: No.

M: Quantum theory and relativity propose time in a circle rather than linear. So that—does this make any sense to you?—the cause and the effect is no longer that causes that; it's A causes B and B causes A.

D: A causes B, and B is caused by A. That makes sense.

M: Does it?

D: Sort of.

M: Because that isn't the way that westerners think.

D: Yeah, yeah. But you know time is a very tricky thing. And there's these stories of time in that Vedic thing. And they say time is a conception to measure eternity. Time is a conception to measure eternity. And they go into how it kinda works. I know it's a trick, but it doesn't really matter. This is where we are. For whatever reason, we're here. And there's things that we try to understand about our world.

M: Do you think, for example, that *Lost Highway* puts time in a circle?

D: It does.

M: That A is the cause of B and B is the cause of A?

D: A mobius strip.

M: Because *Lost Highway* begins with Fred hearing it *["Dick Laurent is dead" spoken through the intercom of his house.]* And it ends with Fred saying it. But he said it a long time ago so there's a sort of strange—

D: Strange loop, yeah.

M: David Albert *[a quantum physicist who holds the Frederick Woodbridge Chair at Columbia University whom Lynch and I have spoken about]* says that he feels that *Lost Highway* is an enclosed loop of time. That you can't get on it and you can't get off it.

D: That's like saying "I want out of the unified field." There's no way. We're in the middle of it. Always have been. Always will be. But we don't know it fully. We've lost our connection to it. So like they say, know it by being it.

## FRAGMENT V

"The world is as you are."

*[The following is, as you can see, not spontaneous speech, nor is this what Lynch said during the interview. A bit more than a year after we spoke, he formulated this summary and asked that I use it in this Appendix instead of many pages of discussion that he preferred not to see published. The actual conversation related to numerous issues other than Transcendental Meditation. But these are Lynch's words.]*

D: The problem today is that people have lost the connection to the big Self, the unified field. The transcendent. That's why Maharishi has brought back this technique of Transcendental Meditation; so that people can establish that connection with the unified field within. The unified field within at the base of all matter and mind is the big Self—the Self of all that is. Every time we human beings experience that deepest level of life—meaning every time we transcend and experience the source of everything—we infuse some of that all-positive consciousness—unity. And we grow in that.

Every human **being** has consciousness, but not every human being has the same amount. The potential for the human being is infinite conscious ness. Most of us only experience waking, sleeping and dreaming, but there are seven states of consciousness that human beings can attain. And the world looks different in each state.

These higher states of consciousness are there for us. We just need to unfold them by regularly experiencing the Transcendent, the unified field, the big Self, Totality. Every day we can experience this field with this technique of Transcendental Meditation. And by experiencing this each day, life just gets better and better and better. The world looks better and better and better.

The highest state of consciousness is unity consciousness and in that state a person experiences Totality. Oneness. Maharishi says it's like 200% of life. 100% of all that is unmanifest and 100% of all that is manifest. This is a state of total fulfillment in infinite bliss—a state of total knowledge. This is supreme enlightenment—the full potential of the human being. The call is, "Come on and enjoy. There's no need to suffer. The individual is cosmic and the nature of life is bliss."

# EXCERPTS FROM MY
# INTERVIEWS WITH
# PROFESSOR DAVID Z. ALBERT

*The following are excerpts from two conversations I was privileged to have with Professor David Z. Albert, Frederick E. Woodbridge Professor of Philosophy and Director of the M: A: Program in the Philosophical Foundations of Physics at Columbia University. Professor Albert's cooperation with me as I wrote this study gave me a perfect mentor: a teacher, an accomplished physicist, a philosopher, and a great admirer of David Lynch. Professor Albert is a tough-minded physicist, who at the same time, enjoys the way that Lynch borrows from physics for a poetics of his own. What Albert objects to strenuously is the presentation of impressionistic statements about physics as if they were science. In the following excerpts from our discussions, one of the major goals was for us to draw clean lines between physics and New Age romanticizing of physics.*

## FIRST MEETING, JANUARY 4, 2010

*Excerpts from an Interview*

### PARTICLES

N: What are the crucial elements of the quantum mechanical view of the world?

A: One of the things that emerges in quantum mechanics that had never emerged in science before is that, up until quantum mechanics, physics had always depended on a certain fantasy to the effect that although everybody was aware that in measuring something or observing something you are necessarily physically interacting with it, there was a fantasy that if you were careful enough, if you were clever enough, if you spent enough money, if you machined things carefully enough, the degree to which you disrupted things by interacting with them could be minimized as far as you like. That is, there is this fantasy in the back of physics of, as it were, opening one's eyes and being able to see what was there before your eyes were open. Of not disrupting the thing in the course of looking at it. And once again, physics before quantum mechanics seemed to allow, seemed to encourage a fantasy like this.

N: The passive observer. The completely objective observer. Is this Cartesian?

A: No. This is pre-quantum mechanics. This is implicit in Newtonian mechanics and in the Maxwellian mechanics of the 19th century. This is the fantasy that decisively collapses in the context of quantum mechanics. And the particular way in which this fantasy collapses is connected with this thing you call the problem of measurement.

N: So later on there are other experiments which disclose the existence of many more particles.

A: That's correct.

N: And 400 particles emerge, or something like that.

A: That's a bit outdated. That's very much in flux. What the elementary constituents of the world are is a subject that is still in flux. But there's more going on in there than just the protons and the neutrons. And those protons and neutrons may be composed of smaller things and exactly what the nature of those things are may be those smaller things are not even particles, maybe they're strings—

N: String theory.

A: Yes.

N: And so what I read was that the scientific mind didn't care for so many particles.

A: Uh-huh.

N: And particles were grouped under the heading of quarks. What does that mean? What is the process by which a bunch of particles like lisons and so forth become quarks?

A: What you are required to do is to figure out how all of these various particles you are seeing could be imagined as being constructed from different combinations of some smaller number of basic elements. So the idea is that you have some small number of basic elements. Of course the number of ways these elements could be combined with each other to form larger things is much larger than the number of elements themselves. And so you begin to search for ways that they can all be understood as combinations of some smaller number of elements. The most successful attempt to do that was back in the 60s and 70s when QED was written, the most successful attempt at imagining a system like that is the so-called quark theory of Murray Gell-Mann. And that's the picture that people were operating with for a long time.

N: Has that changed?

A: Well, now there's a proposal for a yet more fundamental building block, strings, of which the quarks are supposed to be various kinds of excitations of the string. That is, the string vibrating in a certain way is what we mean by a certain kind of quark. And the string vibrating in a different frequency is a different kind of quark. But the only thing one needs to know at the moment is that this is very much in flux.

N: And these particles are held together by gluons?

A: Um hmm.

N: Even the strings?

A: No, if string theory is right, gluons are yet another way in which these strings could be vibrating. Every single particle one talks about is a way in which these strings could be vibrating.

N: You know, vibration is a very big deal with Lynch, so this all becomes very suggestive.

ENTANGLEMENT

N: The issue of entanglement. What I have gleaned is that it has something to do with—

A: With quantum mechanics generally. It has something to do with every particle there is.

N: Is it that two particles created together are entangled?

A: No, they don't necessarily need to be created together. Entanglement has a lot of strange features but the basic one is that you can't describe the situation that this pair of particles is in by saying something about particle number one and particle number two. There's something about the way these particles are related to each other that can't be captured by any mere act of first describing particle number one and then describing particle number two. That's when we speak of them being entangled with one another. The situation of this pair of particles constitutes like I say some way in which they're related to one another that can't be exhausted by just saying everything there is to say about particle number one by itself and then saying everything there is to say about particle number two by itself.

N: [Shows diagram of two partially overlapping circles.] Is it like this? There's an overlapping area?

A: No, it's weirder than that. Any particle can have some states in which entangled particles have some kind of relationship to each other that is a connection that cannot be described, cannot be captured just by describing what particle number one is doing and by describing what particle number two is doing. Going on from there, if you send one particle to one end of the universe and the other to the other end of the universe, if you do something to one, the other one will respond. Separate two such particles and bring them to opposite ends of the universe, and take more precautions, put million-mile-thick lead walls, station snipers, assassins, it will still be the case that there will be correlations in measurements between particle number one and particle number two that cannot be explained by any pre-arranged correlations between the states between the particles. That is it's as if the particles must have been communicating with one another.

N: Could we say that the fact that this is so means that either information is traveling very fast or there's some sort of empathy?

A: Empathy is a little vague, but something of that sort is going on. There's some causal connection between the states of these particles. Let me put it this way, to say that information is traveling very fast is to minimize how weird it is. It's not that it's traveling very fast. It's not traveling at all. It's as if knocking particle one IS knocking particle two. And this is not because particles are traveling at high speeds. If they were moving very fast, there would still be some dependence on how far apart these particles are. That's why I said all that about the lead wall and the snipers. If it was anything traveling, it would be in some way, shape, or form sensitive to conditions in the space between the two particles. This is completely insensitive to those conditions, utterly, absolutely zero sensitivity to those conditions. So it isn't like anything traveling; it's somehow that doing something to particle one is doing something to particle two. Not directly, not in a mediated way, but in an unmediated way. Let me expand on this. It is an inestimably deep feature of the way we approach the world conceptually, every millisecond of our lives that something called locality is true. This is locality. We assume that in order for something here to have an effect on something there it needs to be the case that there is some continuous, unbroken chain of mediating subcauses and effects stretching from here to there in space and time. So for example, if waving my hand here causes somebody to be hit over there, it's because light is bouncing off my hand and traveling and causing a signal. . . . I flip a switch and over there a light goes on, we know that if we rip up the wall we'll find wires, radio signals. So the conviction is that things only directly affect other things that are right next to them. Any effect on anything that is not directly next to you is necessarily indirect. It occurs through the agency of other things between you and them. It's this principle that quantum mechanics apparently violates, that entangled particles violates. So it's much, much weirder than the effect of going fast. It's that the effect doesn't go at all. It's that you have a fundamental violation of this principle of locality. The principle that you can only directly affect things that are right next to you.

N: Let me build on that. Is this true? [Reads] "And since everything was entangled at the moment of the big bang, everything is touching."

A: No. It is true, according to our current theories that everything was entangled at the Big Bang. But all kinds of things have happened since then which to a very large, almost perfect degree washed that effect out in most cases. That had better be true. After all in our everyday experience of the world, I can't be the one who punched you unless I was in the room at the time you were punched.

N: The basis of our legal system.

A: That's exactly right. So it had better not be true that something like that is the case. And yet there are some conditions that can be created in a laboratory in which it is so.

N: And yet we can't explain it because so much has happened since the Big Bang, and we have no idea—

A: No, no. Quantum mechanics makes predictions. Quantum mechanics can give instructions about how to set up an entangled state.

N: You have to set it up, it doesn't just happen.

A: No, sometimes it does just happen naturally. And quantum mechanics gives you tools to predict when to expect it to happen naturally. But it's as obvious as it could be that this is no longer radically true of everything. We're pretty safe in making the assumption that it wasn't me who punched you if I wasn't in the room when you were punched. So it's not true that everything is like this and we have the scientific resources to explain how these effects get washed out. A locution like everything was entangled at the Big Bang will endear itself to New Age sensibilities.

N: Here's another statement: Space is the illusion that there are separate objects.

A: There is entanglement in a situation where the particles interact in a way that takes no account of their spatial relationship where the phenomenon of space disappears.

N: So space becomes an illusion. Under those circumstances.

A: There are scientific proposals on the table, respectable ones, one that I've worked on where one starts with this phenomenon of entanglement and in trying to understand it gets to a place where space does look like a particular kind of illusion generated by the dynamic that we have and where there is only one object in the world. But you have to give a scientific account of how it looks like there are many and why it looks like they have certain spatial relations to one another. But to draw this as a simple and obvious lesson from the basic phenomenon is much, much, much too fast. So there are proposals on the table that are like that, but this as a slogan seems way too fast and another case of this kind of romanticism.

PHOTONS

N: Now I want to talk about photons. Electrons throw them off, right.

A: Right. All charged particles do.

N: [Reads statement from QED] "Photons look exactly the same in all respects when they travel backward in time . . ."

A: [Richard] Feynman developed a very easy-to-remember and easy-to-apply prescription for doing the calculations of quantum mechanics which we need to do to calculate the outcomes of various experiments. And a part of this prescription was to treat these photons as if they were traveling backward in time. I don't think there's any substantive philosophic sense in which they do. This kind of locution is more of a mnemonic device to remind you of how to insert the photons into the calculations. I don't think Feynman himself would defend the proposition of photons actually traveling backward in time and no one thinking about this stuff today is inclined to take that seriously. It's a device that is an aid to how you do a certain calculation. Whether there's a plus sign or a minus sign. When these people talked like this they had no notion who would be listening a couple of years down the road. And from that standpoint the talk is irresponsible, even though it wasn't irresponsible within the context of the audience it was addressed to.

N: The rest of it is that the photons are their own anti-particles.

A: There's a sense in which photons are their own anti-particles.

N: They don't have to travel back in time for that to be the case.

A: Correct. There is elsewhere in general relativity a very real puzzle associated with the fact that general relativity does seem to allow not just for particles for macroscopic material objects—

N: Baseballs?

A: And people. To travel backwards in time in some literal sense. And this is something that seems to come up in Lynch all the time.

N: Indeed it does.

A: Especially in *Lost Highway* which seems—there is this circular rather than linear causal structure. At the end of the day the guy who rings the buzzer is the same guy who rang the bell at the beginning. It was discovered by Kurt Godel, a great logician at the beginning of the twentieth century, who made an astonishing discovery. One of his other discoveries was that he showed that Einstein's equations of general relativity allowed for travel backwards in time. This is always something that people have feared since it seems to lead to logical paradoxes. That is it seems to raise questions like what if I traveled backward in time one hundred years and killed my grandparents. If I did kill my grandparents I didn't kill my grandparents because I didn't exist at all. So there's a real straightforward logical paradox. And there's been a lot of struggling with this both in physics and philosophy. And among the upshots of this struggle has been a realization that if there is a possibility of this kind of travel backwards in time, in such circumstances the causal structures we're going to run into are going to form loops rather than lines. Things are ultimately going to be the causes of themselves. And things are going to have to happen in such a way that they're capable of being the causes of themselves.

There's a beautiful example in a paper by Feynman and Wheeler that tries to come to grips with this possibility of traveling or signaling backwards in time. This paradox I've told you about is called the grandfather paradox for obvious reasons. And they tried to sharpen up the grandfather paradox and here's what they imagined [draws diagram]. Here's a gun. Aimed at a box, with an antenna on top. Antenna to send messages to itself in the past. Box has a mechanical arm with a mechanical wall that can slide in and out of the path of the bullet. The gun is set to go off at six. The box is programmed thus. If the box detects the impact of a bullet at six, it sends orders to itself in the past to close this wall at five. So the bullet never can get to the box. So there's a paradox. If the bullet gets there, it didn't get there. How to solve the paradox? They make this beautiful observation which I've never seen used in any other scientific paper. It goes like this. Imagine I drop this toothpick here at a certain time and I ask how long it takes to reach the floor. The answer is one second. I drop it here instead (over the table). It never reaches the floor. The time it takes to reach the floor is infinity. They make this simple observation. All of our physical theories have as a consequence that final conditions are a continuous function of initial conditions. If there's a place along this line that I can drop this so that it hits the floor in one second, and another place such that it doesn't hit the floor until infinity, there must be places in between where it hits the floor at all times between one second and infinity.

What places are those? They're places right near the edge of the table where it's going to scrape in a certain way or balance for a certain time. Here's a simpler example. I try to balance this pen [picks up my pen] on its tip. There's a certain angle I can hold it where it will hit the table in one second. Two seconds. Then there's a certain place I can put it such that it balances perfectly and doesn't hit the table at all. There must then necessarily be tiny little angles I can hold it at such that it would hit the table not in ten seconds or twenty seconds but in a year, or in a thousand years, or a million years—if there were no atmospheric disturbances in here. They applied this to this situation. There's an oversimplifying assumption here. The assumption is that either the bullet makes direct impact on the sensor in which case the door closes at five. Or it misses the sensor altogether, in which case the door never closes. But if those two possibilities are there, there must be an infinity of other possibilities. What are those? Presumably, that it grazes the edge of the sensor and the door closes late. Envision the following scenario: the bullet just grazes the edge of the sensor. Now we say why did it graze the edge late? Because the wall came down late. Why did the wall come down late? Because the bullet grazed the edge of the sensor. That is, causal questions keep on looping us back to the event that's being explained itself. The causal structures come in circles rather than in lines. I always thought this notion of a causal circle was something the title was alluding to. The highway is lost because it doesn't go anywhere. It circles around. And the movie is full of these causal circles.

N: Now we're dealing with actual physics that can apply to a person. Whereas I think he's also using—. See with Lynch it's all about an above and beneath and we all jumped, me too, to the conclusion that psychology is what we needed to talk about. I'm thinking he's been saying quantum mechanics to me for twenty years. And I never did anything with it. Because that's how your mind is.

A: The particular phenomenon we're talking about here—I'm sure there's much that is quantum mechanical—has nothing to do with quantum mechanics. The reasons we have for believing that time travel into the past wouldn't be a violation of the laws of physics has to do with the theory of relativity. It's a completely different theory from quantum mechanics.

N: So I'm not going to quote back to you your time-reversal symmetry. Because we just did that.

A: Let me just caution you on one thing. Time-reversal symmetry isn't what we were just discussing.

It doesn't have anything to do with time travel. There are three branches of physics. There are the puzzles associated with quantum mechanics. There are puzzles associated with relativity. And there is a third thing that we haven't mentioned yet called the problem of the direction of time, which runs basically as follows. Imagine that you see a film depicting two billiard balls colliding in intergalactic space. Initially you see one billiard ball at rest. Another one comes in, knocks into it. It stops and the other one runs off.

N: Very Newtonian.

A: Very Newtonian. It's a problem that comes up in Newtonian mechanics. It comes up in modern physics as well. Imagine that you were shown this film in reverse. What you'd see is this. The billiard ball comes in from the other end of the frame. Knocks into the ball in the center of the frame, which then rolls off in the other direction. When you're being shown the film in reverse, you're seeing something that is just as much in accord with the laws governing collisions of billiard balls as you see in the film going forward. That is, if you were shown a film and asked to guess whether you were seeing it forward or in reverse, you wouldn't have any grounds for knowing. The process you see in the reverse film is every bit as in accord with the laws of physics as the process you see in the forward film. We describe this in physics by saying that the laws of physics governing collisions of billiard balls are time-reversal symmetric. For any process happening in accord with those laws, the same process happening in reverse is time-reversal symmetric too. The deal is from our examinations of the microscopic fundamental laws of physics, we take ourselves to have very good reasons for believing that all the fundamental laws of physics have this property of time-reversal symmetry. But there's a puzzle. Because our everyday macroscopic experience of the world is exactly the opposite. Because if you see a film of people having lunch or getting murdered or I don't know what, you can damn well tell whether the film is being shown in forward or reverse. There's a puzzle about this because the fundamental dynamical laws that we know about don't seem to underwrite an asymmetry like this. That's what's being referred to as the problem of the direction of time.

N: You know what a palindrome is, don't you? It's when you can read a word both ways like BOB or WOW or MADAM I'M ADAM: That is the linguistic equivalent.

A: Yes, that's right.

N: Because he uses palindromes in *Twin Peaks*, and I've always wondered what the hell that was. Now here comes something from the movie *What the Bleep?* "Only in conscious experience do we go forward in time. In quantum theory you can also go backward in time. Processes in the brain project backwards in time."

A: Bullshit. When you say processes in the brain project backward in time he could mean that we have memories, but if he means something fancier than that, it's just a lie.

QUANTUM MECHANICS AND NEWTONIAN MECHANICS

N: Then there are two sets of laws that govern the universe.

A: Two sets?

N: Quantum mechanics and Newtonian mechanics.

A: Oh. That's not true. Quantum mechanics is supposed to be a complete account of the world. It's supposed to replace Newtonian theory, not supplement it. Quantum mechanics must, if it's going to be a successful account of the world, quantum mechanics reproduces the predictions that Newtonian mechanics makes for those things that Newtonian mechanics is right about like baseballs or planets or eclipses or something like that. Quantum mechanics does as it had better do, if it is going to be correct, make the same predictions as Newtonian mechanics makes about systems like those.

N: Macrosystems.

A: Macrosystem under familiar circumstances.

N: And microsystems there are different predictions.

A: And for microsystems it makes different predictions, but it isn't as though there were two sets of laws. Quantum mechanics presents itself as a complete account.

N: And you agree with that?

A: Yes. There are problems, but I think we're going to come up with a version of quantum mechanics that gets everything right and that's going to include what Newtonian mechanics gets right too.

N: I'm going to read something to you. "In our daily classical world Newton's laws of motion work well. But on a small scale, a different set of laws take over. Quantum laws."

A: No, the "Newtonian laws working well"? That's a little misleading. All that means is that Newtonian laws approximate fairly well the quantum laws for macroscopic systems.

SUPERPOSITION

N: Here are quantum laws: particles may be in multiple places at the same time. . . .

A: It's worse than that. It's putting it poorly to say that they can be in multiple places at the same time.

It's more like this. That they can be in circumstances where asking a question like, "Where is the particle now?" is what philosophers call a category mistake. It's like asking a question like what is the marital status of the number 5. If somebody says "Is the number 5 married?" You say, "No." And they say, "So the number 5 is a bachelor." And you say, "No." And they say, "Oh my god; there's a logical contradiction. The world is breaking down."

N: Superposition.

A: Yes, this is superposition. The right answer is nothing is breaking down. It's just that the number 5 is neither married nor unmarried. Not because it's involved in a logical contradiction but just because the whole question of marital status is inappropriate for things like numbers. Numbers don't have any marital status. And I think I used this example too. If you ask whether a certain tuna sandwich is a Democrat or a Republican, the right answer is you're asking the wrong kind of question. It's one of the strange things in quantum mechanics, this phenomenon of superposition, like you say, that particles can have modes of being available to them in which it fails to make sense to ask whether the particle is here or there. So, it's not like it's in two places. It's much weirder.

N: No place?

A: It's not in no place. Because if you look for it in both places you're guaranteed to find it. So it's not in no place. For example, if you look for it in a third place, you're guaranteed not to find it. So in some sense it's these two places that are relevant, but to ask which of those two places it's in—

N: But you can't say that it's in both places?

A: No. If you look in both places you'll only find it in one. On the other hand, there are reasons for believing that before you look, before you did this violence, there was no fact about which place it was in. . . .

N: It was in both places?

A: Is the number 5 both married and unmarried?

N: But the number 5 has no legal status. But particles do have location.

A: Not in these cases. It has these modes of being open to it where it fails to have a position.

N: And can be perceived in many places?

A: No, if you go look for it, you will do violence to it. You will knock it out of this state, as we were saying before. You can't look at it passively. If you go look for the particle you will do violence to its condition. You will force it to adopt a different mode of being where it's in one place or another. And then you'll find it there.

N: Okay. Just because you brought it up. Let me ask you to talk about this in terms of Fred and Pete [in *Lost Highway*]. Is that the same situation?

A: Fred is the guy—

N: He's the guy we see at the beginning who hears the message, "Dick Laurent is dead."

A: Okay.

N: Pete is the young—

A: Is the young guy who ends up in the prison.

N: The authorities find him there one day.

A: Look once again—

N: Are we talking about superposition?

A: Look, he could have had something like that in mind.

N: But what if he didn't? What if it just is—?

A: It's a tempting analogy. Once again, what I was noticing most is the guy played by Robert Blake, this interesting incident when he's introduced. When he calls himself at the guy's house. This is something you're always going to run into with time travel. If you time travel into the past, there are always going to be moments when two of you are in different parts of the world at the same time.

N: So, that's relativity.

A: It's immediately evocative. So, what is going on in *Lost Highway*, what I was fastening on in terms of physics is much more the general relativity stuff than the quantum mechanics stuff. There's all of this stuff going on that one learns to expect when one begins to think about these closed time line loops. People being in two places at once. Stories causing themselves.

N: Pete and Fred as one. Which seems like superposition. Or at least that I can play with that.

A: You can certainly play with it.

COLLAPSE OF THE WAVE FUNCTION

N: Reads statement: "The threshold (curtain) between quantum and classical world sometimes called the *collapse of the wave function*. In the quantum world, everything is in superposition with multiple possibilities, in the classical world these multiple possibilities seem to collapse into one choice everything is in one particular place."

So as you move from the circumstances that Newtonian physics predicted you have the collapse of something. What I read was the collapse of the wave function.

A: I think it's sloppily put in all sorts of ways, but I think correcting it would take more time than it's worth for your purposes. I think that's OK.

N: So, could we also say that when you move from the circumstances of Newtonian prediction into the circumstances of quantum prediction, that there's an expansion?

A: What do you have in mind? What kind of expansion? Oh, I see, the opposite of a collapse.

N: Yes, exactly.

A: What are you going to do with that if I say yes?

N: I don't know. I mean when you move from Fred to Pete, things seem to expand.

A: Okay. Okay. The following I guess is true. Yes, quantum mechanics presents us with a larger palate of physical possibilities than Newtonian mechanics. So I guess you could say that when you move from the domain of Newtonian mechanics to the domain of quantum mechanics there is an expansion. You could say it and it's an appropriate thing to say.

STASIS

N: I've got Newton's law of motion here and Newton's laws of thermodynamics. What I want to ask is about stasis. There's the Newtonian circumstances and the quantum circumstances. I think stasis is possible within Newtonian circumstances.

A: Yah.

N: In fact, it's entropy, isn't it?

A: I don't know what that means.

N: Newton's second law of thermodynamics says that a closed system will degrade its energy over time.

    Which means that it would be leading toward stasis.

A: Yes. That's true in quantum mechanics too.

N: Is it?

A: That's one of the Newtonian predictions about macroscopic conditions that is essentially correct. And that quantum mechanics reproduces. When you're talking about entropy and approaching an equilibrium state, you're necessarily talking about a macroscopic system. Something like a gas.

N: Is it true of a microscopic system?

A: No. There are different ways that microscopic systems can be stationary. You place a particle in a certain position and there are no forces on it. It just stays there. In quantum mechanics there is no such thing as a particle being at a certain point and having a certain velocity because if it's at a definite point its velocity value is superposed. And if it has a definite velocity, its position is superposed. That's what we mean by the uncertainty relationship of velocity to position. But there are states that you can put particles in in quantum mechanics that won't change over time.

N: Is there such a thing as a closed system outside of Newtonian—

A: Yes, in both cases the following is true. Any system smaller than the universe will never be perfectly closed, there's no way to perfectly isolate any system from influence from the outside, but you can do a better and better job by building thicker and thicker walls and so on. And that's true both in quantum mechanics and in Newtonian mechanics.

N: This is the third law of thermodynamics: As a system approaches absolute zero, all process ceases and the entropy of the system approaches a minimum value.

    I don't know what that means.

A: I don't think you need to know what that means. I don't think that's going to be relevant. If we need to come back to it at a certain point, we will. But I don't think you need to know what that means.

DAVID BOHM AND NON-LOCALITY

N:  Now I want to go to David Bohm.

A:  Does Lynch know about Bohm?

N:  I don't know. I will find out when I interview him. *(He didn't.)*

A:  Because Bohm has this very interesting history. I don't know if you know about him. I knew him at the end of his life. And he was absolutely saintly. But he had—he was—Bohm's model of quantum mechanics was certainly the most important advance in our understanding of quantum mechanics between Bohr in the twenties and Bell in the sixties. He discovered this theory in fifty-three. He was a professor at Princeton. Within a couple of months of the publication of that theory he was called to testify before the House Un-American Activities Committee. He refused very heroically. It was an amazing thing unprecedented in American academia. First of all, the day he refused to testify he was fired. Apparently that evening there was an unprecedented emergency meeting of the trustees of Princeton University which passed an edit to the effect that Bohm could never set foot on the campus again.

 Absolutely astonishing. Anyway, Bohm left the country. His passport was revoked. There was a warrant for his arrest.

N:  Where did he go?

A:  He went initially to South America. Later he went to Israel and was kicked out of Israel under pressure from the American State Department. Ended up in England where he spent the rest of his life. He was a Professor at Birkbeck College. And anyway there were several consequences of all this. One of them was his theory which was revolutionary and enormously important was politically easy to ignore. And it was totally ignored. And the combination of being in this legal trouble and having his great discovery ignored was psychologically devastating. It killed him intellectually in some way. And he associated himself in ways that wasn't worthy of him with all kinds of talk of parallels between quantum mechanics and Buddhism and became a New Age icon. It's a sad story. Bohm expected and had every right to expect that his theory was just going to change the whole landscape and instead it was completely ignored. And he was so devastated by this. Apparently nobody read his theory until [John] Bell read it about ten years later. Bell is the guy who proved that quantum mechanics violates locality. Anyway, Bell seems to be the first person to have read that paper many years later. So Bohm was so devastated—I know someone who did his PhD thesis with Bohm, spent ten years with him at Birkbeck College. Bohm never mentioned this paper. Stopped talking about it completely. It had to be rediscovered through Bell.

N: I'm not really clear what David Bohm's theory is. This is what I got from page 169 of your book:

> The kind of story that contains nothing cryptic and nothing meta-physically novel and nothing ambiguous and nothing inexplicit and nothing evasive and nothing unintelligible and nothing inexact and nothing subtle and in which no questions ever fail to make sense and in which no questions ever fail to have answers and in which no two physical properties of anything are ever "incompatible" with one another and in which the whole universe evolves *deterministically* and which recounts the unfolding of a perverse and gigantic conspiracy to make the world *appear* to be *quantum-mechanical* (Albert, p.169).

What does this mean?

A: Look, Bohm came up with a theory that reproduces all the experimental results of quantum mechanics but that doesn't have any of this weirdness. For example, it never fails to make sense to ask where a particle is. That question always has a definite answer. For which most of the weird things we were talking about—

N: You mean he did the Gerlach boxes and the double slit experiment—

A: He can explain all that—

N: And nothing weird happens?

A: Look, Bohm's theory has one weird feature. There's one weird feature of quantum mechanics he doesn't get rid of. Well, I guess there are two. One is this fantasy of passive observation is still gone. But we now have an explicit mechanical model of why it's gone. Of why we can't avoid messing up systems when we look. And it's not an abstract mathematical model like we were getting from quantum mechanics. It's a very concrete mechanical—

N: Can you tell me?

A: It's a bit of a long story. What he doesn't get rid of is non-locality. And Bell read Bohm's theory. And said, "Well, hey, how come nobody ever told me about this? This violates all the folk wisdom that I've always been given about quantum mechanics." But Bell noticed that the theory is still non-local. And Bell said, "If we could only get rid of that, too. We would really have accomplished something." And Bell started fiddling around with Bohm's theory and tried to modify it in such a way that it would still make all these predictions correctly but wouldn't have this non-local feature. He found he couldn't do it. He tinkered around some more and was finally able to prove that it is simply a mathematical impossibility that there can be any theory that reproduces the experimental predictions of quantum mechanics and is local. So, it's not merely that we now know that quantum mechanics is not local, we know that the world is not local. Because we've done these experiments. They come out this way and we have a proof from Bell that no local theory can explain them. So, other than non-locality, Bohm's theory really does get rid of a lot of stuff. But it's neither here nor there when we apply these theories to art that they are scientifically true or not. There are images that the artist and the critic can play around with.

N: Here's where it does matter. People keep trying to say that Lynch's films, particularly *Lost Highway* and afterward, are dreams and they're not. And that's why I need recourse to that. Because I need to blow that out of the water.

A: Yes, I agree completely. As a matter of fact, if you want to know what I think scientifically—

N: Yes, please.

A: Bohm's theories are a really important reason for thinking that all this talk about superposition may turn out to be unnecessary. May turn out to have been a phase that physics went through. And doesn't need anymore. There are some open questions about Bohm's theory. There are especially questions about whether it can be made consistent with relativity theory. There are all kinds of issues. But it may be that all this stuff is unnecessary.

N: Well this is the reason I am interested in Bohm's theory. There is one film between *Lost Highway* and *Inland Empire* in which—

A: Which film?

N: *The Straight Story*. In which uncertainty seems to all but disappear. I mean you go from *Six Men Getting Sick* [*I describe it*]. From there to *Twin Peaks: Fire Walk with Me*, you have places where quantum mechanical events suddenly erupt. In *Lost Highway* the whole movie is about that.

A: Right. Right.

N: And suddenly you get *The Straight Story* where there's nothing. Nothing.

A: *Straight Story*. It always reminded me of what Flaubert said about his short story, "A Simple Heart." You know this story?

N: I don't know it.

A: It involves a kind of respect for simple people that is radically unlike Flaubert. Everywhere in Flaubert is this loathing of stupidity and unsophisticatedness. And there was some act of purification that he wanted to go through. Write a simple story about a simple person. It's about the entire life from beginning to end of a chambermaid whose one possession that she adores is a stuffed parrot. And that's it. It came to my mind when I saw—

N: Well, that's certainly interesting, but if you want to talk about stuff going on, you have to figure out what happened there. And it seems to me that the paragraph that I just read seemed to describe what happened there. You know, suddenly we have a story in which everything makes sense.

A: That's nice.

N: Etc. Etc. So I feel like I need to do something there.

A: Yes, that is what Bohm's theory feels like in the context of the discourse of quantum mechanics.

N: And so what you're saying is that what he seems to be doing is finding a way to make the predictions of quantum mechanics but without superposition.

A: Correct.

N: But he does have non-locality and he does have a problem with non-locality.

A: And there may be a problem with relativity.

N: It doesn't seem that this is enough. I should know more.

A: Look there's a book by Basil Hiley. I don't like it very much but because he was in the later part of Bohm's life and he's very connected with Bohm's status as a New Age icon. But I think in the early parts of some of these books, you might get an account that is more understandable than in my book.

NEW AGE SCIENCE

A: I'll tell you something presumably irrelevant. The thing that I principally dislike about New Age appropriations of science is exactly that. I mean I think that first of all it attempts to assimilate from science to this or that New Age prejudice or this or that tenet of Buddhism or anything like that seems to me sadly reductive of Buddhism and of science. Science is a genuinely novel way of looking at the world that I think doesn't have precedent before the scientific revolution.

N: Which you think of as when? Seventeenth century?

A: Yes, sixteenth, seventeenth century. And I think that this is not only in New Age stuff. Did you see this play *Copenhagen*? It's this standard—it's committing exactly the same kind of bad taste it seems to me that the New Age people commit with quantum mechanics in a more high-falutin' way, but no better one. There is this attempt to use science for the purposes of finding some kind of human wisdom. Wisdom in the worst sense of the word, a stable place to rest one's imagination. Something comfortable, something timeless. Blah, blah blah. Seems to me that what science has to offer us intellectually is exactly the opposite of wisdom. Science presents us with a picture of who we are that it's really not possible to fully take in and remain a human being. With this mechanical reduction of who we are. I think that the aesthetic sensation associated with taking in scientific theories is something like panic or something like the uncanny or the uncanny in the psychological sense of inanimate things looking animate. That's what I think science does to you if you really open yourself to it. It produces the opposite sensation of being settled. There's a picture of yourself that you recognize as yourself but which you are unable to take in and remain a human being. And you don't know what to do with it.

N: Why? What is it about the quantum picture that is most threatening?

A: It's not just the quantum picture. It's about the Newtonian picture too. It's the picture of us as machines. It's a picture of the world as a place that doesn't have meaning anymore.

N: That doesn't have emotion and empathy.

A: More than that. It just doesn't have meaning. It's not about anything. It's just these balls knocking into each other.

N: Is it close to existentialism?

A: There is this—Heidegger talks about what is usually translated into English as anxiety. Which he thinks is the most philosophically interesting state to be in and in which, according to him, you come directly into contact with the groundlessness of being. And yeah I think that's what you get from science. You know, there's a beautiful little essay by Walter Benjamin called "Notes on Kafka." There's a long essay on Kafka which is less interesting. Look at it if you have a chance. Where he says I know Kafka's about a lot of stuff. It's about bureaucracy and it's about this and about that, but I think it's also about the attempt to inject the picture of the world that we get from modern physics. And it's an incredibly beautiful essay. *[Suggests a book by Arthur Eddington called* The Nature of the Physical World.*]* Benjamin in this essay quotes a long paragraph from Eddington and says, "Look, I've never seen anything in literature that is as Kafkaesque as this passage from Eddington about what the act of walking into a room looks like from the perspective of our microscopic understanding of the physical world." And I think he's absolutely right. If you want to know the literary equivalent of reading physics, I would point to Kafka or to Beckett or to something like that. That's what it feels like to really try to imagine the world as it is as it's being depicted in physics.

N: T. S. Eliot? Before he became Anglo-Catholic?

A: I'm very interested in Eliot. Eliot strikes me as a complicated case. First of all I'm much more interested in Eliot after he became Catholic. I think "Wasteland" is a wonderful poem, but it now looks like it was mostly written by Ezra Pound.... The one academic piece that I read about *Lost Highway* which I thought was really interesting but completely misses the points we're talking about is the Žižek—*(Further discussion of Žižek's misunderstanding of* Lost Highway.*)*

N: Can we talk about *What the Bleep?* There is someone, I don't remember who, who says: "Why does quantum mechanics matter?" And this is what he answers: (paraphrase) "It infiltrates the world of electronics. Why are philosophers passionate about the deconstruction of the assumptions of the world? Quantum mechanics explains it. From the point of view of classical mechanics, we are machines. No conscious experience. Doesn't matter if we die. But quantum says organism. And that kind of environment has a different impact on how we conduct morals and ethics."

And what I really want from you is how he arrives at this. It is so totally different from what you said. So he's got a happy mean. But how did he do it?

A:  I'm a little conflicted. I want to give you honest answers. But I'm aware that what I honestly think is right is infected by my own opinion.

N:  But I am aware too.

A:  So look. So let me tell you a little more about my own orientation. Throughout most of the twentieth century, and this is why I'm writing the kind of book I just described myself as writing. At the end of the nineteenth century, phys-ics had tremendously megalomaniacal aspirations. It was going to explain everything. Psychology, what's psychology? It's just billiard balls bumping into each other. It may be complicated, but in principle it [quantum mechan-ics] can explain everything. That's all there is. This produced in all sorts of people romanticism.

N:  Except romanticism was so much earlier.

A:  But it was after Newton. This produces a very, very deep kind of panic. Very deep feeling that the dignity of being a human being is degraded.

N:  And probably in me.

A:  And me too. So, along comes quantum mechanics. Quantum mechanics was read very widely throughout most of the twentieth century that the previous aspirations of physics were naive and wildly overblown.

N:  Does this have a connection with the objective viewer?

A:  Sure. The collapse of that was the central feature. The fantasies we had about the depth to which the scientific imagination was going to penetrate were exaggerated and naive, and quaint and silly. The natural world, just rocks, turned out to have more mysterious objects than we could have dreamed. Even in looking at a rock, and this is so amazing, the scientific imagination, in a certain way, reaches its limit. And there was always going to have to be this question of the observer standing outside of the thing. And the observer was never going to be able to be incorporated into the physical picture of the world. Of what was being observed. Blah, blah, blah. You had all this coming from people like Bohr and Heisenberg and so on. This was welcome news in all parts of the culture to which science was a threat unnerving. The mega-lomaniac aspirations of science were a threat. Just billiard balls. *[Speculates on the connection between the skepticism about the observer and skepticism about naturalistic narrative which dovetails with my recent thinking about the connection between physics and the development of western narrative.]* The one person who resisted was Einstein.

N: Sweet little Albert?

A: The way Einstein got to be sweet little Albert. Because this is not the way he was. He was this very unruly, sophisticated, Bohemian, ironic, complicated person.

N: That makes more sense.

A: When he was an old man, there were political reasons, cultural reasons, his sympathy with the left, and this was in the fifties and so forth. There were all kinds of reasons he had to be presented to the American public as an otherworldly teddy bear. Among the reasons was that he wasn't getting on board with quantum mechanics. That was the reactionary holdout for the nineteenth-century megalomaniacal aspirations.

N: The unified field theory.

A: Not just the unified field theory but there had to be an understandable mechanical picture at the bottom. Einstein was insisting on this. It's amazing that someone whom everyone acknowledged is the greatest genius since Newton at the end of his life got relegated to this position of a harmless eccentric or a cute eccentric. Now, this all by way of telling you where I am. In the past twenty years or so there's been a small group of people roughly my age who looked again more dispassionately than before at Einstein's argument. And who said, "Look this guy is right." And in combination with things like Bohm's theory . . . , so the thrust of my work and the work of people I respect in this field have been saying, "You know what? Quantum mechanics can be understood in a way that makes it much more continuous with mechanical pictures of the world, with these megalomaniacal aspirations of physics than has been thought through most of the 20th century." And I always thought the interesting project was. . . I always wanted science to be as scary as possible. And as destabilizing as possible. Yes, all this stuff about superposition, all this stuff about the impossibility of objective observation seemed to leave more of a space than there was in earlier mechanical pictures of the world—

N: What did it leave a space for?

A: For meaning, for humanness. For a special role for human beings. For a special role for consciousness. It argued that the world can't be understood as a machine. So, that's what's going on there. So no doubt, to the extent that Lynch is grappling onto quantum mechanics—

N: But what could be more frightening, more destabilizing than *Lost Highway*?

A: That's true . . . . That's why it's lost. It's not connected. You can't get to the highway from anyplace else and you can't get anyplace else from the highway. And this is exactly the causal structure he's playing with. I remember the first time I saw the movie, at the beginning of the movie when Robert Blake makes the phone call to himself—this is exactly what you're trained to expect in what are called closed time-like loops.

## MANY WORLDS / MANY MINDS

N: I'd like to talk about many minds theory.

A: Actually, you're talking to the originator of the many minds theory. One of the co-originators. It's one response to that *[loss of objective observer]* I actually think it's a preposterous response.

Even at the time, I didn't mean it seriously. It was meant to show that a theory with a certain set of properties isn't a logical possibility. It was as if to say, well, here's a way you could do it.

N: A sort of reducto ad absurdum?

A: In a way. It was a response to various debates that were going on at the time, which was about twenty-five years ago.

N: So many minds theory is not the only way you can go once you abolish the objective observer.

A: No, there are several ways to go that are available. There's Bohm's theory. There's theories about the collapse of the wave function. And there are these theories in the so-called many worlds of the Everettian tradition, of which there are a number, one of which is this many minds theory.

We don't know yet which of those is right. Various of these ways make very slightly different experimental predictions. But the experiments in question are very, very technically difficult. We're probably not going to be able to do them for quite a while.

[NOTE: The many worlds theory is an interpretation of quantum mechanics originated by Hugh Everett III, a graduate student working with John Wheeler at Princeton. It's a radical approach that uses neither collapsing wave functions nor observer knowledge. It proposes a deceptively simple alternative: the wave function never collapses. Instead, at every occasion where a quantum event has more than one outcome (e.g., when an electron may strike one atom or another), the universe splits. We have one universe where the electron hits atom A, another where it hits atom B, and so on for all of the possible outcomes. Similarly, if a light photon might be transmitted or reflected, if a radioactive atom might decay or not, the universe splits into alternative worlds, with one new universe for each and every potential outcome. This is the many worlds (MW) interpretation. From the

MW viewpoint, the universe is like a tree that branches and re-branches into myriads of new sub-branches with every passing picosecond. And each of these new branch universes has a slightly different subatomic "history." Because an observer happens to have followed one particular path through the diverging branches of this Universe-Tree, he never perceives the splitting. Instead he interprets the resolution of the myriad of possibilities into one particular outcome as a Copenhagen-style collapse. But the observer plays no active role in the splitting. Events at the quantum level, of course, must lead to consequences in the everyday world. There should be a MW universe in which every physically possible event has happened. There should be MW universes where the dinosaurs dominate the planet . . . Even as you read this sentence your universe may be fragmenting into a number of branches too large to count. . . .]

N: When you demolish the passive, the objective observer, and add superposition and non-locality you make it possible to say, at least from someone's point of view, okay, there's something other than mechanism, possibility, non-rationality or consciousness, which is not mechanism. So that's how they come to the conclusion that quantum mechanics is the savior of—

A: The cold, bad mechanistic images of the world. Right, right.

INFORMATION

N: And now I'm going to quote from John Hagelin: "Quantum mechanics is the play and display of *information and potentiality*, waves of potential electrons." Yes?

A: No. I'm not even sure how to—there isn't so much a thesis here but a smorgasbord of words that have come up in these discussions. I don't know how to say the statement you've just quoted me is right or wrong. I don't understand what it's supposed to mean. He's playing with words. Among the silly things people have said about quantum mechanics is that it shows that potentiality is part of the—so I don't know how to respond to it. It's a salad of various terms that have come up in the discourse strung together in a minimally grammatical way.

N: I don't know whom I quoting here: "The world isn't made primarily of stuff. It is primarily empty. But in the fundamental level of space/time geometry there is fundamental information, the Planck scale. The information has been there since the beginning of the universe."

A: I don't know what this means. I'm a regular guy and as far as I know information is something in books or people's heads. I don't know what this means. Some people want to say the world is made of information. Now it seems to me that the right question to ask is the naive question. Information about what? That's why I say it's not quite grammatical. When you say the world is made of information. Information is not the kind of thing that things can be made of. Information is about things. It's not the constituent of things. Now of course they're saying it exactly for that reason because it sounds weird, I don't know what it's supposed to mean. But you're right in saying, look you want to trace to someplace, it has to do with the collapse of the fantasy of the objective observer.

## PARTICLES AND HUMAN BEINGS

N: Quantum behavior that is true of particles can't be true of human beings, can it?

A: Well, human beings are presumably made of particles.

N: Human beings are made of particles. But basically, as I understand this, the circumstances within which human beings act have little to do with the particle theory so that to apply it to human action is to anthropomorphize the particles.

A: No, I don't know why you say that. Nobody doubts that cars are made of particles—

N: No, let me finish what I'm saying. When Lynch puts two human beings in superposition.

A: Oh, I see what you're saying.

N: He's taking precisely, exactly what the particle theories are not about and applying it to the human condition.

A: Well, yes and no. Look if quantum mechanics is right it entails among other things that not only individual particles but tables and chairs and human beings could in principle be in a superposition. Now there are all kinds of reasons why this doesn't happen under ordinary circumstances. And it's part of quantum mechanics' job to explain why this doesn't happen under ordinary circumstances. And quantum mechanics does provide an explanation. So, yes.

N: Could I understand [those reasons]?

A: It all has to do with how we interact with our environment. There's a whole theory about this called decoherence. Which is the business of explaining how classical-looking phenomena arise under the appropriate circumstances from an underlying quantum mechanical set of laws. In some sense you're right. Quantum mechanics doesn't predict that this would happen to people because of the way that they interact with their environment. In another sense, though, it does in theory predict that if people were put into the right circumstances that would happen.

N: That becomes extremely interesting within the context of my book. It does happen in Lynch when people are in crisis, so they are in certain circumstances.

A: Those wouldn't be the right circumstances, but they could be taken to be metaphors for the right circumstances.

N: It could even be pushed further, but I don't know about that yet.

A: Good.

## SECOND MEETING, FEBRUARY 12, 2010

Post-Bohr Reaction

A: The way quantum mechanics developed the first reaction to it under Bohr was the most radical. And Bohr made all sorts of announcements that what we had learned from the study of subatomic particles was that ordinary notions of reality and so on and so forth had just fallen apart. That even the notion that there is an external world out there before we look in the first place had collapsed. And it's only very recently that people have begun to say—

N: And this is your generation.

A: And this is my generation. We believe that Bohr may have been premature. He may have jumped to conclusions. Maybe we just have to think a little harder about whether this is really compatible with there having been a world out there all along. So it's been a funny kind of evolution. The young Turks of the field have been accusing Bohr of having flown off the handle. So what you're talking about there is aptly characterizing Bohr's picture, which for most of the twentieth century even up to today remains the dominant way of thinking about quantum mechanics. But its hold is weakening as time goes by. People are saying he didn't think hard enough. There's a way of understanding the phenomenon that's compatible with there having been a world out there before we looked. All these things are strange, mind you. There is this nice phrase, which I think was originally about quantum mechanics. I don't know whose phrase it is. That it's beginning to look as if the world is not only stranger than we know, but stranger than we can know. It's not enough to say that the world is strange. It's something that absolutely eludes all of our existing mechanisms in language for getting any kind of conceptual hold on the world at all.

N: And you don't agree with that?

A: I don't agree with that. I think that it turned out to be very premature. Indeed, it's strange. There's non-locality and so on and so forth. But there's much more hope of getting a handle on it than Bohr taught us there was.

## QUANTUM MECHANICS, BUDDHISM, AND PHILOSOPHY

N:  This is from *Bleep*. I don't remember who said it. You're never born and you're never going to die in a quantum universe. The reason that I'm asking is that I relate those words to things that I see at the end of Lynch's films. For example, at the end of *Elephant Man*, a woman's voice says, "Never, Never. Nothing will die. The stream flows. The wind blows. The cloud fleets. The heart beats. Nothing will die." And at the end of *Fire Walk with Me*, the horribly violated girl rises in the Red Room. Nothing will die. Because you were right. I tried to qualify you last time, but you were right. He is not frightened by what he sees. And you have to give him that he sees it in all its complexity and he's still not scared. You're saying, well, 'this is a frightening thing. Very uncomfortable.' And somehow it's not scaring him. There's resurrection. Let me put it that way. At the end of *Mulholland Dr.* the dead girls rise. And the baby in *Eraserhead*, it seems like it doesn't die, it becomes energy or something like that. So when I read this in *Bleep* . . .

A:  . . . It doesn't sound like anything that's a sort of intellectually interesting view of quantum mechanics.

N:  OK. Now, where this leads me in our conversation is to your sense that . . . You don't read out vision. You say Buddhism is here and quantum mechanics is here and you can't find quantum mechanics in Buddhism.

A:  Right, right.

N:  But I thought you said that isn't to say that Buddhism isn't interesting.

A:  I'm interested in lots of religious traditions. But it shouldn't be my view of these things that should be important to you. Here is what I think is interesting about science in a very broad way, and that's why I don't like attempts to amalgamate science and mysticism. Science is this thing that threatens to eat everything. To make everything mechanical, to make everything into a robot. It's something really, really scary about that.

N:  May I interrupt you? I know this is important to you, but I've heard you. And I really did hear you. But what I'm playing with here, and I think it's inescapable, that he really does think, he's fusing—I think what Lynch is doing in his movies is he has got this incredible intuition insight into the double vision that we've been talking about. And he doesn't want to be frightened by it and so he fuses it himself with something mystical, and I think it's probably my job to say what tradition he's fusing it with . . .

A:  Well, you what? When you were saying in quantum mechanics things are also their opposites you know what went through my mind was Augustine. There's this beautiful phrase in Augustine, very intentionally mysterious phrase. Where he's lamenting to God, "O I'm far from you in this region of unlikeness." And even in the Latin, I'm told, the phrase is awkwardly ungrammatical. The right reading of Augustine—here's an example of my respect for religious traditions. I adore Augustine.

N: Really? He doesn't like women.

A: Oh, I don't like him as a person. He's the most unpleasant person in the world. But I think he's a really interesting, smart guy. What it means in the context of Augustine's thoughts is that God is the ground of all things. What does region of unlikeness mean? What is it that things are unlike? I think the correct answer is, "themselves." Things are unlike themselves here far from God. Things only become entirely themselves at home in God. This is what came to my mind when you were talking about things being their opposite.

N: And how does this overlap with quantum mechanics?

A: Only metaphorically. But look, someone like Lynch it seems to me—There's a delicate thing here. If what Lynch gets out of quantum mechanics, OK he's wrong about this, he's wrong about that. But if what he's getting out of quantum mechanics is a reinforcement of his own innate sense that you go underneath things and things look utterly different than they do in the every day. Which is of course a deep sense that he has. And if all he's getting out of quantum mechanics is yes that's what I mean, they're seeing that too that you go underneath things and things look really strange, really, really different and all the stuff that normally holds together our cognitive processes for dealing with the world falls apart, that's great!! And he doesn't need to be right about this detail or that detail, but he's using it as a way to feel out this very deep intuition that he carries around in himself and that he sees in mystical traditions and so on and so forth. That you go behind, you go underneath and it turns out that everything is utterly different.

N: Yes, I agree with you. The other thing is what I'm hoping to find out when I see him is to what extent he is finding anything in quantum mechanics and to what extent it's in the air and he's breathing it. And that's good too. What I'm finding is that all of this is opening Lynch wide in ways that were closed to me before. Including, I think I'm going to talk about decoherence in terms of *The Straight Story*. What gets taken away in order for there to be harmony.

A: That's a great idea . . . There's a nice phrase in the philosophy of science. There's no logic of discovery. Bohr came up with his atomic model because he had a dream that he was standing in the sun and the planets were going around him. And he woke up and said maybe atoms are like this. I don't care. I don't care where it comes from. Whatever Lynch is doing to produce what he produces is fine with me.

WATCHING *INLAND EMPIRE*

A: There's a painting by *[Ludwig]* Wittgenstein that shows one of these etchings of which you've seen many examples. The famous one is the vase and the faces. You can see it as two faces or you can see it as a vase. There's a famous duck/rabbit example like this that Wittgenstein uses where there's a head and two long things coming out of it and you can see it either as the beak of a duck or the ears of a rabbit. And there's something enormously poignant and serious going on among these rabbits in this room but it's being filmed like a sitcom and the audience doesn't appreciate that and is laughing at completely inappropriate moments. And their response is so different from the response of the prostitute who is watching it on TV, weeping.

So first of all there's something very poignant about something terribly serious going on that doesn't manage to quite formulate itself explicitly that many of the witnesses to it don't understand at all. And that's being seen as a duck or a rabbit, you know, as the opposite of what it is. Different people are looking at it and seeing very different things. As in the duck/rabbit.

N: But she does see something poignant.

A: She sees something poignant. She's the one who understands it. The audience doesn't. We're sort of in the middle. We don't understand exactly what she's crying about. But we understand that the canned laughter is inappropriate. And the music is a cue to us that something terribly serious is going on. Something very sad. Not clear what. Something mournful and filled with ideas of doom. I found it enormously poignant.

N: You actually feel it?

A: Yes, very much.

N: So seeing three people dressed as rabbits doesn't create a tension between a sense of the absurd and an emotion of sadness?

A: Yes, it does, but it's this—I don't know why they're behaving—I don't know how to put it. It creates a tension, but the upshot of the tension isn't comedy. It's this feeling that I don't know entirely what's going on. What's going on is a little bit outside of my ken. But that it's something very serious and that's the feeling I get.

*[going forward]*

N: There are two spaces at the beginning. There's the rabbit space—well actually there are more than two spaces, there are three spaces. There's the rabbit space, there's the hotel room in an old Baltic hotel. There's the record player. The beam of life. Then there's the obviously cheap set where the rabbits are. And there's this incredibly old European. So the spaces are contiguous, some of them not—

A: Right, but as the rabbit enters the fancy space—

N: And there's this whole business about him being there and not being there.

A: Right. The light comes up and then he's gone.

N: And then he comes back, the light goes down. . . . So was he there all along?

A: It's certainly easy to read this quantum mechanically.

N: Reads in connection with this: *The denial of absolute simultaneity is intimately connected with denial of absolute velocity; knowledge of absolute velocity would enable us to assert that certain events in the past or future occur Here but not Now; knowledge of absolute simultaneity would tell us that certain events occur Now but not Here* (Eddington).

Does that seem to have something to do with these spaces or not?

A: I mean, it has to do at least in the sense of our standard understanding of these relationships coming apart. In a more particular way than that I'm not sure. But yes, it certainly has to do with taking these ideas in that space is not what we thought it was. That time is not what we thought it was. That is, it feels more in Lynch like the focus is on what it's like to relinquish the old ideas rather than the positive content of what it's like to adopt the new ones.

N: The movement among two patently different spaces seems to make me think of entanglement. Things are happening—

A: That's nice.

N: I don't know where to go exactly with that. But I will know. It's a matter of time.

*[go further with film]*

N: *[about the visitor talking with Nikki]* But what's interesting is that the visitor knows more about Nikki than Nikki knows about the visitor.

A: Right, right.

N: Like the Visitor is entering Nikki's world and the next thing that happens is Nikki enters the Visitor's world. But that's an interesting dynamic. That doesn't necessarily seem to be mirrored in the notion of the double vision because it gives more power to the quantum vision, would you agree with that?

A: Yes.

N: What do you see there?

A: You know, there's this: I mean if I remember there's just this. I mean I completely agree. Here in this house we're dealing with a Newtonian vision. It gets radically destabilized by this woman.

N: But she has come to do it. It is not happening by accident. And the greater power of the quantum reality is interesting.

A: They're not on a par. Like we were saying last time we met, the quantum reality is the fundamental one. That's certainly the way quantum mechanics is presented. The Newtonian world is a set of appearances that quantum mechanics can produce under certain circumstances.

N: Is what you're saying to me that the quantum reality is not a set of appearances, but that the Newtonian world is a set of appearances?

A: Yes, yes. The way quantum mechanics is intended to be understood is as the single universal fundamental theory of the world. Newtonian appearances are a way that the quantum world can behave under certain circumstances. But it's still the quantum world.

N: Is there a link between what culture produces and the Newtonian world?

DECOHERENCE

A: No, what produces it is decoherence and stuff like that. That's how we get the Newtonian world out of the quantum world. But the Newtonian world is very much you know—in people like Heidegger and Kierkegaard and so on you have this big lie which is the lie of the "they." And that's how one can very much see the Newtonian world as the big lie.

N: What seems to me is as we've been discussing it and as everyone discusses it, the quantum world is there, that the appearances that are created under certain circumstances are a matter of removing possibilities. But it doesn't happen by itself. It is a thing that human beings produce. They don't produce the quantum world, but they seem to produce. . . . How else could it happen?

A: No. Like you were saying, it's the phenomenon of decoherence.

N: And decoherence suddenly under certain conditions—

A: Yes. One of the ways that decoherence can happen and this is very much . . . Here's a way to produce decoherence: flood an area with light. That's what happened to the rabbits.

N: Doesn't that sound like Genesis?

A: Sure.

N: The world is flooded with light and suddenly there are these other things. That we didn't see before.

A: Absolutely right.

N: So, the beginning of Genesis is decoherence.

A: That's nice.

N: And it is beyond us. It is not a cultural "they."

A: What's not a cultural "they"?

N: The sudden appearance of creation.

A: Right. Not in quantum mechanics. Decoherence certainly could be used as a metaphor for the cultural "they."

N: Yes, sure, of course.

A: But it's not in any literal sense.

N: *[Refers to William Blake]* So, what he sees is that Nobodaddy dividing up the world geometrically—so that is a distinction between Blake, who certainly sees the unified field but calls it Christ, and what you're saying is that although we can talk about cultural creation of appearances that are Newtonian in character—the mills of industry and things like that—there's something even preceding that.

A: But look it's not the kind of thing you would expect from physics that the culture is what gives rise to the world. It's certain physical circumstances under which things behave Newtonian. And the name of those physical circumstances is decoherence. And what you mean by decoherence is those circumstances in which the environment is peculiarly sensitive to certain features of the physical systems. That is, one way to produce decoherence is to flood the situation with light.

N: That's what the Bible is talking about. That the flooding of light is not a human-produced phenomenon. At certain points, things swerve. This whole thing about flooding things with light is very prevalent in Lynch so now I have a whole new view of it. Good, good. Is there anything else that can cause decreation [decoherence] aside from flooding with light?

A: Yes, flooding the environment with anything that's sensitive to the position of macroscopic objects. If you flood it with dense air. If you flood it with water. Fire not so much. Light is most vivid in that way. It clarifies where things are. And it's by doing something like that that you can impose decoherence.

*[more viewing of Inland Empire, the scene between Nikki and Visitor #1]*

N: How do you react to the folktale?

A: Just that there's something mysterious and menacing about this woman. You could, you know when they do these double slit experiments, these interference experiments, they typically use something like a beam splitter, you pass a ray of light through this beam splitter. Half of it goes through, half of it gets reflected along another path and then they come together and interfere with one another and then you can measure these interference phenomena. I think the story of the boy may be you know and also the story of the girl, there's another way the alley in the back. I suppose you could have these things going through my mind.

N: Well here's what triggered me. Doorway. Reflection. Behind the marketplace. Not in the marketplace, you see that don't you? But evil was born. Why? Is she a reliable person? Do you have any thoughts?

A: No. There's something menacing and interesting and there's something that she knows. There's other evidence like in *Lost Highway* that Lynch is interested in these closed time-like loops that come up in general relativity. In circumstances like that, tomorrow may be among the things you're remembering today. And you have a guilt for something that's going to happen. There is a sense in which this different structure of causation, this loop structure of causation rather than the linear structure of causation that you get with these closed time-like loops; it reminds you of that. Once again this is kind of free association, we need a lot more support from the film—

N: No doubt.

A: —to make something of it, but I felt sure in *Lost Highway* that Lynch had heard about these closed time-like loops.

N: Now I know that Bohr said that quantum mechanics exploded the whole notion of causality.

A: Yes, that's right.

N: So could you tell me a little bit more about that?

A: First of all, the fundamental laws of quantum mechanics appear to be probabilistic rather than deterministic. So, if you say, "Why did the radium decay at just that moment?" there's literally going to be no reason in the way the world was prior to that. Why it decayed at just that moment. There was a certain probability of it decaying at just that moment, there was a certain probability of it decaying at another moment. And that's the moment it decayed. Then if you asked for the reason it decayed at that moment rather than the other moment, there is no answer.

N: If Newtonian physics dealt with a physical problem, it would say . . .

A: It would say here's what—it's a completely deterministic theory.

N: There's a linear progress of events that led to this.

A: That's right. That's one way in which causality breaks down in quantum mechanics. Then there's a breakdown of the kind of causality we're used to of a different kind in general relativity. Where things cause one another in a loop rather than in a line. There are certain circumstances in which a causal sequence of events proceeds in a circle rather than in a line. So if you ask what caused the first event, the answer is the last one. And if you asked what caused the last event, the answer is the first one.

N: I think we've done this before but I think I need a refresher.

A: Remember the example we went through of the gun and the box?

N: Yes, yes.

A: So you say what caused the bullet just to graze the edge of the plate? The answer is the fact that the shield came down late. What caused the shield to come down late? The fact that the bullet just grazed the edge. What caused A? B. What caused B? A.

N: Tautology.

A: Not quite a tautology. But they cause one another in a circle. This is a perfectly logically coherent causal structure. In relativity. It's an alternate to the linear structure that we're used to.

N: Then maybe we'll go forward to the moment when they hear something at the back of the set during the script reading. Then later we see it's her and she knows it. [*Inland Empire*]

N: [*RE: Mulholland Dr.*] At the beginning the first thing we see is a great deal of activity with no context.

A: Right, right.

N: And double figures. And then smoke that turns into a flood of light which now has a new meaning for me.

A: Right, right.

N: And her coming out of the light. I mean it's not like I know what I'm going to do, not like I'm sitting here waiting for you to—

A: Sure, sure—

N: And then it seems to me what I've been thinking lately, in line with very much what you've been saying about what's on top and what's on bottom, the Newtonian view is the high-angle shot, the big picture, the macro picture, and you get a lot of macro pictures in this movie, but you also get she's under the cabinet.

A: You're saying what I would say.

N: But nothing else?

A: No.

    [*the scene at Winkie's about the dream*]

A: There is this haunting notion [*in the dream*] of something else going on behind or underneath.

N: That notion is prevalent in *Mulholland Dr.* Think of Mr. Roque, the mysterious force behind studio politics. To create him, Michael J. Anderson, who is a small person, is put into a huge, false body and lives in a vacuum. What's behind, under, on top of all this? I don't know, I have to think about it. Mr. Roque's construction also suggests that what's behind appearances is death-dealing—

A: Right, right. You can't go on with ordinary life.

N: We've done so much good work, I don't want to push it. Any wrap-up thoughts? What about the excremental nature of the strange figure in the dream behind Winkie's? [He says maybe he'll follow up on that later. As I typed up the conversation, it occurred to me that excrement is inside, usually, but here outside.] Thank you.

# NOTES

## PREFACE

1. Herewith a brief overview of Lynch criticism to date. With his Freudian readings in *David Lynch*, translated by Robert Julian (BFI, 1995), Michel Chion published the first book to apply a psychological theory to David Lynch's art and initiated the "what lies beneath" tradition of Lynch criticism. Chion brought out a second edition in 2008 that extends his approach to the films that had not yet been made when he wrote his first edition. There are also two prominent Lacanian book-length studies of Lynch's films: Slavoj Žižek, *The Art of the Ridiculous Sublime: On David Lynch's Lost Highway* (Walter Chapin Simpson Center for the Humanities/ University of Washington Press, 2000); and Todd McGowan, *The Impossible David Lynch* (Columbia University Press, 2007). My book, *The Passion of David Lynch: Wild at Heart in Hollywood* (University of Texas Press, 1997), was an attempt to move Lynch criticism more into line with Lynch's worldview by presenting Jungian thought as a vision much more sympathetic than Freudian theory to the way Lynch understands life. I also intended to release Lynch from the grip of interpretations overly influenced by literary criticism and social science, which blocked engagement with Lynch's cinema rather than enabling it. Other early approaches to Lynch that have omitted reference to the crucial role of the material world in his cinema and television are: Kenneth C. Kaleta, *David Lynch* (Twayne Publishers, 1992); John Alexander, *David Lynch* (Charles Letts, 1993). Kaleta and Alexander were two of the first critics to publish books in English about Lynch; they primarily took a genre criticism approach to his cinema.

Diverse critiques that were neither psychological nor focused on genre have been published by Fredric Jameson, "Nostalgia for the Present," *The South Atlantic Quarterly* 88 no.2 (Spring 1989): 517–537; Jeff Johnson, *Pervert in the Pulpit: Morality in the Works of David Lynch* (McFarland & Company, 2004); Eric G. Wilson, *The Strange World of David Lynch: Transcendental Irony From Eraserhead to Mulholland Dr.* (Continuum, 2007). Jameson approaches Lynch from a disapproving sociological point of view, castigating him for not taking a stand against the drug dealers depicted in *Blue Velvet*; and Johnson examines his work from a moralizing quasi-political point of view that defines Lynch as an ultra-conservative whose films descend into chaos. Both Jameson and Johnson have imposed on Lynch's art almost laughably irrelevant ideas. Wilson, on the other hand, approaches Lynch from a perspective inflected by the gnostic and American literary traditions; he recognizes the importance of what exists "beyond" in Lynch's films. Acting on a valid intuition of the "beyond" in Lynch, Wilson references other frameworks that resemble in part the Vedas that actually are the texts on which Lynch anchors his mysticism. Greg Olson, *David Lynch: Beautiful Dark* (Scarecrow Press, 2008), and Allister Mactaggart, *The Film Paintings of David Lynch: Challenging Film Theory* (Intellect Ltd, 2010) are more recent entries into the field. Olson's book is primarily an extensively documented biography saturated with a personal affection for its subject; Mactaggart's book is a collage of highly personal responses to Lynch's films, beginning with Mactaggart's favorite scene in *Twin Peaks: Fire Walk with Me* as a jumping-off point and continuing with an array of eclectic allusions to genres, critics, poets, and other filmmakers of interest in whose works Mactaggart intuits correspondences with Lynch.

2. Todd McGowan begins *The Impossible David Lynch* with a fascinating discussion of the role of the observer with respect to art in general and Lynch's films in particular. This highly recommended introduction about the observer could have led McGowan to issues of quantum mechanics in Lynch's cinema, since the position of the observer is also a crucial issue in quantum mechanics. Instead McGowan turned the discussion toward psychology and a purely inner reality. McGowan uses Jacques Lacan's focus on desire to explain the way distance is constructed in Lynch's films, particularly the assertions Lacan makes about desire, fantasy, and human identity: it is only "through fantasy the subject is constituted as desiring." The strange quantum realities that McGowan misinterprets as fantasy in Lynch's films have led to a Lacanian misprision that Lynch is reproducing circumstances in which the real is only available when the characters (and spectators) view events from a distance provided by fantasy. McGowan's misuse of Lacanian postulates in his criticism makes for some interesting speculation, and, unfortunately, many distortions of Lynch's cinema. One particularly problematic aspect of McGowan's Lacanian position is his misinterpretation of the larger-than-life excesses of Lynch's villains as examples of what Lacan says about the excess of enjoyment that accompanies the fantasy nexus to the real. For example, McGowan reads the despicable Marietta Fortune (Diane Ladd) and her criminal associates in *Wild at Heart* as characters defined not by their depraved indifference to life, but their excessive enjoyment of living. To assert that *Wild At Heart* is a film that prizes intensity over ethics and humane behavior, as McGowan does, seriously misreads the film. As we shall see in the Introduction, and as is clear in the transcript of my interview with him in Appendix I, Lynch contextualizes his villains within a cosmic moral framework that extracts retribution, even if it takes another life for them to pay for their bad deeds. The ability of Lacanian theory to block perception of Lynch's work is clear when we consider that McGowan subscribes to a belief that Lynch cherishes the energy of his villains even after witnessing the horrible fate to which Marietta selfishly and stupidly abandons

her boyfriend Johnny Farragut (Harry Dean Stanton). There are similar problems with all of McGowan's readings of Lynch's larger-than-life villains, and no real rewards for accepting these perverse interpretations—except a logical consistency with one interpretation of the writings of Jacques Lacan.

3. Slavoj Žižek's *The Art of the Ridiculous Sublime* takes note of the Lacanian concept of the distance of the observer from *Lost Highway*. Žižek views this issue in extreme terms: "Lynch's *entire* [italics mine] 'ontology' . . . is based upon the discordance between reality observed from a safe distance and the absolute proximity of the real" (Žižek, *The Art of the Ridiculous Sublime*, p. ix). While Žižek is clearly sensitive to the phenomenon of different levels of space in Lynch's cinema, which I am referring to as macrovision and microvision, he has chosen a nonproductive intellectual framework within which to discuss it, since it is not distance that is at stake in Lynch's films; it's uncertainty. When Lynch's characters and the audience feel threatened and/or mystified as the film alternates between an ordinary view of space and a depiction of the quantum behavior of objects and bodies in time and space, all concerned are reacting to the shock of moving from a surface appearance of solidity to the uncertain physics of subatomic particle reality. And, because, like Todd McGowan, Žižek ignores whatever in Lynch's work does not support his Lacanian interpretation, the connections Žižek attempts to make at the end of his monograph about *Lost Highway* between what he sees in Lynch and a way of looking at twentieth-century totalitarian governments shed more heat than light.

4. In fact, Eric Wilson's approach to Lynch from the perspective of gnostic mysticism permits him an interestingly acute sensitivity to many aspects of Lynch's art, for example his attitude toward language and matter. Although Wilson's frame of reference does not permit him to go far enough in his analyses of Lynch's films, it does empower him to cast a very helpful light on Lynch's fear and distrust of words. Similarly, he uses to excellent advantage his intuition that Lynch is in sympathy with the gnostic tradition of envisioning the "the physical world as a stultifying illusion" (Wilson, *The Strange World of David Lynch*, p. 31). For anyone interested in a dialogue with a serious scholar about Lynch, Wilson's commentaries are well worth reading.

5. The traditions of Transcendental Meditation, which Lynch has practiced for almost 40 years, can be helpful for understanding the mind/body connection that is so essential to Lynch's worldview. For interested readers, I present an account of how TM instructors teach meditation. A Transcendental Meditation begins as one is sitting quietly and comfortably with closed eyes. The other primary instructions are to initiate a silent and internal repetition of an assigned mantra and continue it for twenty minutes. At the end of that time, the meditator is instructed to emerge gradually from the meditation over a period of several minutes. During the meditation, thoughts pass through the mind naturally. It is not assumed that the goal is to clear the mind of these thoughts, but rather

that the thoughts are an important release of bodily energy that is part of the process. It is assumed that it is not the content of the thoughts that is significant but rather the integration of mind and body that takes place as the meditator sits still, engaged in his or her mantra and allowing the thoughts to flow. During instruction, meditators are taught that after the mind dives into itself, beneath the level of conscious thought during Transcendental Meditation it is the body that will bring the mind back to the surface, as part of the necessary cycle of release and return. The physicality of the body is, thus, crucial to the dynamic of Transcendental Meditation, not a hindrance of any kind, let alone a necessary evil. Many who have had experience with other meditation practices will be surprised to learn that Transcendental Meditation instructors advise their students to make necessary physical adjustments while they are meditating—such as scratching itches and changing the position of the body if there is discomfort.

Although Lynch reports that his meditation is easy and satisfying, some meditators find that the force of the physical energy released during meditation makes the process uncomfortable, even, in some cases frightening. For very many meditators, the experience of doing nothing, which is pretty much what transcendental meditation involves, is alien to their "normal" stress-filled lives of nonstop activity directed toward some future goal, so that for a while at least the experience of living in the moment and simply being present is upsetting. This paradigm bears an interesting resemblance to the disconcerting experiences Lynchian protagonists must endure before they can achieve a sense of peace and stability.

6. The history of modern physics that I will tap into for the purposes of interpreting Lynch's work is not monolithic, nor will I employ it as though Lynch were a proponent of one school of physics or another. However, the reader may be interested in an overview of the competing perspectives on physics as part of her/his preparation for the journey we are now beginning. Modern physics can be narrated as the drama of a counterpoint between Danish physicist Niels Bohr (and those who share his theoretical assumptions) and German physicist Albert Einstein (and those who share his theoretical assumptions). Even after Einstein changed the course of science with his papers on the relative nature of time, he remained convinced that behind that manifestation was some as yet unknown truth about the material universe that would reaffirm unity and stability. Bohr, on the other hand, gradually became convinced of the fundamental lack of uncertainty in matter. As Bohr also grew to believe in the impossibility of objective observation, his school of modern physics increasingly evoked an uneasy world in which no absolute external reality exists apart from the gaze of the observer. Bohr was so disturbed by his findings that he remarked that, ". . . those who are not shocked when they come across quantum theory cannot possibly have understood it" (Kumar, p. 1). Einstein responded just as sharply, "It was as if the ground had been pulled out from under one, with no firm foundation to be seen

anywhere, upon which one could have built" (Kumar, p. 1). Einstein, however, refused to take quantum mechanics as the final word in physics. While Bohr's (ironic) certainty that uncertainty was the rule of the universe slowly became dogma in modern physics, until he died in 1955 Einstein tenaciously attempted to prove that quantum mechanics was only part of the truth. In 1944, he wrote to Max Born, one of Niels Bohr's circle, "You believe in the God who plays dice and I in complete law and order in a world which objectively exists, and which I, in a wildly speculative way, am trying to capture" (Kumar, p. 331). However, whatever proof of an objective world structured along absolute laws Einstein came up with, Bohr was able to punch holes in it. After Einstein's death, other physicists attempted to pick up where he left off.

In 1951, David Bohm seemed to be on the track of an experiment that would yield such proof. However, when he showed his work to Einstein, the latter wasn't impressed. His attempts to assert an objective reality were further set back by political circumstances unrelated to scientific rigor. Bohm fell under a cloud when he was accused of being a Communist at the height of Senator Joseph McCarthy's Cold War "witch hunts," after which, Princeton University severed ties with him, and he was stripped of his American citizenship. In the 1960s, however, Bohm's work came to the attention of John Stewart Bell, born in Northern Ireland, and Bell took up the cause of searching for unifying principles behind the quantum construction and behavior of particles. The ramifications of Bell's work are still being investigated, but, as yet, there is no definitive proof of the kind of objective law and order for which Einstein so longed. Moreover, it is essential to understand that the mainstream discipline of physics regards the only possible proof of a unified universe to be rigorous experimentation and does not find in mysticism an answer to the questions.

Lynch, on the other hand, has been influenced by Professor John Hagelin, a Harvard-trained, American-born physicist. Hagelin, although at first part of the community seeking answers through rigorous experimentation, left the mainstream of physics in 1984 when he terminated his appointment at Stanford University in California in order to accept an appointment at Maharishi International University in Fairfield, Iowa.

In 1987, Maharishi International University published Hagelin's monograph, titled, *Is Consciousness the Unified Field? A Field Theorist's Perspective*. In this monograph, Hagelin puts forth a cosmology employing his own constructions of string theory and other theories concerning the composition of matter. Hagelin's goal is to demonstrate that beyond the uncertainty of what we have been calling the "marketplace" there exists a consciousness at the core of being. Hagelin identifies this consciousness, which he calls the unified field, as the source of an essential order in the universe, His new theory relegates the uncertainty of quantum particle behavior—which Hagelin does not deny—to a partial aspect of the cosmos. Hagelin is the president of the David Lynch Foundation.

## INTRODUCTION

1. Manjit Kumar, "Uncertainty in Copenhagen," in *Quantum: Einstein, Bohr, and the Great Debate About the Nature of Reality* (W.W. Norton & Co., 2008), pp. 225–249. This chapter gives a reader friendly definition and history of Heisenberg's uncertainty principle.

2. The prelude to Henry's union with The Lady in the Radiator in *Eraserhead* is as powerful a visualization of a deliverance from the marketplace's grotesque illusions as one can imagine. Energy is released as electricity pours from the walls behind which it was formerly constrained, and the matter of which the Baby, his personal albatross, is composed, explodes. Henry is visualized in completely open space, surrounded by radiant, unorganized particles. It is, of course, possible to insist that with all the structure of his world in ruins he has nowhere to go but into his head. However, if we combine Lynch's interest in quantum mechanics with the sense of release—not trauma—that accompanies Henry's exit from a troubled existence into a blissful world of light and the Lady in the Radiator, the influence of quantum science on this film seems to be the more arguable position. Those readers interested in a deeper interpretation of the "baby" as one more illusion of the marketplace, not a literal baby, can refer to *The Passion of David Lynch: Wild at Heart in Hollywood* (University of Texas Press, 1997), pp. 151–152, 160–162.

3. Louisa Gilder, *The Age of Entanglement: When Quantum Physics was Reborn* (Vintage Books, 2009). Gilder provides a thorough, easy-to-read history of the development by quantum physicists of the concept of entanglement. She sets the stage for her discussion of entanglement by exploring the history of quantum mechanics, from 1905 until the present, in a way that offers a large, illuminating portrait of how entanglement fits into the big picture of modern physics. In addition, in the first three pages of Appendix II of this book, you will also find Professor David Z. Albert's extremely lucid description of the circumstances of entanglement.

4. In Appendix II, Professor Albert explains the mind-bending characteristics of particles in superposition. Superposition is generally associated with the paradoxes of a 1935 thought experiment by Erwin Schrödinger about a cat in a box, referred to as Schrödinger's Cat. Schrödinger was able to design a situation in which the cat was both alive and dead at the same time, multiple outcomes that depended on whether or not anyone opened the box (Kumar, pp 316–317).

5. Laura Miller, "'Quantum': When Science Got Spooky," www.salon.com (May 23, 2010). Miller's breezy, playful review of *Quantum*, by Manjit Kumar, which is itself a good popularizing text, demonstrates the penetration of public discourse by non-threatening versions of the rather distressing picture of the universe painted by more austere tracts on quantum mechanics. There is also Charles Seife, *Decoding the Universe: How the New Science of Information is Explaining Everything in the Cosmos from Our Brains to Black Holes* (Penguin, 2007), which takes the sting out of the crumbling of the once-solid Newtonian terrain of matter. The increasing

presence in popular discourse of Miller, Kumar, and Seife, among others, suggests that it will not be long before the subatomic level of matter is as much a subject for parlor talk as is Freud's Oedipus Complex.

6. Footnote 6 of the "Preface" to this book outlines the quantum physics sparring match between Albert Einstein and Niels Bohr. The full story can be found in Manjit Kumar, *Quantum: Einstein, Bohr, and the Great Debate about the Nature of Reality*. In 360 pages, Kumar gives a blow-by-blow account of the rivalry between physicists who expect to find a unifying principle somewhere in the universe and those who don't. At the back of his book, Kumar summarizes his history in an eleven-page time line and provides a thirteen-page glossary containing definitions of the major terms used by modern physicists.

7. Fred Alan Wolf, *Parallel Universes: The Search For Other Worlds* (Simon & Schuster, 1990). In this genial volume, Wolf, an experienced popularizer of hard science, attempts to put forth the "many worlds" theory as the answer to all the major questions posed by quantum mechanics. He usefully identifies those issues for laymen, but most hard-science theorists would insist that the unanswered questions associated with those remain unresolved. However, Wolf does thoroughly outline a theory that makes an interesting sidebar to analysis of Lynch's second-stage films. One of Wolf's more disarming expository tactics is to use witty quotations from unexpected sources on the subject of quantum mechanics. One of his best is from Woody Allen: "There's no question that there is an unseen world. The problem is how far is it from midtown and how late is it open?" (p. 17). Wolf includes a concise account of how Hugh Everett III, then a graduate student in physics at Princeton, came up with the many worlds theory to account for what happens to the endless possibilities for each particle assumed by quantum mechanics (pp. 38–39). He also quotes a statement by David Z. Albert, who was among the first physicists to ponder the "many worlds" theory, suggesting that many "worlds" is an overstatement and that the word "worlds" should be replaced by "points of view" (pp. 274–275).

8. Professor Arkady Plotnitsky has pointed out to me that unity is not necessarily the opposite of uncertainty. There are physicists who believe in a unified universe in which chance rules uniformly throughout. He has directed me toward the following passage in his book *Epistemology and Probability*:

*beginning with the pre-Socratics . . . , there emerged three main conceptions of ontology or reality, defined by this confrontation between chance and necessity or causality. The first ontology, the classical ontology of chance, as just considered, defines chance as only apparent or illusory, while at the ultimate level of reality necessity and order rule. The second ontology is, conversely, defined by the rule or un-rule of chance, which makes all necessity, causality, or order only apparent or illusory. This ontology may be called the Jocasta ontology, since it was arguably first, or in any event most powerfully, expressed by Jocasta, Oedipus's mother and wife in Oedipus the King: ". . . What should a man fear? It's all chance, chance rules our lives. Not a man on earth can see a day ahead, groping through the dark. Better to live at random, best we can" (ll. 1068–1072, Sophocles 1984, p. 215). This view is proved illusory in the play, since the lives of the play's characters are ultimately ruled by fate. However, this view was contemplated by the ancient Greeks. The third ontology is that of the interplay of chance and necessity, which appears to have been introduced by Democritus and developed his followers, such as Lucretius, as the atomist ontology of nature (p. 343).*

In other words, even when chance is in play in a significant way, there may be a unified structure to the universe. However, the Vedic view, to which Lynch inclines, does not admit random elements in the universe. Everything is part of a continuous connection among all elements in a unified cosmos.

9. Arthur I. Miller, *Insights of Genius: Imagery and Creativity in Science and Art* (MIT Press, 2000), p. 156. Miller nicely sums up the double vision of quantum physics, which recognizes that under certain circumstances, Newtonian physics still describes the way objects and bodies work in space: "... we can say that Newtonian mechanics has been superseded in the atomic domain by quantum mechanics and in the domain of high speeds by special relativity. From this we conclude that Newtonian physics has a radius of applicability, not that Newtonian mechanics is wrong or has been discontinued." The radius of applicability is to large objects and bodies and low speeds.

10. *The Tibetan Book of the Dead*, translated by Francesca Fremantle and Chögyam Trungpa (Shambhala, 1987), pp. 13–15. The entire book describes the Bardo between life and death. But these pages are particularly applicable to the transitions that take place in Lynch's films.

11. *Ibid*, pp. 40–42. Numerous passages on these pages are devoted to the many chances that the dying person is offered in the Bardo state for a successful passage from one life to another. There is also a description of the fear and confusion that may interrupt the passage. If the dying person has not been taught properly about the Bardo state he or she will be terrified and will wander in samsara, defined in the glossary as the "cycle of existence, based on ignorance and characterized by suffering." The alternative to samsara (which finds a rough equivalent in Lynch's vocabulary in the "marketplace") is liberation from the cycle of existence toward enlightenment (which in Lynch's cinema is roughly equivalent to "the Palace"). *The Tibetan Book of the Dead* is very specific about the relationship between fear and being locked in downward cycles that move the soul away from enlightenment. The following verse is intended to help us internalize the proper attitude in the transition between life and death: "Now when the bardo of dharmati dawns upon me/I will abandon all thoughts of fear and terror,/I will recognise [sic] whatever appears as my projection/and know it to be a vision of the bardo/now that I have reached this crucial point/I will not fear the powerful and wrathful ones, my own projections" (p. 40).

12. In *The Passion of David Lynch*, I discussed Lynch's cinema as an extension of the filmmaking traditions represented by Alfred Hitchcock and Orson Welles. I should

have included in that list Federico Fellini. As a partial correction of that omission, I include him here. If there are interesting intimations of uncertainty and quantum physics in *Rear Window*, there are equally interesting allusions to the shaken twentieth- century confidence about a solid world of things and bodies in works by Welles and Fellini. The fun house and hall of mirrors scenes in Welles' *The Lady From Shanghai* (1947) clearly reflect a sense of the instability of matter and question our ability to separate the observer from what is being observed. Similarly, Welles alludes to the uncertainty of bodies and things in space in the plot of *Citizen Kane* (1941), a failed attempt on the part of a journalist to unlock the secrets of the mind and heart of Charles Foster Kane through sifting evidence. In forcing the audience into the same position as the investigator, Welles's film involves us in the experience of the assertion of modern physics that the more closely we examine a phenomenon, the more confusing it becomes. We can say the same of the catastrophically failed attempt of journalist Marcello Rubini (Marcello Mastroianni) in Fellini's *La Dolce Vita* (1960) to understand the fragmented realities of post-World War II Rome, which includes the spectator in its final confusion and sorrow. None of these great filmmakers was ready to go as far as David Lynch has in his use of superposition, entanglement, and the "many worlds" theories, but much of what makes the above-mentioned films distinctive is their daring (for their time) challenge to the belief in clarity of perception and control over what we see that is the hallmark of Hollywood filmmaking.

13. As everyone "knows," sequels are made to exploit known successes through repetition, but I am tempted to believe that the two sequels to the original *Matrix* film were prompted as much by the obsessive urge generally demonstrated by popular culture to domesticate all reference to cutting-edge physics. Where popular culture has alluded to modern physics, it has generally found a way of disavowing the more frightening aspects of quantum realities as fantasies or appearances that can ultimately be explained. Much of the time this has meant presenting its mysteries as part of the content rather than creating fiction in which the determining shape of the rhetoric leaves us uncertain in any way. So *The X-Files* (1993–2002), which was ostensibly about incomprehensible occurrences, rarely took the chance of creating an episode in which the audience wasn't given the position of controlling observer, and when that did happen in the series, it took the form of comedy, as for example the funny episode 20 from season 3, "Jose Chung's From Outer Space," in which we are presented a set of events from multiple perspectives and literally do not know what happened when all is said and done. *The X-Files* never plunged us beneath the surface of social appearances to a level at which objects and bodies behaved like subatomic particles.

14. Allister Mactaggart, *The Film Paintings of David Lynch: Challenging Film Theory* (Intellect, 2010), p. 225.

15. We can see how crucial the "physics lesson" in the Red Room is to David Lynch if we compare the written script Mark Frost prepared for Episode 29 and the

actual show as it appeared on air, restructured and directed by Lynch. In Frost's original script, for most of the action, Dale Cooper's adversary is the towering, controlling figure of Windom Earle, who is extremely cerebral and poses mental challenges to Cooper as if he is playing chess with a number of pawns. Earle threatens Annie, Cooper's innocent girlfriend, in a cruel act of revenge against Cooper for his infidelity with Earle's wife Caroline. Finally, Earle is captured by BOB, who appears as a demonic dentist and tries to inject Cooper with some diabolical liquid when Laura appears to oppose him. This kind of fantasy was not at all the kind of series finale Lynch had in mind. In the on-screen episode, Cooper isn't involved in a traditional conflict with nasty villains. Lynch's script revisions caused the emphasis to be on the subatomic landscape of uncertainty in which they are all struggling: Cooper, Annie, even Earle, and BOB. Those interested in an extended discussion of Lynch's rejection of Frost's script for Episode 29 may wish to consult my article: "Desire Under the Douglas Firs: Entering the Body of Reality in *Twin Peaks*," *Film Quarterly*, vol. 46 (Winter 1992–1993), pp. 22–34.

16. In Lynch's pre–*Lost Highway* feature films, changes that resemble reincarnation take place only in *Eraserhead* and the *Twin Peaks* cycle. As in the second-stage films, in each of these cases the pertinent character moves into another state of life during a flurry of light and sound that is very much in the spirit of the Bardo state as described in *The Tibetan Book of the Dead*. In *Eraserhead*, the metamorphosis begins when Henry, marooned in his seedy apartment, furtively cuts the swaddling of the Baby and then stabs the innards exposed when the bandages are completely severed. On the soundtrack, we hear loud reverberating sound layered with wind and machine-like noises, and all the electricity in the room spontaneously flashes and then pours out of the wall sockets. Henry is backlit against the explosion of a sphere known as the planet, and a figure known as the Man in the Planet (Jack Fisk) throws a rusty switch as sparks shoot from it. Henry is out of his former site of misery; he has moved into a different level of existence, a place of misty brilliance, in which an eager and affectionate Lady in the Radiator is waiting to embrace him.

The possession of Agent Cooper by BOB and the murder of Laura Palmer at the end of *Twin Peaks: Fire Walk with Me* are also shot as Bardo states in which lights, sound, the appearance of strange figures, like the Little Man from Somewhere Else, mark the transition from one state of being to another. After Cooper receives the "physics lesson" discussed in this chapter, which demonstrates how one thing may be two or more things, Bardo-like flashing lights, intense sounds, and the demonic figure of BOB accompany Cooper as he loses his way in the Red Room, and discovers that it and all the characters in it are simultaneously two or more rather than only one. The discovery wounds him and leads to his final existence in the Red Room and in *Twin Peaks* as two rather than one. When this superposition is reflected in the mirror of his hotel room as he sees BOB instead of himself in its glass, we aren't sure whether, as the Log Lady said in her prologue, he was two all along and the reflection lets us see it, or whether he has split in the Red Room. Was the Bardo state Cooper's transformation or was it ours?

After Leland/BOB sets Laura, wrapped in plastic, adrift on the river near Twin Peaks, he walks into the Red Room through the circle of trees in Glastonbury Grove. Leland and BOB stand in superposition in the Red Room—one in two places—as their bodies and those of the Little Man defy gravity, the arrow of time (the direction in which events usually take place), and other classical rules of objects in space. When we see Laura, Agent Cooper, and Laura's angel in the same room where all these subatomic events have taken place, lights and music accompany their release into another cycle of life, clearly not samsara—back into the cycle of suffering—but toward enlightenment.

## CHAPTER 1

1. Wayne C. Booth, *The Rhetoric of Fiction* (The University of Chicago Press, 1961). Booth's is the standard of commentary on the unreliable narrator in fiction. He identifies unreliability as a highly complex quality in the point of view of a first person narrator, associating it with irony and distance from the norms of the author of the book. "Our terminology for this kind of distance in narrators [distance from authorial norms] is almost hopelessly inadequate. For lack of a better term, I have called a narrator reliable when he speaks or acts in accordance with the norms of the work (which is to say the implied author's norms), unreliable when he does not. . . . It is most often a matter of what [Henry] James calls *inconscience*; the narrator is mistaken, or he believes himself to have qualities which the author denies him. Or, as in *Huckleberry Finn*, the narrator claims to be naturally wicked while the author praises his virtues behind his back." (pp. 158-9). One clarification: since the arc of most narratives is the discovery of truths not known at the beginning of the story, a character may be reliable who is wrong at the beginning but who makes discoveries that bring him/her into line with the beliefs of the implied author. Unreliability is a matter of the character making the wrong discoveries continually as he/she moves through the narrative. An unreliable narrator may also be a deliberate liar. Unreliable narrators are deluded, deceitful, or mistaken from start to finish, or become increasingly wrong as they go along. Books with unreliable narrators call for highly active participation on the part of the reader, just as films built on an unreliable character's point of view require highly active spectatorship.

Of course, films do not usually have narrators, first person or otherwise, but generally contain a character through whose eyes we see the action. In *Lost Highway*, Fred Madison's is the point of view, but he operates at a distance from Lynchian norms, which Lynch tells us behind his back. Very many character points of view in Lynch's films are unreliable, and their unreliability tells us much about the shape of the universe by means of the limitations of the particular point of view. In Lynch's second stage films, we will find this to be the case with Alvin Straight (Richard Farnsworth) in *The Straight Story*, and Betty Elms/ Diane Selwyn (Naomi Watts) and Adam Kesher (Justin Theroux) in *Mulholland Dr.*, but we will not find it to be the case with Nikki Grace/Susan Blue (Laura Dern) in *Inland Empire*.

2. Lynch's belief that "the world is as you are" certainly suggests the ability of the individual consciousness to shape perceived reality, but it would be wrong to infer that Lynch would agree that all perceived realities are equally valid. As Lynch sees it, there is a unified field, the consciousness at the heart of being, the central reality of existence, that is the fount of love, creativity, and peace. To the extent that the character's point of view is able to access that universal power, it is in touch with reality and able to partake of positive energy. In the Lynchian worldview, if the individual consciousness is cut off from the unified field, it falls into negativity, delusion, and self-destructiveness. On its own, the individual consciousness does not create reality, although being in touch with reality permits all kinds of secondary creativity, like creating art, creating technology, creating food. In Lynch's second-stage films, with the exception of Nikki Grace in *Inland Empire*, all his protagonists are cut off from the unified field, with various consequences.

3. The transformation of Fred into Pete has been a source of confusion in all published criticism on *Lost Highway*. The confusion is caused by critical reluctance to regard this transformation as an external reality, or to recognize the existence of what Lynch portrays as very real responses to Fred's metamorphoses from the police and the courts and from Pete Dayton's parents. In fact, none of the critics whose ideas I am about to summarize deal at all with the actual presence of the Daytons, the detective, and the penal system in *Lost Highway*. The most convoluted and impressionistic attempt to avoid the complexities of the modern understanding of the physical world in which Fred/Pete exists is to be found in *The Art of the Ridiculous Sublime: On David Lynch's Lost Highway*, by Slavoj Žižek (Walter Chapin Simpson Center for the Humanities/University of Seattle, 2000). Žižek interprets the "two versions of the male hero," as he puts it, by wrestling with the question of whether he himself can identify which part of this transformation is fantasy, and which reality. To his credit, he arrives at the conclusion that this kind of polarization is pointless and reductive, but then goes on to assert that the most productive way to see Fred's metamorphosis is as a demonstration of the circularity of the psychoanalytic process. He states: "That is to say, a crucial ingredient of Lynch's universe is a phrase, a signifying chain, which resonates as Real that insists and always returns," as the film begins with the spoken words, "Dick Laurent is dead" and then ends with the death of Mr. Eddy (p. 17). Žižek then concludes that "the entire narrative of the film takes place in the suspension of time between these two moments" (p. 17). But is there really no motion of time in *Lost Highway*? It is possible to account for the

circularity of the phrase, "Dick Laurent is dead," in a way that is more reflective of what actually happens in Lynch's film. For example, we may say that time has a linear forward motion and at the same time a circular motion so that we are always returning to the "here" with more depth, if we use the vocabulary of modern physics as a referent. But Žižek is so caught up in Lacanian theory that he sees Fred only as an illustration of the Lacanian precept that one can never encounter his/her own reality. Oddly, Žižek also implies that some motion does take place. Because the sentence about Laurent is repeated, Žižek believes that Fred has made some progress in understanding himself, or as Žižek puts it, "in the end he is able to pronounce the symptom consciously as his own" (p. x). But how the second announcement of the death of Laurent implies that Fred understands himself better is not immediately clear, especially since as the film ends he is in the process of another upheaval that points toward a worsening, not an improvement, of his situation.

In their discussions of *Lost Highway*, most other critics, unlike Žižek, do opt for a polarized reading of reality versus fantasy in interpreting Fred's transformation into Pete. In *The Impossible David Lynch* (Columbia University Press, 2000), Todd McGowan reads Pete as Fred's fantasy escape from the tortures of desire. "Fantasy, though it is opposed to 'reality,' nonetheless provides an underlying support for our sense of reality. Without this support, we can no longer be sure of our bearing within the social reality—our sense of the meaningfulness of that reality" (p.155). McGowan's Lacanian belief that it is only through fantasy that human beings can know reality leads him away from Lynch's worldview of an open universe of unlimited possibility to a Lacanian interpretation of *Lost Highway* as a completely closed world in which Fred's assumption of a fantasy identity as Pete keeps him stuck within his head, replaying the same desires he had as Fred. Lacanian psychoanalytic theory also leads McGowan to an unexplored convolution. At the same time that McGowan asserts that fantasy is our only support for a meaningful sense of reality, he also asserts that in fantasy one "inevitably encounters the deadlock [the unsatisfying pursuit of desire] in a new form. One fantasizes oneself a different person, but the traumatic disruption of the 'impossible' object cause of desire—remains" (pp. 155–156). It is not immediately apparent how this repetition of the same compulsive desire enables us to maintain a connection with reality.

The polarities of fantasy and reality identified by Eric G. Wilson in *The Strange World of David Lynch* (Continuum, 2007) are to be understood within a theological tradition of discovery by negation. As Wilson puts it, "Such a quest requires us to reverse our traditional expectations. Instead of assuming that small insights lead to the great glimpse, one must conclude that large confusion concludes in sacred vision" (p. 112). Wilson's emphasis on confusion is understandable, since Lynch's protagonists, Fred Madison in particular, do manifest a great deal of confusion. And Lynch's use of the unreliable point of view might be interpreted as discovery by negation. But confusion in *Lost Highway* is a result of the obstacles put in Fred's way by the marketplace; it is not his means to enlightenment. And Fred's unreliability is founded in his illusory certainties. Unreliability is not a means of discovery, but the inverse. Wilson's misperception about how confusion works in Lynch's films leads him to misread Pete Dayton as a fantasy of freedom. "However, Fred is unable to hold for long [sic] this vision. It seems that he is forever doomed to repeat the same round of solipsism, transcendence, and the return to selfishness" (p. 114). Wilson's way of dealing with the circularity in the film is to imagine Pete as a clearly better option that eludes Fred, but that is a dubious conjecture. Pete is just as confused and locked into compulsion Fred is. Moreover, since all this confusion makes it impossible for Fred to see the limitlessness of the universe—the closest thing in *Lost Highway* to a "sacred reality"—does Fred's negativity conclude in or block sacred vision?

In *The Film Paintings of David Lynch: Challenging Film Theory* (Intellect, 2010), referring to the Fred/Pete nexus, Allister Mactaggart straightforwardly confesses "that even with multiple viewings of the fixed cinematic text of *Lost Highway* my confusion never clears" (p. 106). In this very personal study, the critic attempts to make sense where he can by exploring other texts that Pete/Fred reminds him of, principally Freud's study of a patient he calls the Wolf Man, first published in "From the History of an Infantile Neurosis" in 1918. Mactaggart tries to dispel as much confusion as he can by comparing the problem of time in Freud's study with the problem of time in *Lost Highway*, but he arrives at little beyond a statement of resemblances. (In general, Mactaggart's book is a memoir of watching Lynch's films and all the associations with the rest of his reading they conjured for him.) But this much Mactaggart feels he does understand: "Fred's inability to face up to his actions leads to his phantasmic shift into the character of Peter Drayton [sic] while in prison awaiting execution in the electric chair. The traumatic effect of his actions is just too much for him to bear and he enacts a new fantasy scenario as a way to disavow the horror of the brutal murder of Renee" (p. 105). At no point does Mactaggart deal with how the reality of Pete's parents and friends fit into Fred's fantasy.

4.   The method of shooting Fred walking through the corridors in his home, without any light to draw a line between his body and his environment, is atypical, as cinematographer Ben Wolfe remarked to me when we watched *Lost Highway* together. Filmmakers usually want to define boundaries. Lynch, however, in *Lost Highway*, specifically ordered cinematographer Peter Deming to lose that kind of definition. In Stephen Pizzello's article, "Highway to Hell," in *David Lynch Interviews*, edited by Richard A. Barney (University Press of Mississippi, 2009), Pizzello extensively quotes Peter Deming about how he worked to achieve the various gradations of darkness that Lynch wanted. "David feels that a murky black darkness is scarier than a completely black darkness; he wanted this particular hallway [in the Madison house] to be a slightly brownish black that would

swallow the characters up. After we had finished the shot and sent it to the lab, I called the color timer and told him, 'As Bill Pullman walks down the hall, he should vanish completely because if I see him down there I'll never hear the end of it'" (p. 176). Although Deming does not say it, the call was necessary because, unless otherwise instructed, labs always try to "fix" film frames so that they reflect the industry bias for preternatural, pristine clarity, a bias Lynch does not share—unless it suits a particular purpose in a particular film.

5. Unpublished script. David Lynch and Barry Gifford. *Lost Highway*. June 1995, p. 8.

6. I spoke with Lynch about this scene before I had seen *Lost Highway* for the first time, but after I had read the script he gave me. I noted that there was nothing on the pages to indicate what Fred saw in this scene, and asked Lynch what Fred saw in place of Renee's face. Lynch was tickled by my question, knowing that I had quite a surprise in store for me when I did see the film, and he playfully refused to tell me anything about the face. In *The Passion of David Lynch*, having seen the film a couple of times, I opined that what Fred saw was a projection of his own fear and anger. Like so many other interpretations of the Mystery Man as a figment of Fred's inner reality, this interpretation lacked any ability to deal effectively with those scenes in which the Mystery Man is present in external reality, for example at Andy's party and when he speaks with Mom Dayton on the phone.

7. Louisa Gilder, *The Age of Entanglement: When Quantum Physics Was Reborn* (Vintage Books, 2009), p. 3.

8. I should make it clear that Lynch enjoys a good procedural now and then. He very much enjoyed the television series *The Shield* (Creator Shawn Ryan, 2002–2008). But he esteems more highly mass media entertainment that partakes of the uncertain and dreamlike nature of a complex reality, like *The Sopranos* (Creator David Chase, 1999–2007), which he told me he thought was very good indeed.

9. *The Tibetan Book of the Dead*, translated with commentary by Francesca Fremantle and Chögyam Trungpa (Shambhala, 1987), p. 41. The description of the Bardo state is very evocative of Fred's transition into Pete, though it specifically denies the external reality of the physical manifestations, which I am arguing is not true of Lynch:

*A great thunder will come from within the light, the natural sound of dharmata like a thousand thunderclaps simultaneously. This is the natural sound of your own dharmati, so do not be afraid or bewildered. You have what is called a mental body of unconscious tendencies, you have no physical body of flesh and blood; so whatever sounds, so whatever sounds, colors, and rays of light occur, they cannot hurt you and you cannot die. It is enough simply to recognise them as your projections. Know this to be the bardo state.*

*O son of noble family, if you do not recognise them in this way as your projections. . . . the sounds will bewilder you and the rays of light will terrify you . . . and you will wander in samsara.*

10. The talk the Daytons have with Pete about their pact with each other that they will never talk about "that night" on the lawn is immediately preceded by a scene of furtive sex in a motel between Pete and Sheila, sex that is both violent and unsatisfying. The aura of forbidden lust bleeds forward into the next scene as the Daytons speak to their son, wracked with shame and convulsed with a need for secrecy. This aura is augmented by the sudden appearance of lighting; the three Daytons sit in the darkness, each emerging from his or her own background patch of murkiness in partial light, each filled with a pain fraught with the kind of remorse associated with extreme transgression, primarily because no one will identify it. Pete, who was involved in the fusion with Fred on the lawn but has repressed his memory of it, and Bill and Candace Dayton are each struck dumb for their separate reasons by an action that cannot be named—code for homosexual violation.

11. Confusion abounds about the doubleness of Alice and Renee. Slavoj Žižek embeds his ideas about Alice and Renee in Lacanian theories about the way the femme fatale in film noir exists to support patriarchy, since she becomes its most formidable adversary and erasing her from the scene guarantees the safety of the patriarch (p. 10). However, it is not entirely clear that the death of the femme fatale in true noir film does secure the safety of male-dominated society, as she tends to leave behind some traces that suggest that the instability she causes endures forever. Moreover, the patriarch as Žižek identifies him in *Lost Highway*, the Dick Laurent/Mr. Eddy character, dies either at the end of the film or at the beginning of the film, depending on how you look at it. Žižek asserts that *Lost Highway* is a meta-commentary on the femme fatale, but, as if he were talking about two different movies, isolates this issue from the issue of Fred encountering himself. His overdependence on psychoanalytic theory has reduced Žižek to seeing *Lost Highway* in fragments, instead of as the organic structure Lynch created.

For Todd McGowan, using his Lacanian framework, Alice and Renee appear to be among the most intense centers of Fred's fantasy escape from his frustrated desire. Like Žižek, McGowan also understands Alice and Renee in terms of Fred's Oedipal hostility to the patriarch, Laurent/Eddy. But his use of psychoanalytic theory is dubious. For example, when he explains that the patriarchal phallus, Mr. Eddy, gets in the way of Pete enjoying Alice, it may fit Lacanian/Freudian theory about the patriarch, but it has no connection to Lynch's film (p.170). Eddy threatens Pete after he discovers that Pete and Alice have been cheating on him, but if this produces fear, it is not what cuts off Pete's supply of sexual gratification from Alice. It is Alice herself who ejects Pete from his imaginary Eden, and Alice's taunting of Pete with her "You'll never have me" elusiveness has nothing to do with Mr. Eddy as phallic threat.

Allister Mactaggart is as confused about Alice and Renee as he is about other aspects of this film. In a crucial part of his commentary, he writes about the scene in the desert in which Alice tells Pete he will never have her. Mactaggart is under the impression that Alice turns into Renee in this scene, which she doesn't, and that when Pete turns back into Fred, which he does, he follows Renee into the Mystery Man's shack (p. 81). This is quite a problematic mistake since when Fred finds the Mystery Man alone in the shack, he asks where Alice is, sparking an important interchange between the two about Fred's identity. Fred's confusion is connected with his search for the missing Alice, whom the Mystery Man insists doesn't exist. Insisting that there is no one but Renee, the Mystery Man challenges Fred to deal with his own identity. But neither woman is present.

## CHAPTER 2

1. http://www.desmoinesregister.com/article/99999999/FAMOUSIOWANS/41221018 /Straight-Alvin. The historical Alvin Straight received much coverage locally for his 240-mile ride on a 1966 John Deere mower to Wisconsin from Laurens, Iowa to visit his ailing brother, starting on July 5, 1994. Straight died in 1996, but his story was still being told in venues like the *Des Moines Register.com* in 2004, which reported some details that never made it into *The Straight Story*. The change of Straight's brother from Henry to Lyle is not the only alteration Lynch made when he told the story. Lynch also chose not to extend the story past Straight's arrival at his brother's home, which would have allowed him to include the offers that were made to Alvin to appear on David Letterman's *Late Show* and Jay Leno's *The Tonight Show* (http://www.highbeam.com/doc/1G1-69578136.html). According to the *Wisconsin State Journal* of November 14, 1996, the name of the town in which Henry Straight lived was Blue River, which Lynch changed to the more resonant Mt. Zion. However, Lynch did use the actual name of Straight's wife, Frances (http://www.myhavelockpaper.info). According to the *Havelock Times* of July 30, 2010, during the annual Laurens Celebration and Wine Festival there is still an Alvin Straight Memorial Lawnmower [sic] ride in the local parade.

2. Decoherence, also known as collapse of the wave function, explains why we only see one possible shape for matter when quantum mechanics has proven that there are an infinite number of possible shapes. As we see in Appendix II, in the transcript of my discussion about physics with Dr. David Z. Albert on January 4, 2010, "quantum mechanics presents us with a larger palette of physical possibilities [for the behavior of particles, objects, and bodies] than Newtonian mechanics . . ." (p. 11). Yet, so far, the large range of possibilities has only been observed on the particle level and in the laboratory. In ordinary life we see only one possibility, the possibility described by Newton, which is why physicists often say that Newtonian mechanics still works for all phenomena on the level of day-to-day living. So, there must be a perceptive process by means of which we ordinarily perceive only one possibility, by means of which we eliminate all the other possibilities that quantum mechanics speaks of, by means of which we eliminate the

uncertainty principle from ordinary perception. That perceptive process, that process of eliminating the infinite possibilities of matter in the world around us, is called decoherence, or the collapse of the wave function. Decoherence is, as Albert says, a theory about how we interact with our environment (Appendix II). Decoherence means that we see things as Newton described them even though things and bodies are behaving in the limitless way that quantum mechanics has demonstrated. Alvin, alone among Lynchian protagonists, sees things only in a Newtonian way, hence the appropriateness of the title *The Straight Story*. As Albert says, "You know *The Straight Story* makes you think of Newtonian mechanics as opposed to general relativity. Where it's all curvature" (Appendix II, conversation of February 12). Curious readers can find further discussion about decoherence in Appendix II, including some exploration of "Let there be light" from the book of Genesis in the Old Testament of the Judeo-Christian Bible as a possible model of decoherence.

3. In *The Impossible David Lynch* (Columbia University Press, 2007), Todd McGowan discusses Alvin's trip to see his brother in terms of Lacanian fantasy, but in this particular interpretation he is not very distant from my interpretation of Alvin's point of view as one that resembles the phenomenon of decoherence in physics. Physics never occurs to McGowan, but he does not look at Alvin from the perspective of realism, which was the usual way in which journalists described him. In McGowan's vocabulary, however, Alvin's way of dealing with physical difficulty is completely internal. As McGowan sees it, Alvin commits to fantasy more fully than any previous Lynch character. For this reason, McGowan finds himself agreeing with Jeff Johnson, who in *Pervert in the Pulpit: Morality in the Works of David Lynch* (McFarland & Company, 2004) said that "Lynch's vision of America in *The Straight Story* [is] even more mythical than the Republican National Committee's" (p. 178). However, where McGowan understands the phantasmic nature of Alvin's point of view as Lynch's conscious portrayal of fantasy as part of a triumph over adversity, Johnson sees what he calls the mythical view of America as disingenuous falsification on Lynch's part. Johnson's reductive and overly literal reading drives him to itemize all the "flaws" in Midwestern life that he believes Lynch has deviously omitted in order to celebrate Alvin: tornadoes, draughts, floods, minorities, migrants, cops, robbers, violence, homelessness, and drugs. Where, Johnson wonders, in this portrait of Alvin's trip, are the cynicism, petty viciousness, and backbiting that are actually a part of life in the American heartland? Of all the critics, Johnson is the most simplistic and bewildered as he attempts to deal with the moment of Alvin's escape from the endless possibilities of a limitless world by imposing on the terrain his own brand of decoherence filled with love and determination. In *The Film Paintings of David Lynch: Challenging Film Theory* (Intellect, 2010), Allister Mactaggart comes close to Johnson's reductivism, as he characterizes Alvin's story as a straightforward, sentimental narrative (p. 57). However, it is more likely that Lynch would call *The Straight Story* an emo-

NOTES TO PAGES 71-77

tional film, as we see in an interview with Michael Sragow, where Lynch denies
that Alvin's story takes place in a Lynchian fantasy of the Midwest (p. 212). Lynch
speaks emotionally of the film in the same interview (Sragow, "I Want a Dream
When I Go to a Film," in *David Lynch: Interviews*, ed. Richard A. Barney. University
Press of Mississippi, 2009, p. 203).

4. Rose is quite relaxed when she finds herself talking at cross-purposes with people.
Alvin, on the contrary, is extremely impatient when people don't understand
him instantly. He is irritated by the ordinary nonsense that people engage in
with each other as they are trying to figure out what's going on, as for example
when Dorothy and Bud find him on the floor of his kitchen or when the old men
in the hardware store are curious about his purchases. He can be quite impatient
with things too, as when he shoots the Rehds mower that failed him on his first
attempt to travel to Lyle. Alvin is extremely grumpy and troublesome when he's
in the doctor's office as the nurse and the doctor attempt to help him. It's hard to
see how he has earned the right to counsel other people to behave civilly and co-
operatively with family or anyone else, given his discomfort with being a part of
a community. On the other hand, we can easily imagine Rose quoting homilies,
if the notion took her. She is at ease with the messiness of human communica-
tion. We see this most vividly when she is in the supermarket buying provisions
for her father's trip. Because Rose is purchasing cold cuts in bulk, the checkout
girl says to her, "Having a party?" But Rose interprets the remark as a statement
that the girl is having a party herself, which leads to a "Who's on first?" comedy
of errors. But Rose remains affable through it all.

5. The low-key scene with the runaway, pregnant girl leaves much unstated, even
as Alvin is spouting sensible advice to her, and that openness apparently creates
opportunities for critics to read all kinds of reactions into Alvin. Todd McGowan
believes that Alvin is humiliated when the girl calls his mower and trailer a hunk
of junk (p. 188), which seems dubious considering his constantly reiterated sense
of humor about his slapdash arrangements.

6. The bicycle rally that Alvin encounters was inspired by the prevalence of such ral-
lies in the area where Alvin is traveling, as we see in *The Havelock Times*. Different
critics have different takes on Alvin's relationship with the cyclists he meets.
McGowan sees it as a somewhat hostile contest between Alvin and the young
men. He says that at first the speed of the cyclists overwhelms Alvin, but that
he gets his own back when he reminds the boys that they will be old someday
(p. 186). In the interview with Michael Sragow (pp. 200–212), Lynch says that the
boy gains insight from Alvin's words, but is enigmatic about whether Alvin had
a good youth to look back on (p. 211). And Sragow opines that *The Straight Story*
is the opposite of a generation gap movie (p. 212).

7. The appearance of the "Deer Lady" is almost universally seen by critics as a re-
surgence in an otherwise non-Lynchian film of a true Lynchian element. While I
don't believe that *The Straight Story* is non-Lynchian, but merely a Lynchian look

233

at decoherence in an uncertain world, I do agree that the scene with the "Deer Lady" is an anomaly in this film, one of the few places in Alvin's tale where we get a vivid look at the uncertainty that plays so big a part in most of Lynch's other work. But oddly, McGowan, who believes that Alvin's fantasy trip "stages trauma only in order to solve it," while Lynch's other films don't provide solutions, regards the deer lady scene as just such an solved traumatic incident. It isn't clear just what solution McGowan had in mind. The deer lady drives off still in the desperate situation of not knowing where the deer come from and not being able to avoid hitting them. Does the fact that Alvin eats the deer she killed resolve the trauma? Each reader will come to his/her own conclusion. In "David Lynch: A 180 Degree Turnaround," an interview with Michael Henry published in *David Lynch: Interviews* (pp. 213–220), Lynch reveals that although there was an actual deer lady in the area over which Alvin traveled, the real Alvin never met her (p. 215). This raises interesting questions about why it was important for Lynch to stage a meeting between the two. I would say it was to bring into the film the presence of what lurks beneath the surface, even though it never becomes a threshold for Alvin, who holds himself distant from it, and continues on his linear way.

8. During Michael Sragow's interview with Lynch, Lynch comments on the scene between Verlyn Heller and Alvin in a bar in Clermont, where Alvin is camping out in the front yard of the Riordan house. "There's a bunch of things going on there ... Because Verlyn tells his story first and it's deeply disturbing. So for Alvin to tell his story is almost like a gift to Verlyn. Now when Verlyn goes home he won't feel bad and think, Jeez, I told Alvin about this terrible thing and he just sat there. Instead, Alvin shares with him and puts himself in the same horrible, vulnerable memory spot. And, in a way, that's beautiful" (p. 211). Typically, Lynch avoids speaking of why a scene is in one of his films or what it means, but rather gives insight into the emotional reality of his characters.

9. Most critics speak emotionally of the touching reunion of the Straight brothers at the end of the film. Michael Sragow is representative in discussing the emotionality of the moment when Alvin calls Lyle's name and there is no answer, and the audience can see that Alvin fears he is too late, until he hears Lyle's response (p. 203). But in *Pervert in the Pulpit*, Jeff Johnson has an against-the-grain reaction to the reunion: beyond the "surface image of the estranged and now reunited brother achieving a peace beyond words," Johnson finds that "the closing shot implies that Alvin, who didn't have a debilitating stroke, and who refused to walk and who has just ridden lawn mower [sic] over three hundred miles [sic] has had the last laugh and Lyle seethes with hatred and futility" (p. 144). There's no accounting for Johnson's misreading of deep feeling as hatred. It's part of the marketplace.

## CHAPTER 3

1. *The Tibetan Book of the Dead: The Great Liberation through Hearing in the Bardo.* Translated with commentary by Francesca Fremantle and Chögyam Trungpa. (Shambhala, 1987), p. xvi. For readers who want to explore the place of emptiness within the mystic perspective, which is more characteristic of the way Lynch sees it than the way it operates in the Hollywood marketplace in *Mulholland Dr.*, the following passage may be helpful: ". . . Buddhism looks for the basic cause of sin and suffering and discovers this to be a self or ego as the centre [sic] of existence. . . . Since we experience the whole of life from this falsely centralized viewpoint, we cannot know the world as it really is. . . . The remedy is to see through the illusion to attain the insight of emptiness—the absence of what is false. Inseparable from emptiness is the luminosity—the presence of what is real, the basic ground in which the play of light takes place." In *Mulholland Dr.*, when Betty and Rita see illusion unmasked at Club Silencio, they go into convulsions of terror. This is quite a different experience of emptiness than the one described here in *The Tibetan Book of the Dead.*

2. Stephen W. Hawking, "Black Holes Ain't So Black," in *A Brief History of Time: From the Big Bang to Black Holes* (Bantam Books, 1988), pp. 99–113. In these pages, Hawking gives a lengthy, challenging, but ultimately comprehensible account of the phenomenon of the black hole that does not employ mathematical equations as part of the explanation. Hawking explains the many ramifications of the existence of the black hole as "a set of events from which it is not possible to escape to a large distance. . . . It means that the boundary of the black hole, the event horizon, is formed by the paths in space-time of rays of light that just fail to get away from the black hole, hovering forever on the edge" (p. 99). Since the characters that go into the blue box/black hole do emerge from it in another form, it is of interest that Hawking speaks of the theoretical transformation of anyone or thing entering a black hole. "The existence of radiation from black holes seems to imply that the gravitational collapse [of anything entering the black hole] is not as final and irreversible as we once thought. If an astronaut falls into a black hole, its mass will increase but eventually the energy equivalent of that extra mass will be returned to the universe in the form of radiation. Thus, in a sense, the astronaut will be 'recycled'" (p. 112).

3. In addition to the fact that both films are concerned with the dark side of Hollywood, there are a number of allusions to Billy Wilder's *Sunset Boulevard* in *Mulholland Dr.*, including a street sign and a waitress's ID badge that each read, "Sunset Boulevard," and several shots of the apartment complex in which Betty's Aunt Ruth lives that are reminiscent of Wilder's shots of Norma Desmond's (Gloria Swanson) mansion. Moreover, at the beginning of *Sunset Boulevard*, Joe Gillis (William Holden), a fugitive, initiates the action of the film by taking refuge in Desmond's home. In some ways, it can also be said that "Rita," also a fugitive, initiates the action of *Mulholland Dr.* by seeking refuge in Aunt Ruth's apartment.

However, although Lynch has often publicly acknowledged his admiration for *Sunset Boulevard*, he has never said that it was an influence on *Mulholland Dr.* He has said on numerous occasions that the actual street Mulholland Drive, high above Los Angeles, has inspired him as a place of mystery and danger. For one such comment, please see John Powers, "Getting Lost Is Beautiful," in *David Lynch: Interviews*, ed. by Richard A. Barney (University Press of Mississippi, 2009), p. 224.

4. http://en.wikipedia.org/wiki/Mulholland_Drive_film. The Wikipedia article on *Mulholland Dr.* is a good source of the misreadings of Lynch's film by critics who bifurcate the film into an initial dream followed by a depressive reality. Beyond Wikipedia, there is Eric G. Wilson's chapter on *Mulholland Dr.* in *The Strange World of David Lynch: Transcendental Irony from Eraserhead to Mulholland Dr.* (Continuum, 2007) which is unable to come to a conclusion about which is the dream and which is reality in Lynch's film, but Wilson does believe that some division of that kind can be made (pp. 146–153). According to Jeff Johnson in *Pervert in the Pulpit: Morality in the Works of David Lynch* (McFarland & Co., 2004), "[Betty's] dreams of innocence and purity linked to her overbearing awareness of Abrahamic justice cannot save her from her need to be punished. A victim of her own morality, she possesses an acute sense of guilt that drives her to self-immolation" (p. 134). In other words, the beginning of *Mulholland Dr.* is a wish-fulfillment dream that dissipates guilt. When she awakes at the end of the film, she kills herself because she can no longer hide from her remorse about killing Camilla Rhodes. It's a strange division, since Diane has Camilla killed in the second part of the film, not the first. This poses the question of why she would feel guilty before she has her dream. In *The Impossible David Lynch* (Columbia University Press, 2007), Todd McGowan divides the film into an initial fantasy section followed by a second section that is "Diane's World of Desire" (p. 196). In Richard Barney, "*Mulholland Drive*, Dreams, and Wrangling with the Hollywood Corral," in *David Lynch: Interviews*, ed. by Richard Barney (University of Mississippi Press, 2009, pp. 240–241), in an interview with Lynch, Barney tentatively explores a circularity he sees in the shot that pushes into the pillow at the end of the initial montage, a dolly shot that reminds him of the circularity of *Lost Highway*. But when Lynch neither confirms nor denies this intuition, Barney drops it.

5. Martha P. Nochimson, *The Passion of David Lynch: Wild at Heart in Hollywood* (University of Texas Press, 1997), pp. 16–19. Interested readers may wish to refer to these pages for an extended discussion of "letting go"—or as Lynch sometimes calls it "the will to lose one's will"—as the foundation of Lynch's artistic process, and as the ideal spectatorial process.

6. Sogyal Rinpoche, *The Tibetan Book of Living and Dying*, Revised and Updated Edition, ed. by Patrick Gaffney and Andrew Harvey (Harper One, 2002), p. 37. "Nothing has any *inherent* existence of its own when you really look at it, and this absence of independent existence is what we call emptiness." The interconnection of all things is a Buddhist belief that is a part of the positive definition of emptiness

or nothingness that Lynch reflects in *Mulholland Dr.* The events in Ed's office, in a darkly comic way, assert this interconnectedness of an entire environment. *Mulholland Dr.* is structured by interconnections. We see them in the dancers and the radiant images of Betty and Irene and her companion in the initial montage. (Note that the image in the claustrophobic bedroom in that montage is one of disconnection.) There are also the explosive unforeseen connections between the young speeding joyriders and the limousine in which "Rita" is riding; and the connections among all the inhabitants of Los Angeles implied in the high-angle shots that show the city as a collection of many related lights and buildings. Then there is the strange Louise Bonner, who seems to have extraordinary knowledge about the connections in Betty's life; and the instant rapport Betty builds with Woody Katz at her audition for Wally Brown. There is, above all, the crucial sudden connection that Betty and Adam simultaneously feel. In the scenes at the Sierra Bonita complex, we see an interconnectedness between Diane Selwyn and her neighbor in the confusion about who lives in which apartment. The film blurs the boundaries between Betty and "Rita" when "Rita" puts on a blonde wig. And, of course, the entire narrative design of the film is based on the collage method that Lynch uses to track narrative interconnections.

7. I spoke with Lynch in New York, when *Mulholland Dr.* was being presented at the New York Film Festival (January 13, 2001), and he was especially emphatic about the importance of the two readings of the audition scene, first in Aunt Ruth's kitchen, and then in Wally Brown's office. However, he would not say anything about the nature of the importance. As I state above, I believe that the audition reading with Rita points toward the depthlessness of their relationship; there is nothing between the two of them that can engender something new and vital. This not only is information we need to consider when we think about their sexual tryst, but also when we think about the open-ended nature of the circumstances Wally creates and the closed circumstances that are imprisoning Adam Kesher.

8. Lafayette "Monty" Montgomery worked with Lynch as a producer for five of his projects: he was a producer for Lynch in 1988 for a short film he made in France that was commissioned as part of a series for French TV called *Les Français vus par . . .* ; in 1990, he was executive producer for Lynch for *Industrial Symphony No. 1: The Dream of the Brokenhearted*; also in 1990, he was an associate producer for Lynch for the pilot episode of *Twin Peaks*; in the same year he was Lynch's producer for *Wild at Heart*; and in 1993, he was the executive producer for all three episodes of Lynch's TV miniseries *Hotel Room*.

9. Richard A. Barney, "*Mulholland Drive*, Dreams, and Wrangling With the Hollywood Corral," in *David Lynch: Interviews*, ed. by Richard A. Barney (The University Press of Mississippi, 2009), pp. 232–245. In this interview, in speaking to Barney about the Cowboy whom Kesher is forced to meet in a strange corral on a dark, dead-end street, Lynch comments on how corrals have been a source for him of analogies

for restrictions on artists in Hollywood. "And I always use the analogy of the corral as either a big corral in terms of not so many restrictions or a small corral with more restrictions and less room to move. You know, corrals, even small corrals—this is sort off the subject—are restrictions and restrictions are mostly just that but sometimes really good things can come out of restrictions" (p. 238). One of Lynch's most interesting traits is the way he turns concepts around to see them in a 360-degree complexity. It suggests how foolish it is to try to pigeonhole Lynch into a reductively schematic interpretation. It also suggests how uneasy Lynch is giving any definitive statement about interpretations of images in his films. In *Mulholland Dr.*, however, it seems pretty clear that the image of Kesher being penned into a corral by Cowboy on a cul-de-sac speaks to a specific instance when restrictions are extremely destructive.

10. Nochimson, *The Passion of David Lynch*. For a general description of Lynch's eye-of-the-duck scene, see p. 26. For explorations of the eye-of-the-duck scene in *Blue Velvet*, see pp.114–115; in *The Elephant Man*, pp. 145–146; in *Eraserhead*, pp. 159–160; in *Wild at Heart*, pp. 57–59.

11. Although the worldview of *Barton Fink* is pessimistic—quite unlike that of *Mulholland Dr.*—there is a certain resemblance between the two films in that neither one blames the problems that artists encounter in Hollywood on the personal characteristics of those in charge—the ruthlessness of studio boss Jonathan Shields (Kirk Douglas in *The Bad and the Beautiful*, for example)—but on the entire zeitgeist of the culture, which brackets what studios can and can't do because they are a part of the larger social system of constructed relations and values.

12. Astonishingly, in previous books about Lynch, the critics, for the most part, do not appear to recognize how the striking scenes in Club Silencio bear on their theories about *Mulholland Dr.* Todd McGowan has little or nothing to say about Club Silencio, despite the fact that his thesis is about fantasy and so much that happens at Silencio bears on reality and its possible alternatives. Jeff Johnson says that the scene in Silencio is a "comment on moviemaking in general and Diane's attempt to disguise, dismiss or explain her reality in a dream" (p. 136). This perfunctory reading does not account for Betty's extreme reaction in the club, the reason for juxtaposing Silencio with the lovemaking scene, or the relationship between the Silencio scenes and the mysterious appearance of the blue box as the girls sit in the audience. Eric G. Wilson suggests that the scene in which Betty and Rita are at Club Silencio could be another dream, separate from what he sees as Betty's initial dream, a dream that both Betty and Rita are dreaming. He then goes on to say that in Club Silencio we see all we can ever know of reality: ". . . the graspable world is a dream, a distorted copy of an inaccessible and silent original; however some dreams are capable of unveiling the ineffable nature of this abysmal original" (pp. 150–153). While this is an interesting statement in itself, it's not clear how it applies to the film, and to the changes through which Betty, Rita, and Adam go. In the Wikipedia article about *Mulholland Dr.*,

Robert Sinnerbrink and Andrew Hagerman are quoted in reference to the reappearance at the end of the film of the lady with blue hair who sits silently in a box over the stage at Club Silencio. Each reads philosophical import into the fact that she has the final word of the film, "Silencio." Sinnerbrink states, "The concluding images float in an indeterminate zone between fantasy and reality, which is perhaps the genuinely metaphysical dimension of the cinematic image." Hagerman notes that "the ninety-second coda that follows Betty/Diane's suicide is a cinematic space that persists after the curtain has dropped on her living consciousness, and this persistent space is the very theatre where the illusion of illusion is continually unmasked." Both are interesting speculations that do not explore why Lynch has chosen to put these ideas in this film in this manner. In David Lynch's famous "10 Clues to Unlocking This Thriller," he refers to Club Silencio in the 7th clue: "What is felt, realized, and gathered at the Club Silencio?" *David Lynch Swerves* is the first commentary to offer a sustained answer to this question.

13. The relationship between the scene at Winkie's and the rest of *Mulholland Dr.* has not previously been illuminated in any coherent way. In Lynch's "10 Clues," he enigmatically directs us to: "Note the occurrences surrounding the man behind Winkie's. [sic]" Apparently, the scene is a hot-button issue for him, though. When in my 2001 interview with him I asked if Dan dies from the sight of the man behind Winkie's, Lynch was pretty scathing, suggesting that he could not see any other interpretation—possibly the only time he has been deeply impatient with me. There is little of interest about the Winkie's scene in the extant criticism of the film. Eric G. Wilson simply summarizes the scene. Jeff Johnson says that it echoes Betty's mental instability and that it is a projection of Diane's having hired a hit man to kill Camilla (p. 136). Todd McGowan has nothing to say about it.

14. *The Tibetan Book of the Dead*, p. 1; *The Tibetan Book of Living and Dying*, pp. 11–12.

15. *The Tibetan book of Living and Dying*, p. 39.

16. The blue box has proven to be such a staggeringly mysterious element in *Mulholland Dr.* that few have dared to interpret its presence, essential as the discussion of that image would seem to be to any credible account of the film. Jeff Johnson has avoided it, as have Eric G. Wilson and Todd McGowan. In the plot summary on Wikipedia, the blue box is barely mentioned. When the scene in Club Silencio is referred to, the full extent of the summary's acknowledgement of the box is this: "Betty finds a blue box in her purse that matches Rita's key." In Richard A. Barney's interview with Lynch, "*Mulholland Drive* (sic), Dreams, and Wrangling with the Hollywood Corral," he never once mentions the blue box. The ability of cutting-edge physics to account for the function of the blue box in this second-stage Lynchian film is especially vivid proof of how crucial it is to import quantum mechanics into a critical discussion of Lynch's films.

17. There has been no previous commentary on the shot patterns Lynch uses when we observe the transition between Betty and Diane, between what is generally

NOTES TO PAGES 120-126

called the first part of the film and the second. (I have described the film as a three-part structure, of which the first part is the initial montage.)

18. David Lynch, *Catching the Big Fish: Meditation, Consciousness, and Creativity* (Jeremy & Tarcher/Penguin, 2006), p. 115.
19. *The Tibetan Book of Living and Dying*, p. 33.
20. *Ibid*, p. 12.

## CHAPTER 4

1. In Appendix I, I quote Lynch talking about the creative process as a part of every-one's life. Here is an excerpt from that part of our discussion:

> D:  ... *I love when an idea comes along. You know, there's ideas for everything. You don't do anything without an idea. The thought comes first. I'm going to go to the store and get a loaf of bread. Where did that come from? It bobbed up. It's kind of a desire and a thinking at the same time. And you're off to the store. You go down the aisle and you see the bread. There's a lot of different kinds of bread. Boom! This is the one you want and you get it. You follow through on that idea and you get that loaf of bread. So the same thing happens when you get an idea for cinema and you know it's for cinema. You fall in love with it because you love the idea itself. And then you love what cinema can do with that idea. And it's like there are some ideas that—They're not bad, but they don't feel like things you want to use cinema for.*
>
> M:  *Are you saying to me that a cinematic idea for you is a natural extension of the way you live anyway? You have an idea and you get a loaf of bread. And you have an idea and you build a film world. So, art and shopping are parallel ideas?*
>
> D:  *For everybody, not just for me.*

2. For an extensive discussion of non-locality, please see Manjit Kumar, *Quantum: Einstein, Bohr, and the Great Debate About the Nature of Reality* (W. W. Norton & Company, 2008), pp. 341–346.
3. The many worlds theory became a part of the conversation among physicists in 1957 with the work of Hugh Everett III at Princeton. It is sometimes known as the relative state formulation. This theory puts a new spin on decoherence (collapse of the wave function), the moment when the infinite possibilities of the particle level of physical reality become one possibility in the eyes of an observer. According to Everett, when decoherence occurs, it's not that we resolve to a single possibility but that the universe splits and creates enough worlds to house all the possibilities. (See Wikipedia, http://en.wikipedia.org/wiki/Many-worlds_interpretation.) The name many worlds theory was coined in the 1960s and 1970s by Bryce Seligman DeWitt. In private conversation with me, Professor David Z. Albert said that he was among the group of physicists that played with the many worlds concept at that time, but that he doesn't take it seriously as hard physics. In contrast, Fred Alan Wolf takes it very seriously,

exploring this concept as the key to explaining some of the so-far inexplicable aspects of quantum theory (Fred Alan Wolf, *Parallel Universes: The Search for Other Worlds* [Simon & Schuster, 1988]). The counterpoint between these two positions is not an issue with respect to *Inland Empire*. Lynch is not making a scientific statement by borrowing the many worlds paradigm. He uses it because it works as part of the poetic vocabulary necessary to his film.

4. I am quoting from my interview of March 18, 2010 with David Lynch.

5. In the film, the Hollywood power players hold a cheap idea of storytelling. After Nikki turns into Nikki/Susan, Devon Berk becomes very nervous about Kingsley Stewart's story about the murder of the two lead actors in the film of which *Blue Tomorrows* is purportedly a remake. Or at least, this is what is elliptically communicated in a tense, visually dark scene between Berk and the producer of *Blue Tomorrows* (Neil Dickson). In the face of Devon's obvious anxiety, the producer maintains that Hollywood is full of stories, and that there's no proof that the stories surrounding the production of *Vier Sieben* are true. As he speaks, the producer trivializes the idea of the story: "Stories are stories. Hollywood is full of them . . . stories which grew out of the imagination. We're surrounded by these screwball stories every day. They shouldn't be taken as truth or given credence and jeopardize Nikki's performance." However, *Inland Empire* seeks to show us that the distinction the producer makes is bogus. When all is said and done in Lynch's film, the non-local intersection of stories of the marketplace and fictional narratives are all part of the adventure of life, and are part and parcel of how we reach full humanity.

6. Lynch has used television screens, or screens that resemble them, in many of his films: *Dune*; *Blue Velvet*; *Twin Peaks*; *Twin Peaks: Fire Walk with Me*; *Industrial Symphony No. 1: The Dream of the Broken Hearted*; *Lost Highway*, and *Inland Empire*. In *Dune* and *Twin Peaks*, Lynch uses screens in a generally literal way, as media devices. But in the other films listed, he tends to employ the screens for more complex and original purposes: as a way of visualizing the roots of the bound and defined material world of the marketplace in the limitless particle level, or to represent the co-presence of difference frames of space-time. In some of his films, Lynch uses screens for both of these purposes. We find the presence of a screen to multiply time-space frames in *Blue Velvet*, when Jeffrey Beaumont's mother watches a man on a staircase at the same time as we watch Jeffrey on a staircase. Similarly, in *Industrial Symphony*, we see events happening simultaneously from different angles on a big television screen and on the stage. In *Twin Peaks: Fire Walk with Me*, we see two different versions of time-space on a television monitor and in the FBI offices, when Philip Jeffries suddenly appears and just as suddenly disappears. In *Lost Highway*, the uses of screens are many. As Fred attempts to escape from the Mystery Man outside his shack in the desert, and the Mystery Man gives chase with a camcorder fixed at his right eye, we see a version of a very bad tape recording of Fred, which displays an image of Fred driving away that sits on the border

between particle and defined image. On the home entertainment screen (which may be a rear-projection television) in Andy's house in *Lost Highway*, we see an alternate view of Alice in another time and space. We also see different versions of Fred and the Mystery Man in real life and on the screen of the Mystery Man's phone in *Lost Highway*; and we see contrasting time-space areas when the Mystery Man shows the dying Mr. Eddy scenes from somewhere else. The multiplication of time-space areas is even more complex in *Inland Empire* with the screen the Lost Girl looks at, which shows many time-space frames; at the end of the film it displays images of the Lost Girl and Nikki, while at the same time displaying direct images of the two women in the Lost Girl's Room.

Lynch uses screens to depict the contrast between the boundless particle level of the material world and the defined world of matter in the marketplace in the main title of *Twin Peaks: Fire Walk with Me*, which shows the snow on a television set as a prelude to the formed landscape and objects of the story to come. In *Inland Empire*, before the Lost Girl can see anything on her screen of the shaped and formed world, she sees the boundless, particle-like snow there.

7. In Episode 16 of *Twin Peaks*, after the death of Laura's cousin Maddy—when Agent Cooper is close to finding Laura's killer, but isn't sure what to do—there is an explicit reference to the kind of faith Lynch asks of us in *Inland Empire*. Hawk, the sheriff's deputy, calms Cooper, and reassures him that he doesn't need to know where he is going. "You're on the path. You don't need to know where it leads. Just follow." It is of great interest that Lynch did not write this episode, nor was he working closely with *Twin Peaks* when this episode was written and produced. Yet, it does in many ways embody Lynch's ideas. This can't be said for a great many of the episodes of the second season, but his spirit seems to be all over Episode 16. The combined sense of indeterminacy and karma in Hawk's endorsement of Cooper is precisely the balance of uncertainty and destiny that pulsates behind *Inland Empire* and pulls the audience forward, if it will "let go."

8. The hyper-invasive aggression that characterizes the Lynch villain is manifest in the frenzied control he is determined to have, and in his implacable intention of "getting in," as the Impassive Man puts it in the Anger Room. In *Dune*, the Baron Harkonnen (Kenneth McMillan) tyrannizes and exsanguinates his victims. In *Blue Velvet*, Frank Booth is a domineering rapist. The horror of BOB (Frank Silva) in the *Twin Peaks* cycle is his goal of entering his victims—and Laura dies because she won't allow him "in." The Mystery Man (Robert Blake) in *Lost Highway* is a variation on BOB. If we stretch a point, we can say that the Cowboy in *Mulholland Dr.* is too, as an invader of an unwilling and resentful Adam Kesher through his hands-on manipulation of Kesher's thought process as he corrals him.

9. When I spoke with Lynch about the first version of *Blue Tomorrows*, calling it a "draft," he responded, "What kind of draft? Draft beer? A draft in a room?" He was emphatic about rephrasing what I had in mind so that it reflected the idea

that revelation was taking place, not change or evolution. Yet many will take a position midway between the two. Need these different stages of the story in *Blue Tomorrows* be thought of purely in terms of revelation? After all, we don't see only sudden revelatory leaps. We also see more gradual motion among different forms of the film-within-a-film.

10. ". . . partial, tantalizing but troubling, vivid information which we can't yet use . . ." is a pretty apt way of describing Lynch's creative process when he is putting together a film. In private conversation, Catherine Coulson told me that Lynch told her when they were working together on *Eraserhead* that an image had come to him of her carrying a log and that he knew that one day he would use her in a film as a "log lady." That image stayed with Lynch for about fifteen years until it found its way into *Twin Peaks*. Similarly, he spontaneously put together a video project with Laura Dern years before he began to see it as part of his *Inland Empire* project, and only after he had put that fragment into his new film did he began to think that the images of the rabbits that had been on his website years before also belonged to the *Inland Empire* that was emerging in his imagination. On March 18, Lynch repeated for me a description of how *Inland Empire* came into being. It involved numerous particles, or as we may say, bubble worlds, roiling about as separate ideas until they made themselves known to him as connected elements of what would eventually be the whole film.

11. The portrayal of the creative process in American film tends toward the simplistic and the irrelevant, casting the artist's primary struggle in terms of either the sociology of industry or the pathology that the artist as manufacturer or rebel faces. People who "put on a show" in Busby Berkeley's Warner Bros. gold-digger extravaganzas in the 1930s and in the MGM Mickey Rooney/Judy Garland comedies of the 1940s, are always fighting for production money or against repressive morality. If American film is not depicting artistic wars between industry and morality, it tends to depict artists involved in a central battle with internal pathology. For example, in *Black Swan* (Dir. Darren Aronofsky, 2010), when Nina Bayer (Natalie Portman) interprets the role of Odette/Odile in an updated version of *Swan Lake*, her inner process is negatively evoked as interchangeable with mental illness. Federico Fellini's *8½* (1963), not a part of the Hollywood legacy, is one of very few films other than *Inland Empire* that portrays the artistic process in a positive way. While acknowledging the opposition the artist encounters from moralists and moneymen, and the mental turmoil that his protagonist feels, Fellini portrays those interferences as a kind of white noise that is irrelevant to the artist's central struggle, which is to dance with uncertainty toward the outcome of the process.

12. We have already discussed superposition in the chapters about *Lost Highway* and *Mulholland Dr.*, but, for the convenience of the reader, I review its definition here. The simplest way of talking about superposition is to say that on the particle

level of matter, any one particle may exist simultaneously in all possible positions without it being possible to say which of the states is the "real" particle. In speaking of superposition, quantum scientists tend to refer to a thought experiment by quantum scientist Erwin Schrödinger called "Schrödinger's Cat," which he developed in 1935. As he developed the experiment, it presents us with a situation in which a cat, which we are unable to see but know is hidden in a container, is both dead and alive at the same time. For further reading on this paradox, please see Manjit Kumar, *Quantum*, pp. 316–317.

13. Many critics talk about the presence of the light girl (pure, wholesome, innocent) and the dark girl (sensual, dangerous) in Lynch's films, as for example Sandy and Dorothy in *Blue Velvet* and Betty and Rita in *Mulholland Dr.* For a correlation in physics, we might refer to the pairing of particle and anti-particle that is theorized on the atomic level of matter. In *Inland Empire*, however, Nikki, as a result of her work making *Blue Tomorrows*, is able to be in both positions, which correlates in quantum physics with superposition, and becomes Lynch's most highly evolved metaphor in his second-stage films for the probable, complex nature of human experience in the marketplace.

14. The melting of the Phantom, which can be compared with the melting of the Wicked Witch of the West (Margaret Hamilton), is one more place in Lynch's work that allows his fans and critics to debate the influence on him of *The Wizard of Oz* (Dir. Victor Fleming, 1939). Another film in which an allusion to the MGM classic is patently present is *Wild at Heart*, when Sailor Ripley (Nicholas Cage) has a vision of Glinda the Good Witch (Sheryl Lee), who tells him to return to Lula (Laura Dern). Fans have also found more dubious references to *The Wizard of Oz* in *Blue Velvet* (Dorothy Vallens's name) and in *Twin Peaks: Fire Walk with Me* where the name "Judy" has been assumed to be a reference to Judy Garland. When Philip Jeffries makes his mysterious appearance in the FBI office in that film, his first words are that he is not going to talk about "Judy." Later, a monkey says the name "Judy." In *Mulholland Dr.*, the fast food restaurant is called Winkie's, the name of the land ruled by the Wicked Witch of the West in Oz. In private conversation with me, Lynch has told me how much he likes that movie, but mostly the black and white part of it, particularly the tornado. This did not give me any insight into the way the film might be read into Lynch's films and television, except possibly that it isn't necessarily a good idea to look for clues to Lynch's films in the parts of films he likes. I can't think of a place in his work that refers back to the frames of the tornado.

For Lynch's own words about Sailor's vision of Glinda in *Wild at Heart*, please see David Breskin, "David Lynch," in *David Lynch: Interviews*, ed. Richard A. Barney (University Press of Mississippi, 2009), p. 95–96, and Michael Ciment and Hubert Niogret, "Interview With David Lynch," also in *David Lynch: Interviews*, pp. 114–115. At least one critic, Michael Sragow, has seen an influence from *The Wizard of Oz* in *The Straight Story*, when Alvin tells the runaway girl to go home. And Lynch is tickled by this interpretation, "Good deal! I never thought of that. I'm sure Mary and John [the writers] never thought of that. But maybe there's something of *The Wizard of Oz* that's in every film. It's that kind of a story." (Michael Sragow, "I Want a Dream When I Go to a Film," in *David Lynch: Interviews*, p. 210.) I'm pretty sure that Lynch was talking about ALL films, not all of his films. Does this observation shed light on his work? It might have some bearing on the idea that I explore about *Blue Tomorrows*, that Lynch is expressing a belief in *Inland Empire* that all stories are made up of many influences from antecedent stories.

15. In the very last frames of *Inland Empire*, Nikki Grace's living room is filled with a large, motley assortment of people. Who is there? The assembled group of people is preceded by the woman with one leg about whom Nikki/Susan told Mr. K and the sister of the Marine who killed several children in the first grade. She pronounces Nikki's home, "Suweet!" Then we see the woman and her monkey from a story told by a homeless person comforting Nikki/Susan as she is dying on the Walk of Fame; then we see Laura Harring and Scott Coffey, two of the actors previously wearing rabbit suits in the Rabbit Room. We see a man sawing wood who has not previously appeared in this film but who resembles a figure Lynch used in *Industrial Symphony No. 1: The Dream of the Broken Hearted*. The sisterhood of abject women who turned up suddenly in Nikki/Susan's living room are dancers in these final frames. They are followed by another group of dancers, this time black women we have never seen before. A number of unidentified people sit quietly in the vicinity. Among them are fictional characters, some familiar, others not; actors appearing for the first time in *Inland Empire* without their rabbit suits, and an old image from a work Lynch produced over a decade previously. By situating Nikki among images created by Lynch, he might be reminding us that *Inland Empire* is a movie, at the same time that he is celebrating Nikki's artistic and personal victory.

There are many reasons that Lynch might want to remind his audience that they are looking at a movie. One is that he frequently reminds critics that they are looking at a movie and not life when he is asked questions about why the characters do what they do. Perhaps he wants to remind us that we should not ask about, or apply psychological models to, his characters as if they were real people under analysis. A third reason is that he may be creating a distance from his film as a concluding gesture, since he is well known for creating too much closeness to his work, which prompted *Village Voice* film critic Amy Taubin to liken his movies to a hypodermic to the subconscious. Similarly, an online review of *Inland Empire* by Kate Rennebohm tells us that her friend was so profoundly drawn into the film that she said, "I think I actually lost track of who I am." (Kate Rennebohm, "Look at Me and Tell Me if You've Known Me Before: Exploring Affect After *Inland Empire*," http://www.synoptique.ca/core/articles/rennebohm_david_lynch/)

16. During our conversation on March 18, Lynch spoke of Mother Divine, an important figure in Vedic literature. There is a Mother Divine program sponsored by the Maharishi Transcendental Meditation organization, purely for women, to help them find the Mother Divine within themselves. She is considered the female aspect of the Hindu Godhead. The prayer to Mother Divine speaks of power, intelligence, forgiveness, peace, faith, mercy, beauty, and consciousness . . . a source of stability and blessing in the cosmos (http://www.sacredwind.com/divinemother.php). I would suggest that, for Lynch, Mother Divine is a reference to the sustaining aspects of femininity that he showed in abundance in his first-stage films, standing in opposition to the image of the siren, with her teasing "You'll never have me" call. At the end of the film, when Lynch asserts Nikki's newly found vitality and radiance, it is possible to connect it with the power of Mother Divine, though we should remember that it is easy to push references to the faith of an artist too far.

17. Although Lynch has directly said to me that his films are not about his beliefs, those interested in Lynch's films, television, and artwork are advised to become acquainted with the David Lynch Foundation, though not in order to make a reductive evaluation of his films based on his social attitudes. It seems to me that more knowledge about his recent engagement in social programs casts important doubts on groundless opinions often ventured about Lynch and his work because he is courageous enough to depict human nature at its most depraved as well as at its most admirable. We hear all the time that Lynch sees the world as a dark, hopeless place. Yet we get quite a different picture of Lynch from his foundation, established in 2005, as a way for Lynch to try to affect the culture with direct action. It is of interest that his method of reaching out is to give at-risk populations a way to reach inside themselves, where change, as he sees it, begins. Lynch has made available scholarships for any who are in need to learn how to meditate, his contribution to eliminating the stress and stress-related disorders that he believes are at the core of the upheaval, anger, crime, and violence he sees around him. However, he has special programs that seek to involve particularly vulnerable groups: inner-city students, veterans with PTSD and their families, and American Indians, for example. More information about Lynch's foundation is available at the foundation website: http://www.davidlynchfoundation .org/about-us.html. Might a more fully rounded understanding of the man leave many critics and moviegoers free to divorce the disturbing power of his work from inaccurate personal characterizations of this director and concentrate on his aesthetic as an artist?

18. There has been a marked change in the way Lynch uses darkness between his first- and second-stage films. In his first-stage films, Lynch used darkness in opposition to the conventions of Hollywood, for which the dark was traditionally

a source of moralistic anxiety about the presence of evil. By contrast, Lynch's darkness was an analogy for the fertile source of potential creativity, sexuality, and love in the subconscious. For more discussion of the darkness in Lynch's first-stage films, please see Martha P. Nochimson, *The Passion of David Lynch: Wild at Heart in Hollywood* (University of Texas Press, 1997), pp. 32–34, 107. In his second-stage films, however, as Lynch moves his metaphorical emphasis from the subconscious to the external space around the characters, marketplace darkness is associated with the traumatic discovery of the unnerving boundless possibility beneath the surface of things, while marketplace light is associated with decoherence, and the reassuring surface illusion of limited, well-defined objects and bodies. For a discussion of decoherence, please see Chapter 2, "*The Straight Story*: 'And You'll Find Happy Times.'" But there is always, in addition, a sense of a greater, absolute light from above the marketplace that implies the heart of being in the unified field.

19. On March 18, Lynch conveyed to me the image of the creation of the world he gleans from studying *The Holy Vedas*; it is reminiscent of the beginning of the main title of *Inland Empire*. Out of cosmic consciousness, which is being, sound, light, words, and things, comes into existence a magical process that is both sequential and simultaneous.

20. *Inland Empire* is full of all kinds of light: the starbursts of light from the reality above contrast with fascinatingly lit scenes in which different forms of illumination speak of marketplace light that casts illusion. But there are also lights in the marketplace that present as starbursts resembling cosmic, star-like radiance. This could be a matter of Lynch creating a way in which there are parallels between the marketplace and the unified field beyond it, as expressed in a saying he likes: "As above, so below." The most interesting instance of that kind of parallel appears in the frames relating to the soundstage on which Nikki, Devon, Kingsley, and Freddie gather for the first reading of Scene 35 from *Blue Tomorrows*. Before Nikki enters, there is a large starburst of light above the studio building, but there is also a smaller starburst emanating from a light standing in the soundstage, near the table around which she and the others sit. It is as though a pathway of lights toward something important for Nikki is being indicated on two levels of existence. There are also a number of marketplace starbursts on lampposts and on table candles in the scenes in Poland, and on the lampposts on the Walk of Fame in Hollywood, which suggest some less-compelling form of the cosmic starbursts. In contrast to the large, cosmic starbursts, which are clearly, I think, intentionally indicative of a "guiding light," these secondary lights might be portentous, or they might be purely a coincidental result of how the camera registers the light in those particular scenes. I have never discussed this matter with Lynch.

## AFTERWORD

1. Coming to grips with their experiences of the "beyondness" that emerges full throttle in Lynch's art because of his challenge to ordinary limits is a frequent stumbling block for the critics. In *The Strange World of David Lynch: Transcendental Irony from Eraserhead to Mulholland Dr.* (Continuum, 2007), Eric G. Wilson is right to search for a way to understand his intuition of a religious spirit. He understands well that there are issues about the solidity of materiality in Lynch's films, but he makes his frame of reference the Transcendental writers of the American nineteenth century. These writers were also interested in Eastern philosophy and religion and did intuit a simultaneous coexistence and interpenetration of the bound and the limitlessness in human life, but were not in a position to take those insights to the lengths that Lynch takes them. Modern physics was not available to them. Similarly, by referring to gnostic wisdom as a reference point for Lynch's films, Wilson can be extremely acute about the illusory aspects of the physical world in Lynch's cinema, but he cannot tap into the limitless possibilities inherent in the primary structure of the world of matter that is so crucial to Lynch's metaphors. In the "Introduction" to Slavoj Žižek's *The Art of the Ridiculous Sublime: On David Lynch's Lost Highway*, a monograph published by the Walter Chapin Simpson Center for the Humanities in 2000, Mark Wieczorek perceptively emphasizes the importance to Žižek's thinking of his statement, "Lynch's entire 'ontology' is based upon the discordance between reality, observed from a safe distance, and the absolute proximity of the Real" (p. ix). In this statement, Žižek demonstrates that he is aware of the problem of the real in Lynch, but mistakes it for a question of a disconnect between objective and subjective observation. His reading ignores the core issue of limits and limitlessness that we have seen play such a crucial role in Lynch's cinema. Although it is also true that in Lynch's films, contact with the real is a question of perception, distance is not the issue, but rather the courage to face the traumatic instability of cultural parameters.

   By contrast, Jeff Johnson's intuition of limitlessness in Lynch has led him to circle the wagons of convention tightly around himself in his misguided book, *Pervert in the Pulpit: Morality in the Works of David Lynch* (McFarland & Company, 2004). Johnson shows an almost morbid sensitivity to the great changes that took place between Lynch's first- and second-stage works, but, able to appreciate only traditionally structured forms of morality and narrative, he misinterprets the changes. Johnson misreads Lynch's vision of a limitless universe and his successful but hard-won struggles to find narrative forms to express his vision as a collapse into chaos, precisely the opposite point of view that Lynch has in all his films.

2. Good conventional mass market films and television about the beyond blur the boundaries between normality and the exceptional to some extent, suggesting

**248**

on occasion that human existence is both bound and limited. *The X-Files* (Creator Chris Carter, 1993–2002), for example, by and large, protects normality as the primary reality of human culture, but often suggests that it is too narrow, and quite frequently that it is destructive in its narrowness. Thus evidence of a beyond may be a cause for fear, but it also makes room for the validity of hero Fox Mulder's (David Duchovny) declaration of independence from normality, and the validity of the love of Dana Scully (Gillian Anderson) for Mulder's salutary rebelliousness that others see as peculiarity, insanity, or willful perversity. *Edward Scissorhands* (Dir. Tim Burton, 1990) tap dances on the borderline, depicting a world in which normality produces small minds, but also the lovely Kim (Winona Ryder) who, in her love for Edward Scissorhands (Johnny Depp), demonstrates a capacity to see and feel beyond ordinary boundaries. But ultimately, in Burton's film the two are separate, incompatible realms. We and Kim must stay within the parameters of normality; it is our destiny. There is a sadness attached to being confined to the marketplace, but it is a lyrical sadness, not the tragedy that Lynch depicts it, a tragedy that rules out the possibility of any real connection with reality, love, and creativity.

*Pleasantville* (Dir. Gary Ross, 1998) goes further than *Scissorhands* in merging the beyond with the "normal." What might have been a fantasy entrance into a 1950s sitcom and return to normality for a brother and sister is expanded to allow the energies of the "abnormal" experience to alter the definition of normality. *Pleasantville* dips its toes into the vocabulary of altered materiality that Lynch uses so fully. *Dark City* (Dir. Alex Proyas, 1998) is an even more extreme example of the lure among Lynch's contemporaries of generic use of cinematic vocabulary to convey a modern sense of an uncertain world of matter. In *Dark City*, John Murdoch (Rufus Sewell) is confronted by a group of men with the power to alter the contours of reality, both physically and psychologically, without the knowledge of the person who is the object of their manipulations. Normality is a total invention in this film. However, Proyas's film is anything but Lynchian. The chaos that ensues because of the impossibility in Murdoch's world is reminiscent, not of Lynch, but of the perversions involved in Club Silencio's fearmongering.

The history of the vampire film charts both the evolution of commercial cinematic treatment of the beyond and the inability of the artists involved to deal with the material implications of viewers' increasing preference for the monster over the normal person. Originally, in *Nosferatu: eine Symphonie des Grauens* (Dir. F. W. Murnau, 1922) and the early American vampire movies, notably *Dracula* (Dir. Todd Browning, 1931), the monster represents a contamination that must be erased to serve the needs of the normal. But by the 1970s, Dracula had become acceptable as a possible object of romantic fascination, as in *Dracula* (Dir. John Badham, 1979), or amusement, as in *Love at First Bite* (Dir. Stan Dragoti, 1979). In both of these films, the monster, while remaining a demon of sorts, is dramatized as the most attractive man in the film, "gets the girl," and escapes with her from dreary ordinary life. Neither Badham nor Dragoti, however, seem to have had any awareness that if extraordinary life is to exist as a valid alternative to normality, so must extraordinary materiality. Similarly, in current vampire film and television, like *True Blood* (Creator Alan Ball, 2008–) and *Twilight* (Dir. Catherine Hardwicke, 2008), physicality plays all kinds of tricks, as relativist stories present protagonist monsters who constitute a new normality that challenges old concepts of value. Yet uncertainty and probability don't destabilize the material security of these landscapes.

# BIBLIOGRAPHY
# AND FILMOGRAPHY

## BIBLIOGRAPHY

Albert, David Z. In-person Interviews. January 4, 2010; February 12, 2010; May 7, 2010.
———. *Quantum Mechanics and Experience*. Harvard University Press, 1993.
Avadhanulu, RVSS. *Science and Technology in Vedas and Sastras*. Shri Veda Bharathi, 2007.
Benjamin, Walter. "Some Reflections on Kafka." In *Illuminations*. Edited and with an Introduction by Hannah Arendt. Translated by Harry Zohn. Schocken Books, 1969, pp. 141–146.
Bertone, Gianfranco, ed. *Particle Dark Matter: Observations, Models, and Searches*. Cambridge University Press, 2010.
Bohm, David. *On Creativity*. Second Edition. Routledge, 2004.
———. *Wholeness and the Implicate Order*. Reissue Edition. Routledge, 2002.
Cavelos, Jeanne. *The Science of* Star Wars: *An Astrophysicist's Independent Examination of Space Travel, Aliens, Planets, and Robots as Portrayed in the* Star Wars *Films and Books*. St. Martin's Griffin, 2000.
Chion, Michel. *David Lynch*. Second Edition. British Film Institute, 2008.
Coulson, Catherine. Interview, by telephone. June 25, 2010.
*The Cinema of David Lynch: American Dreams, Nightmare Visions*. Edited by Erica Sheen and Annette Davison. Wallflower Press, 2004.
*The City of K: Franz Kafka & Prague*. Catalogue for the exhibition at the Kafka Museum in Prague. Edited by Juan Insua. Translation Editor, Alexandra Bonfante Warren. Centre Cultura Contemporanea, 2002.
*David Lynch: Interviews*. Edited by Richard A. Barney. University Press of Mississippi, 2009.
Debroy, Bibek and Dipavali Debroy. *Holy Vedas*. Commonwealth Publishers, 1989.
Deleuze, Gilles. *Cinema 2: The Time-Image*. Translated by Hugh Tomlinson and Robert Galeta. University of Minnesota Press, 1989.
Doane, Mary Ann. *The Emergence of Cinematic Time: Modernity, Contingency, the Archive*. Harvard University Press, 2002.
Eddington, Arthur S. *The Nature of the Physical World*. The Macmillan Company, 1929.
Elsaesser, Thomas and Malte Hagener. *Film Theory: An Introduction Through the Senses*. Routledge, 2010.

Feynmann, Richard P. *QED: The Strange Theory of Light and Matter*. Princeton University Press, 1985.

Gilder, Louisa. *The Age of Entanglement: When Quantum Physics Was Reborn*. Vintage Books, 2009.

Gillot, John and Manjit Kuman, eds. *Science and the Retreat From Reason*. Monthly Review Press, 1997.

Goswami, Amit. *The Self-Aware Universe: How Consciousness Creates the Material World*. Tarcher, 1995.

Hagelin, John. "Is Consciousness the Unified Field?: A Field Theorist's Perspective," *Modern Science and Vedic Science*, Vol. 1, No. 1 (January, 1987): pp. 29–87. A Publication of Maharishi International University; Fairfield, Iowa.

Hawking, Stephen. *A Brief History of Time*. Bantam, 1988.

Hughes, David. *The Complete Lynch*. Virgin Publishing LTD., 2002.

Johnson, Jeff. *Pervert in the Pulpit: Morality in the Works of David Lynch*. McFarland & Company, Inc., 2004.

Kafka, Franz. *The Basic Kafka*. Washington Square Press, 1979.

———. *The Castle*, the Definitive Edition. Translated by Willa and Edwin Muir. Alfred Knopf, 1954.

———. *The Trial*. Translated by David Wyllie. Echo Library, 2007.

Kumar, Manjit. *Quantum: Einstein, Bohr, and the Great Debate about the Nature of Reality*. W. W. Norton & Co., 2010.

Lim, Dennis. "David Lynch Goes Digital: Why *Inland Empire* is better on your TV than it was on the big screen," *Slate.com* (August 23, 2007).

———. "David Lynch Returns: Expect Moody Conditions, With Surreal Gusts," *The New York Times* (October 1, 2006).

Lynch, David. *The Air is On Fire*. Thames & Hudson, 2007.

———. *Catching the Big Fish: Meditation, Consciousness, and Creativity*. Jeremy P. Tarcher/Penguin, 2007.

———. *Images*. Hyperion, 1994.

———. In-person Interviews. March 29–31; April 1, 1993; January 13, 2006; March 18, 2010.

Lynch, David and Barry Gifford. *Lost Highway*, unpublished script dated June 1995.

Rodley, Chris, ed. *Lynch on Lynch: Revised Edition*. Faber & Faber, 2005.

Lucretius Carus, Titus. *On the Nature of the Universe*. Translated by Sir Ronald Melville. Oxford University Press, 1999.

Mactaggart, Allister. *The Film Paintings of David Lynch: Challenging Film Theory*. Intellect Ltd., 2010.

McCloud, Scott. *Understanding Comics: The Invisible Art*. Second Printing. Kitchen Sink Press, 1993.

McGowan, Todd. *The Impossible David Lynch*. Columbia University Press, 2007.

Mermin, N. David. *It's About Time: Understanding Einstein's Relativity*. Princeton University Press, 2005.

Miller, Arthur I. *Insights of Genius: Imagery and Creativity in Science and Art.* The MIT Press, 2000.

Mindell, Arnold. *Quantum Mind: The Edge Between Physics and Psychology.* Lao Tse Press, 2000.

"Mulholland Dr." on Wikipedia (http://en.wikipedia.org/wiki/Mulholland_Drive_%28 film%29]).

Nader, Tony. *Human Physiology: Expression of Veda and the Vedic Literature.* Maharishi Vedic University, 2001.

Nochimson, Martha. "'All I Need Is the Girl': The Life and Death of Creativity in *Mulholland Drive,*" in *The Cinema of David Lynch: American Dreams, Nightmare Visions.* Edited by Erica Sheen and Annette Davison. London: Wallflower Press, 2004, pp. 163–179.

———. "Desire Under the Douglas Firs: Entering the Body of Reality in *Twin Peaks,*" *Film Quarterly*, vol. 46 (Winter 1992–1993)

———. *The Passion of David Lynch: Wild at Heart in Hollywood.* University of Texas Press, 1997.

———. Review of *Lynch on Lynch, Film Quarterly.* Edited by Chris Rodley (Summer 1999).

———. Review of *Lynch on Lynch, Quarterly Journal of Film and Television.* Edited by Chris Rodley. Second Edition. Faber & Faber (Fall 2005).

———. Review of *Inland Empire. Cineaste* (Summer 2007).

———. Review of *Mulholland Drive, Film Quarterly* (Fall 2002).

———. "Sunlight Will Out of Darkness Come: *The Straight Story,*" *Senses of Cinema*, an online journal (2000): http://www:sensesofcinema.com/2000/7/straight.

———. "*Twin Peaks*: Still a Slice of Robust Cherry Pie," *Wrapped in Plastic* (April 2000).

Odel, Colin and Michelle Le Blanc. *David Lynch.* Oldcastle Books, 2007.

Olson, Greg. *David Lynch, Beautiful Dark.* Scarecrow Press, 2008.

Overbye, Dennis. "A Scientist Takes on Gravity," *New York Times.com* (July 12, 2010) http://www.nytimes.com/2010/07/13/science/13gravity.html?_r=1&pagewanted= all

Panek, Richard. *The 4 Percent Universe: Dark Matter, Dark Energy, and the Race to Discover the Rest of Reality.* Houghton Mifflin Harcourt, 2011.

Plotnitsky, Arkady. *Complementarity: Anti-Epistemology After Bohr and Derrida.* Duke University Press, 1994.

———. *Epistemology and Probability: Bohr, Heisenberg, Schrödinger, and the Nature of Quantum-Theoretical Thinking.* Springer, 2009.

———. *The Knowable and the Unknowable: Modern Science, Nonclassical Thought, and "The Two Cultures."* University of Michigan Press, 2002.

Prigogine, Ilya, in collaboration with Isabel Stengers. *The End of Certainty: Time, Chaos and the New Laws of Nature.* Free Press, 1997.

Prinz, Jesse J. *Gut Reactions: A Perceptual Theory of Emotion.* Oxford University Press, 2004.

Rancière, Jacques. *The Emancipated Spectator.* Verso, 2009.

———. Translated by Gregory Elliott. *The Future of the Image.* Reprint. Verso, 2009.

Rennebohm, Kate. "Look at Me and Tell Me if You've Known Me Before: Exploring Affect After *Inland Empire*," http://www.synoptique.ca/core/articles/rennebohm_david_lynch/.

Rinpoche, Sogyal. *The Tibetan Book of Living and Dying*, Revised and Updated Edition. Edited by Patrick Gaffney and Andrew Harvey. HarperOne, 2002.

Rogers, Tom. *Insultingly Stupid Movie Physics: Hollywood's Best Mistakes, Goofs and Flat-Out Destructions of the Basic Laws of the Universe*. Sourcebooks Hysteria, 2007.

Rosenblum, Bruce and Fred Kuttner. *Quantum Enigma: Physics Encounters Consciousness*. Oxford University Press, 2011.

Russell, Bertrand. *The ABC of Relativity*. Mentor, 1959.

Seife, Charles. *Decoding the Universe: How the New Science of Information is Explaining Everything in the Cosmos, from Our Brains to Black Holes*. Penguin, 2006.

Sobchak, Vivian. *Carnal Thoughts: Embodiment and Moving Image Culture*. University of California Press, 2004.

Simons, Jan. "Complex Narratives," *New Review of Film and Television Studies*, 6:2, 111–129.

Smolin, Lee. *The Trouble With Physics: The Rise of String Theory, the Fall of a Science, and What Comes Next*. Mariner Books, Reprint Edition, 2007.

Stenger, Victor. *The Unconscious Quantum: Metaphysics in Modern Physics and Cosmology*. Prometheus Books, 1995.

Stewart, Mark. *David Lynch Decoded*. AuthorHouse, 2008.

*The Tibetan Book of the Dead: The Great Liberation through Hearing in the Bardo*. Translated and with commentary by Francesca Fremantle and Chögyam Trungpa. Shambhala, 1987.

Thorne, Kip S. *Black Holes and Time Warps: Einstein's Outrageous Legacy*. W. W. Norton & Company, 1995.

van Alphen, Ernst. *Francis Bacon and the Loss of Self*. Harvard University Press, 1992.

*Veda as Word*. Edited by Shashiprabha Kumar. Special Centre for Sanskrit Studies, Jawaharlal Nehru University, D.K. Print World Ltd: First Edition, 2007.

*Vedic World View & Modern Science*. Edited by Radhavallabh Tripathi. Pratibha Prakashan, 2006.

Verma, Keshav Dev. *Vedic Physics: Towards Unification of Quantum Mechanics and General Relativity*. Motilal Banarsidass Publishers, 2008.

Verma, Dr. Shiriam. *Vedas: The Source of Ultimate Science*. Nag Publishers, 2005.

Wheeler, J. Craig. *Cosmic Catastrophes: Exploding Stars, Black Holes, and Mapping the Universe*. Second Edition. Cambridge University Press, 2007.

Williams, Linda. *Hard Core: Power, Pleasure, and the "Frenzy of the Visible."* Expanded Paperback Edition. University of California Press, 1999.

Wilson, Eric G. *The Strange World of David Lynch: Transcendental Irony from Eraserhead to Mulholland Dr.* Continuum, 2007.

Wolf, Fred Alan. *Parallel Universes: The Search for Other Worlds*. Simon & Schuster, 1988.

Žižek, Slavoj. *The Art of the Ridiculous Sublime: On David Lynch's Lost Highway*. Walter Chapin Simpson Center for the Humanities/University of Seattle, 2000.

## FILMOGRAPHY

### BY DAVID LYNCH

*Eraserhead*, 1977

*The Elephant Man*, 1980

*The Short Films of David Lynch* (With commentaries by David Lynch)
Including:

    *Six Men Getting Sick* (1967)

    *The Alphabet* (1968)

    *The Grandmother* (1970)

    *The Amputee* (1973)

    *The Cowboy and the Frenchman* (1987)

    *Lumière* (1995)

*Dune* (1984)

*Blue Velvet* (1986)

*Twin Peaks* Gold Box Set (1990–1992)

*Wild at Heart* (1990)

*Hotel Room* (1993)

*Industrial Symphony #1: The Dream of the Broken Hearted* (1990)

*Twin Peaks: Fire Walk with Me* (1992)

*Lost Highway* (1997)

*The Straight Story* (1999)

*Mulholland Dr.* (2001)

*DumbLand* (2002)

*Rabbits* (2002)

*Inland Empire* (2006)

Lady Dior-Lady Blue Shanghai 3—The Poem (2010). Available at: https://www
.facebook.com/video/video.php?v=1402355429745

Dior "Lady Blue" The Movie Part 1. Available at: http://www.youtube.com/watch?
=7gmisZ1nyRM

Dior "Lady Blue" The Movie Part 2. Available at: http://www.youtube.com/watch?
v=O_a8RopPjvc

### ABOUT DAVID LYNCH

*Pretty As a Picture: The Art of David Lynch* (Dir. Toby Keeler, 1997)

*I Don't Know Jack* (Dir. Chris Leavens, 2002)

### OTHER FILMS AND TELEVISION

*2046* (Dir. Wong Kar-wai, 2004)

*8½* (Dir. Federico Fellini, 1963)

*Across The Universe* (Dir. Julie Taymor, 2007)

*The Adventures of Baron Munchausen* (Dir. Terry Gilliam, 1988)

*Altered States* (Dir. Ken Russell, 1980)

*Battlestar Galactica* (Creator Ronald B. Moore, 2004–2009)
*Brazil* (Dir. Terry Gilliam, 1985)
*Dark City* (Dir. Alex Proyas, 1998)
*Donnie Darko* (Dir. Richard Kelly, 2001)
*Dracula* (Dir. John Badham, 1979)
*Edward Scissorhands* (Dir. Tim Burton, 1990)
*L'Enfer d'Henri-Georges Clouzot* (Dirs. Serge Bromberg, Ruxandra Medrea, 2009)
*Eureka* (Creators Andrew Cosby and Jaime Paglia, 2006–)
*eXistenZ* (Dir. David Cronenberg, 1999)
*Feet First* (Dir. Clyde Bruckman, 1930)
*The Imaginarium of Doctor Parnassus* (Dir. Terry Gilliam, 2010)
*Inception* (Dir. Christopher Nolan, 2010)
*La Jetée* (Dir. Chris Marker, 1962)
*Last Year at Marienbad* (Dir. Alain Resnais, 1961)
*The Matrix* (Dir. Andy Wachowski, Lana Wachowksi, 1999)
*The Matrix: Reloaded* (Dir. Andy Wachowski, Lana Wachowski, 2003)
*Matrix Revolutions* (Dir. Andy Wachowski, Lana Wachowski, 2003)
*Memento* (Dir. Christopher Nolan, 2000)
*Minority Report* (Dir. Steven Spielberg, 2002)
*No Such Thing* (Dir. Hal Hartley, 2001)
*Nosferatu, eine Symphonie des Grauens* (dir. F. W. Murnau, 1922)
*Numb3rs* (Creators Nicolas Falacci, Cheryl Heuton, 2005–2010)
*That Obscure Object of Desire* (Dir. Luis Buñuel, 1977)
*Out of the Blue* (Dir. Dennis Hopper, 1980)
*Paprika* (Dir. Satoshi Kon, 2006)
*Pi* (Dir. Darren Aronofsky, 1998)
*Pleasantville* (Dir. Gary Ross, 1998)
*Quantum Activist* (Dirs. Renee Slade and Ri Stewart, 2009)
*Safety Last!* (Dir. Fred C. Newmeyer and Sam Taylor, 1923)
*The Saragossa Manuscript* (Dir. Wojciech Has, 1965)
*Solaris* (Dir. Andrei Tarkovsky, 1972)
*Stalker* (Dir. Andrei Tarkovsky, 1979)
*Synechdoche, New York* (Dir. Charlie Kaufman, 2008)
*True Blood* (Creator Alan Ball, 2008–)
*Twelve Monkeys* (Dir. Terry Gilliam, 1995)
*Twilight* (Dir. Catherine Hardwicke, 2008)
*Uncle Boonmee Who Can Recall His Past Lives* (Dir. Apichatpong Weerasethakul, 2010)
*What the Bleep? Down the Rabbit Hole* (Dirs. William Arntz, Betsy Chasse, Mark Vicente, 2006)
*Whatever Works* (Dir. Woody Allen, 2009)
*The X-Files* (Creator Chris Carter, 1993–2002)
*Youth Without Youth* (Dir. Francis Ford Coppola, 2007)

# INDEX

Big Bang, 186–187
Birds, The, 163
Birkbeck College, 196
black hole, 13, 91–92, 96, 108, 113–120, 167, 168, 235n2. See also darkness
Black Swan, 243n11
Blake, Robert, 9, 35, 36, 62, 193, 203, 242n8
Blake, William, 162–163, 212
Blue Tomorrows. See Inland Empire, film-within-a-film (On High in Blue Tomorrows)
Blue Velvet: critic on, 215n1; Dorothy Vallens in, 14, 22, 169, 244nn13–14; drug dealers in, 215n1; ending of, 14; eye-of-the-duck scene in, 105; Frank Booth as villain in, 6, 242n8; Jeffrey Beaumont in, 6, 22, 99, 160; Jeffrey and Sandy in, 14, 49, 65; journey from here to here in, 22; light girl (Sandy) and dark girl (Dorothy) in, 244n13; marketplace in, 6; screens in, 241n6; threshold experience in, 6; and The Wizard of Oz, 244n14. See also specific actors
Bohm, David, 196–199, 203, 219n6
Bohr, Niels, 19, 201, 206, 208, 213, 218–219n6, 221n6
Bond, Maya, 100
Booth, Wayne C., 225n1
Born, Max, 219n6
boundlessness. See light; limitlessness; Many Worlds theory
Bouquet, Carole, 21
Bowie, David, 7
Browning, Todd, 249n2
Buddhism, 196, 207–208, 235n1, 236–237n6
Buñuel, Luis, 20, 21
Burton, Tim, 249n2
Busey, Gary, 41, 45
Butler, Lucy, 41

Cada, James, 76
Cage, Nicholas, 14, 65, 244n14
Carpenter, Joseph A., 69–70
Carter, Chris, 249n2
Castellanos, Vincent, 97
Cavelos, Jeanne, 161
Chion, Michel, 215n1
Citizen Kane, 223n12
Coen, Joel, 107
Coffey, Scott, 128, 131, 245n15
Cohen, Leonard, ix, xvi
collapse of the wave function, 194, 203, 232n2. See also decoherence
collective unconscious, 15
consciousness: connection of, to big Self, 182; Hagelin on, as unified field, 219n6; individual consciousness, 31, 32, 36, 37, 226n2; Lynch's belief in universal consciousness, 11, 31; self-referential consciousness, 179; as source of everything, 179; states of, 182; in The Tibetan Book of the Dead, 17; and Transcendental Meditation, 182, 217–218n5, 246n16; unity consciousness as highest state of, 182; Vedas on universal center of, and unified field, x–xi, 15–16, 31, 226n2; and Vedic story of creation, 247n19
Cooke, Herb, 111
Copenhagen, 199
Coulson, Catherine, 243n10
Crary, Erik, 146–147, 156
creativity and creation: darkness as analogy for, 247n18; Fellini on, in 8½, 243n11; in Genesis, 211, 212; in Inland Empire main title, 126–127, 247n19; Inland Empire on, 243n11; and "letting go," 97, 125, 167, 176, 236n5, 242n7; Lynch on, 125, 142–143, 174–178, 240n1, 243n10; in Mulholland Dr., 99, 101–102, 104,

Eppolito, Lou, 37
*Eraserhead*: Baby's explosion in, 207,
220n2, 224n16; Coulson's work with
Lynch on, 243n10; ending of, 14;
external uncertainty in, 7–8; eye-
of-the-duck scene in, 105; frame of
normality in, 7; Henry Spencer in,
6, 14, 160, 220n2, 224n16; journey
from here to here in, 22; Lady in the
Radiator in, 6, 14, 220n2, 224n16;
lights, colors, and sounds in, 220n2,
224n16; and quantum mechanics,
6, 220n2; uncertainty of matter in,
5; Vedic influences on, 159–160, 161.
*See also specific actors*
Everett, Chad, 101, 102
Everett, Hugh, III, 203, 221n7, 241n3
existentialism, 200
*Existenz*, 20, 21

Facebook, 9
fantasies. *See* dreams and fantasies
fantasy films, 146, 163–164
Farley, John, 80–81
Farley, Kevin P., 80–81
Farnsworth, Richard, 60, 73, 76, 79, 84,
87, 226n1
Fellini, Federico, 152, 223n12, 243n11
femininity: in Lynch's first-stage films,
49, 246n16; and Mother Divine,
246n16
femmes fatales: in *The Lady From
Shanghai*, 52–53; in *Lost Highway*,
44–54; in noir film, 230n11; in
*Sunset Boulevard*, 92. *See also* sirens
Feynman, Richard, 188, 189
film-about-making-films genre, 92, 107–
108, 124, 235–236n3, 238n11. See
also *Inland Empire*; *Mulholland Dr.*
filmography of David Lynch, 255
Fine, Sylvia, 60
*Fire Walk With Me. See Twin Peaks: Fire
Walk With Me*

Fischler, Patrick, 110–111
Flaubert, Gustave, 198–199
Fleming, Victor, 150, 244n14
Four Quartets (Eliot), 24
*Français vus par, Les*, 237n8
Freud, Sigmund, xiii, 19, 215n1,
228n3
Frost, Mark, 223–224n15
fugue state, 31

Garland, Judy, 150, 243n11, 244n14
gender. *See* femininity; femmes fatales;
masculinity; sirens
Genesis, Book of, 211, 212, 232n2
George, Melissa, 103
Getty, Balthazar, x, 9
*Gilda*, 99
Gilder, Louisa, 38, 220n2
gluons, 185
Gnostic theology, xiv, 216n1, 217n4,
248n1
Grace, Wayne, 101
Graham, Heather, 23, 168
"Grandmother, The," 159
Green, Johnny, 60
Gregory, Dick, 41
grotesque, 147–148, 151, 168–169
Gruszka, Karolina, 125, 129

Hagelin, John, 204, 219n6
Hagerman, Andrew, 238–239n12
Hamilton, Margaret, 150, 244n14
"Happy Times," 60, 80
Hardwicke, Catherine, 250n2
Harker, Wiley, 79
Harring, Laura Elena, 90, 128, 131,
152, 245n15
Harvard University, 219n6
Hawking, Stephen W., 235n2
Hayworth, Rita, 52, 99
Hedaya, Dan, 103
Heidegger, Martin, 200, 211
Heisenberg, Werner, 5, 123, 201

Hencz, Jan, 130
Henry, Michael, 234n7
Heuring, Lori, 103
Hiley, Basil, 199
Hinduism. *See* Vedic philosophy
Hitchcock, Alfred, 19–20, 163–164,
    222–223n12
Hitler, Adolf, 15
Holden, William, 235n3
Hollywood: creative process in
    American films, 243n11; and
    disaster films, 20; and film-about-
    making-films genre, 92, 107–108,
    124, 166, 235–236n3, 238n11; and
    film conventions for limitlessness,
    163–164, 248–250n2; and horror,
    science fiction, and fantasy
    films, 146, 163–164, 248–250n2;
    as marketplace in *Inland Empire*,
    123–125, 135–136; as marketplace
    in *Mulholland Dr.*, 27, 89–92, 97–98,
    102–110, 113, 115, 117, 120–121, 168,
    237–238n9; and noir film, 230n11;
    and vampire films, 163, 164, 249–
    250n2; and western films, 83, 85,
    103–104. *See also specific Hollywood
    film actors*
Holy Vedas. *See* Vedic philosophy
Homer, 50–51, 52
Hope, Bob, 112
Hopkins, Anthony, 10
Hopper, Dennis, 6
horror films, 146, 163–164, 248–250n2
*Hotel Room*, 237n8
*Huckleberry Finn* (Twain), 225n1
Hurt, John, 10

"I'm Deranged," 32–33
India, 15. *See also* Vedic philosophy
*Industrial Symphony No. 1: The Dream of the
    Brokenhearted*, 237n8, 241n6, 245n15
*Inland Empire*: David Z. Albert on, 209–
    212, 214; alley behind marketplace

in, 134, 135, 143; audience's
relationship with, 131, 133–134,
138, 144, 146, 148, 157, 164–165,
167, 169, 209, 242n7; compared
with other Lynch films, 124, 125,
131, 132, 138, 147, 226nn1–2;
entanglement in, 10, 125–127;
faith in, 127–129, 131, 132, 151,
156; final frames of, 152–153, 154,
157, 245n15; higher power of love
and positive energy in, 151–154,
156–158; Hollywood marketplace
in, 123–125, 135–136, 140–141,
148, 156–157, 241n5; journey from
here to here in, 24, 25, 51, 143, 147,
151–152, 226–227n3; lights, colors,
starbursts, and sound in, 16, 17,
127, 147–151, 153–154, 247n20;
limitlessness in, 4, 13, 25, 123,
127, 151–153, 167, 242n6; linear
versus non-linear time in, 138–147,
153; Lynch on, 145, 176–178,
242–243nn9–10; Lynch's script for,
176–178; magic in, 146; main title
of, with image of creation, 126–127,
247n19; and Many Worlds theory,
13, 143, 145, 153, 168, 241n4,
243n10; music in, 128–129, 135,
152, 155; non-locality in, 125–130,
133, 135, 137–147, 151–152, 241n5;
parables of marketplace and palace
in, 133–134; "Polish Poem" song
in, 128–129, 135; and quantum
mechanics generally, 12, 122, 123–
124, 145; responsibility for others
("unpaid bill") and generosity in,
125, 127, 128, 132, 135, 138, 151–152,
154, 156, 168; review of, 245n15;
screens in, 242n6; sexuality in, 140–
143, 145, 147, 152–155; still shots
from, 2, 128, 129, 130, 134, 137,
141, 144, 149, 152, 155, 156, 157;
superposition in, 142–143, 244n13;

Maharishi Transcendental Meditation, 246n16. *See also* Transcendental Meditation

Majchrzak, Krzysztof, 127–128, 130, 152

Many Worlds theory: David Z. Albert on, 122–123, 203–204, 221n7, 240n3; and decoherence, 240n3; and entanglement, 13; and *Inland Empire*, 13, 143, 145–146, 153, 168, 241n4, 243n10; and *Lost Highway*, 13; Lynch on, 145, 243n10; of physics, 12–14, 122–123, 203–204, 221n7, 240–241n3. *See also* limitlessness

marketplace: alley behind, 134, 135, 143; and being stuck in appearances, 111; and black hole in *Mulholland Drive*, 13, 91–92, 96, 108, 113–120, 166–167, 168; in *Blue Velvet*, 6; decreation of, 91, 113, 117, 166; in *Dune*, 6; in *Eraserhead*, 220n2, 224n16; fictitious normality of, 163; Hollywood marketplace in *Inland Empire*, 123–125, 135–136, 140–141, 148, 156–157, 241n5; Hollywood marketplace in *Mulholland Dr.*, 27, 89–92, 97–98, 102–110, 113, 115, 117, 120–121, 168, 237–238n9; and illusions of materialism in American society, 3–5, 10–11; instability of, in Lynch's second-stage films, 160–162; liberation from, xv, 14, 30–32, 102, 112, 121, 125, 129, 143, 151–154, 157, 167, 169–170, 222n11; in *Lost Highway*, 27, 30, 32, 41, 43–57, 62, 228n3; love in, 154–155; and macro and micro visions of materiality, 16, 108; meaning of term in Vedic philosophy, 4–5; obligation within, 135; the Palace versus, 16, 17, 18, 130, 222n11; and quantum mechanics, 5; reduction of everything to nothingness in,

57, 112, 113; samsara compared with, 222n11, 229n9; screens as imagery associated with, 241–242n6; and self-involvement, 167–168; and sexuality, 43–54; and superposition, 45; in *Twin Peaks: Fire Walk With Me*, 7; uncertainty of, 12, 97–98, 131, 167, 219n6; and "unpleasure" moments in Lynch's films, 168–169

Marquette, Jacques, 85

masculinity: compromised manhood of Fred/Pete's threshold experience, 43–44; domination as sign of, in Lynch's first-stage films, 49; Hollywood cliché of, 104; and masculine entitlement in *Inland Empire*, 154; and patriarchy, 92, 136, 230n11; in *The Odyssey*, 51

Massee, Michael, 34

Mastroianni, Marcello, 152, 223n12

*Matrix* trilogy, 20, 223n13

Maya, 54

McCarthy, Joseph, 219n6

McGill, Everett, 71

McGowan, Todd, xiii, 215n1, 216–217n2, 227n3, 230n11, 232n3, 233–234nn5–7, 236n4, 238–239n12–13, 239n16

McMillan, Kenneth, 242n8

meditation. *See* Transcendental Meditation

microvision, 16, 19–20, 23, 192, 217n3

Miller, Ann, 100

Miller, Laura, 220–221n5

Minnelli, Vincente, 107

modern physics. *See* physics; quantum mechanics

Molina, Angela, 21

Montgomery, Lafayette "Monty," 103–104, 116, 237n8

Mother Divine, 246n16

*Mulholland Dr.*: David Z. Albert on, 214; allusion to *The Wizard of Oz* in,

quantum mechanics (*continued*)
causality and nature of time
in, 21–22, 54, 89, 181, 213–214;
and collapse of wave function,
194, 203, 232n2; and confusion
when looking at phenomena,
5; and decoherence, 60, 64, 67,
205, 211–214, 231–232n2, 241n3;
Einstein versus Bohr on, 218–219n6,
221n6; and entanglement, 8, 38,
125–126, 179, 185–187, 220n3; and
information, 204–205; macrovision
and microvision in, 16, 19–20,
64, 192; New Age science versus,
187, 196, 199–203; Nochimson's
interview with David Z. Albert
on, xvi, 28, 60, 122–123, 183–214;
Nochimson's interview with Lynch
on, 178–181; non-locality of, 28, 29,
120, 196–199, 204; overlap between
Vedic philosophy and, in Lynch's
films, xiv–xv, 5, 12, 16, 18, 24, 26–27,
159–170, 180–181; and particles,
183–185, 205–206; and photons,
188–191; probabilistic nature of
laws of, 213; public interest and
popularizing texts on, 10, 220–
221n5, 221n7, 223n13; as referent
for critique of Lynch's films, xiv–xv,
5, 6, 8, 11–12, 16, 18–23, 162–168,
208–211, 220n2; relationship
between Newtonian physics and,
16, 60, 180, 184, 191–192, 194–195,
210–211, 213, 222n9, 231–232n2;
and stasis, 195; threatening nature
of, 112, 200; and time-reversal
symmetry, 23, 190, 191; and
uncertainty principle, xiv–xv, 5, 8,
33, 94, 219n6, 231–232n2; *What the
Bleep?* film on, 191, 200–201, 207. *See
also* Many Worlds theory; physics;
superposition
quarks, 184–185

Rakshasas (diabolical beings), 54, 91,
131–132, 147
*Rear Window*, 19, 223n12
Reeves, Keanu, 20
relativity theory, 188, 190, 194, 198, 199,
212–213, 214, 222n9, 232n2
Rennebohm, Kate, 245n15
Resnais, Alain, 20
Rey, Fernando, 21
*Rhetoric of Fiction, The* (Booth), 225n1
*Road to Morocco*, 112
Rogers, Tom, 161
Rollins, Henry, 40
Rooney, Mickey, 243n11
Roselius, John, 37
Ross, Gary, 249n2
Rossellini, Isabella, 169
Ryder, Winona, 249n2

Salon.com, 10
samsara, 222n11, 229n9
Schrodinger, Erwin, 220n4, 244n12
Schrodinger's Cat, 220n4, 244n12
science, 26, 199–200, 207. *See also* New
Age science; Newtonian physics;
physics; quantum mechanics
science fiction films, 163, 248–250n2
Seife, Charles, 220–221n5
Sewell, Rufus, 249n2
sexuality: darkness as analogy for, in
Lynch's films, 247n18; in *Inland
Empire*, 140–143, 145, 147, 152–155;
in *Lost Highway*, 3–4, 33, 34, 43–54,
57, 58, 109, 230–231nn10–11; and
marketplace, 43–54, 154–157;
in *Mulholland Dr.*, 103, 108–109,
117, 237n7; pornographic way of
experiencing, 52, 53, 56, 58; of
sirens in classical culture, 50–51,
52. *See also* femmes fatales; love
Shakespeare, William, 146
*Shield, The*, 229n8
Silva, Frank, 62, 242n8

"Simple Heart, A" (Flaubert), 198–199
Sinnerbrink, Robert, 238–239n12
sirens, 50–51, 246n16. *See also* femmes
fatales
"Six Men Getting Sick," 159, 198
Skype, 9
Slaughter, Lou, 56
smartphone, 9
*Solaris*, 20–21
"Song to the Siren," 44, 46, 52
Sophocles, 221–222n8
*Sopranos, The*, 229n8
space: David Z. Albert on, 186, 187, 190,
202, 204, 209–210; and "alley behind
the marketplace," 134, 135, 143;
and "AXXON N." door in *Inland
Empire*, 2, 9–10, 18, 141–142, 143,
150; and Bardo state, 17–18, 41,
112, 222n11, 224n16, 229n9; Betty's
illusory grasp of, in *Mulholland Dr.*,
100; and black hole in *Mulholland
Dr.*, 13, 91–92, 96, 108, 113–120, 167,
168, 235n2; BOB/Leland Palmer as
two bodies occupying same space,
7; confined space in *Mulholland Dr.*,
94–95; and dancers in *Mulholland
Dr.*, 93–94; of death-row cells in *Lost
Highway*, 40–42; and Eddington's
doorway, xvi, 1, 2, 3, 8, 14, 45,
50, 53, 74, 127, 178–179, 200; in
*Eraserhead*, 220n2; folding space
in *Dune*, 180; illusions of, 60;
in independent American and
European films, 20–21; and journey
from here to here in Lynch's
second-stage films, 24–26; and Lost
Girl in *Inland Empire*, 132; Lynch
on, as consciousness, 179; Lynch's
use of generally, 61–62, 217n3;
and macrovision/microvision, 16,
19–20, 23, 64, 108, 192, 217n3; and
magical ritual by Nikki/Susan in
*Inland Empire*, 146; in *Matrix* trilogy,

20; and metamorphosis of Fred
into Pete in *Lost Highway*, x,
xi–xii, 30–32, 40–44, 71, 147,
164–165, 168, 226–228n3, 229n9,
230n10; multiple time/space frames
in *Inland Empire*, 126–127, 142–143,
209–210; Newtonian physics on,
124, 222n9; Palace as space beyond
marketplace, 16, 17, 18, 130, 133–
134, 222n11; and Phantom in *Inland
Empire*, 131–132; and screens, 241–
242n6; and sexually abject women
in *Inland Empire*, 145; shifts in time
and space in *Mulholland Dr.*, 113–115,
117; in *The Straight Story*, 62–66, 68,
71–72, 77, 80, 81–85; threshold as
passage between two perceptions
of same space, 2; in *Twin Peaks:
Fire Walk With Me*, 225n16. *See
also* decoherence; entanglement;
limitlessness; Many Worlds theory;
marketplace; superposition;
thresholds; time
Spacek, Sissy, 63
spectatorial process. *See* audience
Sragow, Michael, 233n3, 233n6,
234nn8–9, 244–245n14
Stafford, Jo, 60, 80
Stanford University, 219n6
Stanton, Harry Dean, 61, 87, 135–136,
144, 168, 217n2
Stewart, James, 19
Stole, Mink, 39, 40
*Straight Story, The*: David Z. Albert on,
198–199; allusion to *The Wizard
of Oz* in, 244n14; audience's
relationship with, 67, 78, 83,
84–85, 87, 234n9; beginning
images of, 71; compared with *Inland
Empire*, 124, 131; cowboy stereotype
in, 83; decoherence in, 64–67,
87–88, 208, 232nn2–3, 233–234n7;
final frames of, 86–87, 234n9;

Straight Story, The (continued)
lighting and high-angle filming
of, 64–66, 81, 83; lightning storms
in, 72; limitlessness in, 25, 61–62,
165–166, 232–233n3; linear plot
of, compared with other films
by Lynch, 60–65; love within
illusions of bounded culture in,
62–63, 65–67, 86–87, 165–166;
Lynch on, 165, 232–233n3, 233n6,
234n8; machines in, 66–71, 166;
miscommunication in, 69–70,
233n4; music soundtrack in, 71–72,
74, 80, 83, 88; overlapping images
of earth and sky in, 82–83; reversed
trajectory of eastward motion in,
83–84; reviews of and critics on, 63,
232–233n3, 233–234nn5–7, 234n9;
roots of, in true story, 60–61, 62,
231n1; steely determination in, 27;
still shots from, 68, 73, 76, 77, 79,
82, 84, 87; threshold experience in,
4; uncertainties and incompleteness
in, 63–70, 74–81, 84–88, 233–234n7.
See also specific actors; Straight Story
characters and scenes, general
Straight Story characters and scenes,
general: bicyclists on tour, 75,
76–77, 233n6; Danny and Darla
Riordan, 75–76, 78–79; "Deer
Lady," 76, 77–78, 166, 233–234n7;
doctor visit by Alvin, 70, 73, 233n4;
Dorothy, 70, 75, 233n4; four
stages of discontinuities in Alvin's
progress, 67–70; hardware store
scene, 70–71, 233n4; historical tale
of Marquette, 85; idyllic scenes
of Alvin's progress, 11, 67, 72, 81;
Laurens as seen from the air, 81–82;
Lyle's stroke, 61, 67–68, 72; Olson
twins, 80–81; parable of the sticks,
75; priests, 81, 84–86, 87; reunion
between Alvin and his brother Lyle,

4, 60–63, 65–66, 84, 86–87, 138, 165–
166, 234n9; Rose and her children,
63, 65, 70–72, 74–76, 81, 233n4;
runaway unmarried, pregnant girl,
63, 74–75, 233n5, 245n14; Verlyn
Heller, 79, 85, 234n8. See also
Straight Story, The, Alvin in
Straight Story, The, Alvin in: advice and
wisdom during his travels, 63, 72,
74–76, 80–81, 233n5; arrival in Mt.
Zion, 84–88; careening down steep
hill, 68, 69, 76, 78, 79; dream as
momentarily sustaining, 91; family,
74–76, 81; habit of looking to the
stars, 81–84, 87; history, 71, 76–77,
79–81, 85–86, 87, 165, 233n6, 234n8;
hometown friends, 69–71, 131,
233n4; limitations, 68; and Lyle,
75, 81, 85, 87; and retribution, 25,
27; on the road, 69, 71–81; small-
town life, 66, 69–71, 73, 166, 233n4;
unreliable point of view, 87, 226n1;
and women, 75–76
string theory, 23, 179, 184–185, 219n6
Sunset Boulevard, 92, 235–236n3
superposition: David Z. Albert on,
192–194, 220n4; in Inland Empire,
142–143, 244n13; in Lost Highway,
x, xi–xii, 9, 13, 41–42, 45, 48–49, 55,
193–194; in Lynch's films generally,
205; and marketplace, 45; in Matrix
trilogy, 20; meaning of, 8, 9, 180,
243–244n12; as metaphor, 162; in
Mulholland Drive, 9, 13, 90, 92–93,
108, 109, 117; and possibility, 204;
in That Obscure Object of Desire, 21; in
Twin Peaks, 9; in Twin Peaks: Fire Walk
With Me, 224–225n16
Swanson, Gloria, 235n3
Swenson, May, 168

Taggart, Rita, 101
Tarkovsky, Andre, 20–21

Twin Peaks (continued)
of Laura and Cooper in, 38; screens
in, 241n6; self-involvement of
marketplace in, 167–168; Sheriff
Harry S. Truman in, 7; Special
Agent Dale Cooper in, 7–8, 9, 10,
22–23, 30, 38, 65, 99, 160, 167–168,
224n15, 242n7; superposition in, 9,
224–225n16; threshold experience
in, 7–8, 22–23; uncertainty in, 7–8,
242n7; Windom Earle in, 224n15.
See also specific actors
Twin Peaks: Fire Walk With Me: allusion
to The Wizard of Oz in, 244n14; angel
for Laura in, 23, 24, 169, 225n16;
beginning of, 16; circular time in,
21–22; creation mythologies evoked
in, 16; critic on, 21–22, 216n1;
eating garmonbozia in, 23; end of,
207; FBI Agent Philip Jeffries in, 7,
241n6, 244n14; journey from here
to here in, 23; Laura Palmer's sexual
assault and murder by Leland/
BOB in, 7, 23, 24, 168, 224n16;
lights and colors in, 224–225n16;
Little Man from Somewhere Else
in, 23, 224n16, 225n16; Lynch as
character Gordon Cole in, 7; main
title of, 242n6; marketplace in,
7; Nochimson's critique of, in The
Passion of David Lynch, ix, x; and
quantum mechanics generally,
198; Red Room in, 23, 24, 83, 207,
225n16; screens in, 241–242n6;
visionary capability of Laura Palmer
in, 160. See also specific actors

Ulysses, 50–51, 52
uncertainty: Eliot, Beckett, and Kafka
on, 12, 14, 26, 32, 40, 42; and
entanglement, 8–9; in Eraserhead,
7; in Hitchcock's Rear Window, 19;
in Inland Empire, 123, 124, 126,

129, 142, 143–144; in Lost Highway,
33–34, 39–41, 55; Lucretius on,
122, 123–124, 126; in Lynch's first-
and second-stage films, 14–15;
Lynch's positive vision of, 12; of
marketplace, 12, 97–98, 131, 167,
219n6; and maturation process,
144; metaphor of uncertainty
principle, 162; in Mulholland Dr., 94,
95–98; and observation as changed
by observer, 19, 33, 183–184; and
quantum mechanics, xiv–xv, 5,
8, 94, 219n6, 231–232n2; in The
Straight Story, 63–70, 74–81, 84–88,
233–234n7; and superposition, 8,
9; thresholds and uncertainty of
matter in Lynch's films, 3–11; in
Twin Peaks, 7–8, 242n7; uncertainty
principle in modern physics, 5,
219n6; and unified universe ruled
by chance, 221–222n8
Uncle Boonmee Who Can Recall his Past
Lives, 20, 21
unconscious. See collective unconscious
unified field, 15–16, 31, 127, 177, 179–
182, 202, 212, 219n6, 226n2, 247n18,
247n20. See also limitlessness
"unpaid bill," 135, 138, 151, 154, 168
unreliable narrator/point of view, 31,
87, 225–226n1, 227–228n3

vampire films, 163, 164, 249–250n2
Vedic philosophy: on cosmic
"beyondness" and boundlessness,
xiv–xv, 5, 16, 28–32, 159–160;
creation story of, 16, 127, 247n19;
and deceptiveness of appearances,
5, 16; and karmic debt, 135; and
Lady in the Radiator of Eraserhead,
6; Lynch's belief in, x–xi, 4–5,
14–18, 26–27, 159–161, 163, 182;
marketplace as opposite of cosmic
reality of, 5, 12; and Maya, 54;